THE COMPENDIUM OF
AMERICAN RAILROAD RADIO FREQUENCIES
13TH EDITION

RAILROAD REFERENCE SERIES NO. 15

BY GARY L. STURM AND MARK J. LANDGRAF

Editor: George Drury   Cover Design: Kristi Ludwig

On the cover: Delaware & Hudson train 555 is shown at Mohawk Yard in Scotia, New York, on May 14, 1994, behind six Montreal-built diesels belonging to D&H's parent CP Rail. Photo by William R. Mischler.

Warning

It is a federal crime, with severe punishment and/or fines, to: (a) divulge what you hear to anyone who is not a party to the broadcast; (b) make use of any broadcast information for your own personal gain; or (c) make use of any broadcast information for illegal purposes or to commit a crime. Any such violations may be investigated by the FBI and prosecuted by the U. S. Department of Justice.

Many states have laws prohibiting the installation of a scanner in an automobile, or in some cases, just the possession of a scanner. You should consult your local authorities for an interpretation of your state's laws.

Publisher's Cataloging in Publication
(Prepared by Quality Books Inc.)

Sturm, Gary L.
　　The compendium of American railroad radio frequencies / by Gary L. Sturm and Mark J. Landgraf. — 13th ed.
　　　　p. cm. — (Railroad reference series ; no. 15.)
　　　　ISBN 0-89024-231-3

　　1. Radio stations—United States—Directories. 2. Radio stations—Canada—Directories. 3. Railroads—United States—Communications systems. 4. Railroads—Canada—Communications systems. I. Landgraf, Mark J. II. Title. III. Title: American railroad radio frequencies. IV. Series.

TK6555.S77 1995　　　　　　　　　　　　385'.2042
　　　　　　　　　　　　　　　　　　　　QBI94-21309

Printed in U.S.A.

INTRODUCTION

Welcome to the COMPENDIUM OF AMERICAN RAILROAD RADIO FREQUENCIES. Data in this book comes from license and allocation information of the Association of American Railroads and the Federal Communications Commission, railroad industry communication professionals, and many railroad enthusiasts. The authors combine more than 40 years' experience in monitoring, analyzing, and consulting in railroad radio systems.

This book includes frequencies for railroad lines in the United States, Canada, and Mexico. Frequencies used in Mexico are different from those used the United States and Canada and are listed in the International section, along with frequencies used in Australia, England, Ireland, Germany, New Zealand, and Sweden.

A HISTORY OF RAILROAD USE OF RADIO

Radio emerged as a communication link in the railroad industry around 1910, when a Union Pacific switch engine was equipped with equipment so the crew could receive orders by radio. Prior to the use of radio, dispatchers used written train orders to communicate with engine and train crews. Crew members communicated with each other using hand signals by day and lanterns by night. Telegraph served as the communication link between stations.

A few eastern lines experimented with two-way radio systems in the medium-wave band in the 1920s. The Federal Radio Commission (which became the Federal Communications Commission in 1934) allocated a band exclusively for railroad use between 2250 and 2380 kilohertz (KHz). It was one of several frequency groups just above the AM commercial broadcasting band — 540 to 1600 KHz — that were developed for industrial and public-safety use.

Wireless communication was successfully used in the railroad industry in 1937 when the Bessemer & Lake Erie introduced carrier induction train phones, a half-radio, half-telephone communication system. This device transmitted a low-power, low-frequency signal to any continuous metallic structure, which could be rails, telephone lines, or catenary. The system was successful because it remained stable in a rough operating environment.

The Pennsylvania Railroad installed inductive phones on its main line between Harrisburg and Pittsburgh in 1942. Space was limited on steam engines and cabooses, so antennas took the form of large vertical disks. Other roads using inductive phones were Kansas City Southern and Denver & Rio Grande Western.

Disadvantages of the inductive phone system included a short range in air, large antennas, and heavy power requirements. Caboose batteries were quickly exhausted and portable operation was impossible. Train crews noticed interference where phone and telegraph lines were used as the conducting medium, particularly when two or more users transmitted simultaneously.

Two-way radio in the VHF band of 30 to 300 megahertz (MHz) using a new mode called frequency modulation (FM) provided needed improvement, but despite some commercial development, the equipment was unreliable. During World War II the system was improved, and there were experiments in the use of higher frequencies, where antennas could be more compact and better suited to mobile service.

The Federal Communications Commission (FCC) allocated VHF frequencies from 158.1 MHz to 162.0 MHz to the railroads in 1944. It stipulated that channels were to be spaced 0.06 MHz apart, making 66 channels available. Among the first railroads to use this technology were the Erie and the Denver & Rio Grande Western.

Communications systems developed under this plan were referred to as "four-way radio." Medium-wave radio was two-way in its end-to-end usage, and inductive phone was "three-way" with the use of base stations, but those two systems did not provide access off-line. The VHF-FM system allowed use by automobiles, maintenance equipment, and portable devices.

The Association of American Railroads (AAR) was designated to be the coordinator for frequency assignments at the start of VHF-FM frequency development. The AAR surveyed the railroad industry to establish operating areas and terminal locations. Chicago, where many railroads converged, was used as the control point in resolving conflicts. From this survey a scheme was developed which continues today, the AAR Frequency Allocation Plan.

Advances in this technology were recognized in 1949 by the World Administrative Radio Conference (WARC), an international body which coordinates radio usage treaties. WARC officials adopted narrow-band FM for the VHF communication system, allowing channel spacing to be cut in half to 0.03 MHz (30 KHz).

When channel spacing was reduced and the number of channels increased, pressure was placed on the FCC by non-railroad VHF users for more frequencies. The FCC decided to reduce the U. S. railroad band to its present size, 160.230 to 161.550 MHz. Since the development of railroad radio use was still in its early stages, the railroads saw no problem in the decrease in available channels from 66 to 45.

The band reduction and the adoption of narrow-band FM meant that equipment in use had to be replaced or modified, and some users had to change frequencies. One interesting exception which remains today is 161.610 MHz, which was "grandfathered" to the now-defunct Chicago, Rock Island & Pacific.

In 1959 WARC decided to again cut in half the spacing between channels to 15 KHz, which is the current form of the VHF railroad band. Some railroads had to modify and replace equipment to meet these new specifications. The system in use today has 91 frequencies from 160.215 to 161.565 MHz, plus the 161.610 MHz channel in limited use as allowed in 1949.

WARC also recognized the international commercial marine bands of 160.625-160.975 and 161.475-162.025 MHz during its 1959 meeting. The existing use of radio by U. S. and Canadian railroads had to be accommodated by a footnote in the resulting treaty. This exception put railroad radio use at risk during the 1979 WARC meeting when maritime interests asserted their needs. It could be a source of future problems as radio band space becomes scarce.

The general adoption of UHF radios for two-way communication in 1959 resulted in less generous treatment of the railroads. Only six frequencies comprising three paired channels — 452.900/457.900, 452.925/457.925, and 452.950/457.950 — were allocated to exclusive railroad use. WARC decided in 1979 to allow 12.5 KHz spacing between UHF channels, but added only two more channel pairs,

4

452.9125/457.9125 and 452.9375/457.9375. This change did not require equipment replacement.

TODAY'S TRENDS

The railroad mergers of the 1970s and 1980s resulted in major changes in channel use. Entire radio systems were converted to reflect new ownership. While consolidation idled many active channels in some areas, the trend has reversed in the 1990s, with a movement toward regional and divisional channel assignments.

Radio has been responsible for the disappearance of the caboose in mainline freight service. Radio-relayed indication of trainline air pressure (end-of-train telemetry) and electronic inspection of mechanical condition by automatic wayside defect detectors, which relay train-condition messages to the crew by radio, have eliminated the need for crew at the rear of trains.

Centralized traffic control (CTC) has eliminated the need for stations housing agents, telephones, typewriters, and pads of train-order forms. Rules have been modified to allow train crews to take operating orders directly from the dispatcher by radio in a system called Direct Train Control.

There has also been a decline in railroad-specific radiotelephone systems known as PBXs, which flourished during the 1980s. With the advancement of cellular phone systems railroads are relying more on the phone companies.

NEW SYSTEMS

Railroads are showing increasing reliance on digital (computer) communication. Burlington Northern is advancing a number of systems, including an automatic train location program that transmits a short burst of digital information along with voice transmission. BN is also exploring control of track switches by radio command from the locomotive.

"Voiceless" radio dispatching of trains is still in its infancy. The system includes computer terminals in locomotives, on which track layout, orders, and procedures are displayed.

TYPES OF RADIO SYSTEMS

In one-frequency simplex the radios transmit and receive on the same frequency, but cannot do both at the same time. Two-frequency simplex uses one frequency in one direction and another for return communications. It is normally used for base-to-mobile communications. The transmit and receive frequencies in the base station are reversed from those in the mobile unit.

The repeater has a receiver connected to a transmitter, which allows automatic retransmissions from mobile units to stronger, wider-coverage base stations. Thus, mobile units can communicate with each other over the entire range of the base station rather than being limited to line-of-sight range.

A variation of the repeater system is the PBX system combining range-extension with the repeater, including automatic connections to telephone systems.

AAR CHANNEL IDENTIFICATION NUMBERING SYSTEM

For many years, when a run-through train passed from one railroad to another its radio had to be changed to the frequency of the new railroad. This has been changed by the introduction of the 97-channel synthesized locomotive radio. Now when a run-through train enters tracks owned by another company, the engineer dials the appropriate channel number for that railroad.

The AAR has assigned channel numbers to each of the 96 radio frequencies used in the United States and Canada. Channels 2-6 are used for rail operations only in Canada; railroads in the U. S. use channels 3-6 for truck operations. Most new radios have an indicator window that displays a four digit number like 8080 — the first two digits are the transmission channel and the last two digits are the receiving channel. For example, 8080 represents 161.310 MHz transmission frequency and 161.310 MHz receiving frequency. Here are a few examples:

Ch.	Freq.	Ch.	Freq.	Ch.	Freq.	Ch.	Freq.
02	159.810	26	160.500	50	160.860	74	161.220
03	159.930	27	160.515	51	160.875	75	161.235
04	160.050	28	160.530	52	160.890	76	161.250
05	160.185	29	160.545	53	160.905	77	161.265
06	160.200	30	160.560	54	160.920	78	161.280
07	160.215	31	160.575	55	160.935	79	161.295
08	160.230	32	160.590	56	160.950	80	161.310
09	160.245	33	160.605	57	160.965	81	161.325
10	160.260	34	160.620	58	160.980	82	161.340
11	160.275	35	160.635	59	160.995	83	161.355
12	160.290	36	160.650	60	161.010	84	161.370
13	160.305	37	160.665	61	161.025	85	161.385
14	160.320	38	160.680	62	161.040	86	161.400
15	160.335	39	160.695	63	161.055	87	161.415
16	160.350	40	160.710	64	161.070	88	161.430
17	160.365	41	160.725	65	161.085	89	161.445
18	160.380	42	160.740	66	161.100	90	161.460
19	160.395	43	160.755	67	161.115	91	161.475
20	160.410	44	160.770	68	161.130	92	161.490
21	160.425	45	160.785	69	161.145	93	161.505
22	160.440	46	160.800	70	161.160	94	161.520
23	160.455	47	160.815	71	161.175	95	161.535
24	160.470	48	160.830	72	161.190	96	161.550
25	160.485	49	160.845	73	161.205	97	161.565

Road	Window number	Transmission frequency	Receiving frequency	Example
BRC	2626	160.500	160.500	Road and dispatcher
BAR	3838	160.680	160.680	Yard
FEC	2844	160.530	160.770	Road and dispatcher
B&M	9470	161.520	161.160	Ch 1 dispatcher
B&M	8686	161.400	161.400	Ch 2 road and yard

TERMS USED IN THIS BOOK

Road: The road channel is the most important channel for the railroad (and rail enthusiasts). Train crews operating on the main line use this channel to communicate with each other and with stations. Typical uses of radio include instructions for delivery of cars, issuance of train orders, and warning of unusual or emergency conditions.

Vehicles of supervisory and maintenance personnel are equipped with radios so they can use the road channel to advise train crews of conditions that need to be corrected. Employees who work along the track often contact the dispatcher by radio to determine when trains will pass their locations so they can clear the tracks.

Maintenance of way: Section crews, track supervisors, and communications, signal, and engineering department employees have radios in their vehicles. They communicate with trains and the dispatcher on the road and dispatcher channels. Some railroads assign a frequency to maintenance workers for communication with each other.

Talking hot box detectors (HBD) and **dragging equipment detectors (DED):** A number of railroads have installed electronic hot box detectors, dragging equipment detectors, and wide-load detectors along the right-of-way to transmit warnings of defects. Talking HBDs and DEDs ("talkers") are a recent innovation. They digitally analyze the information they collect and issue a status report using a recorded or synthesized voice broadcasting on the road channel. Talkers usually identify the railroad, town, state, milepost, track number, train condition and direction, and number of axles. They are spaced approximately 20 miles apart on most main lines.

Talkers provide important information to train crews; they tell railroad enthusiasts where trains are located. When you hear a talker reporting from a milepost location, it is helpful to know what milepost you are near.

Locotrol: Slave units, which are engines in the middle or at the rear of a train, work automatically in response to controls transmitted by radio from the lead locomotive. They save the cost of a helper-locomotive crew and improve braking speed and efficiency. Commands are transmitted to the slave unit as digital code. The radio transceiver on the slave unit receives these commands, acknowledges receipt to the lead locomotive, controls the slave locomotive, and notifies the lead unit that the command has been carried out. Several sets of slave units may operate at the same time in the same vicinity without interfering with each other.

The FCC has allocated two exclusive frequency pairs, 452.925/457.925 MHz and 452.950/457.950 MHz, for slave and hump locomotive speed control, and they may be used only for that purpose. These frequencies carry only coded digital information; their use indicates a train with slave units is nearby.

End-of-train telemetry: Railroads have replaced cabooses with electronic devices on the rear of the train that monitor the condition of the train and relay that data to the locomotive. End-of-train monitors (ETM) are mounted on the coupler on the last car and attached to the brake hose. Even when the train is not moving they transmit a signal about every 40 seconds; if the train status changes, a signal is sent immediately.

To facilitate run-through trains, the AAR has assigned ETMs a single radio frequency of 457.9375 MHz at a maximum power output of 2 watts. The signal will travel 3 to 5 miles under favorable conditions, but information cannot be discerned without special digital electronics. Most U. S. railroads use the AAR frequency, but Norfolk Southern uses 161.115 MHz at 5 watts.

Yard: As trains approach major yards, crews switch their radios from the road channel to the yard channel to contact the yardmaster for instructions. The yard channel is also used to communicate instructions for breaking up trains. A special yard channel, the pulldown channel, is used when trains are assembled.

Hump: In hump yards cars are pushed over a hill where they are uncoupled and roll down into classification tracks. Switches direct them into different tracks, and automatic retarders reduce their speed so they can couple to other cars without excessive impact. In some hump yards radio is used to relay voice instructions to the engine crew and to issue instructions for trimming the yard — pushing cars that have not rolled far enough and retrieving cars that have gone down the wrong track. In other hump yards the hump locomotive is controlled remotely by radio. This system is compatible with that used for slave locomotives and uses the same frequency.

Car department: At each yard or terminal, the cars of departing trains must be inspected to ensure safe operating condition. This is the job of the car or mechanical department. Most large yards have at least one channel assigned exclusively to the car department. Some larger yards use repeaters for greater coverage.

Diesel shop: Many large railroads have their own locomotive rebuilding facilities. These shops are usually quite active and often have pakset/repeater systems (walkie-talkies) similar to the car department systems, but on their own channels.

Stores department: The supply room at a large repair facility is often a separate department called the stores department. Repair parts and materials used by shop workers are kept here. Some of the larger stores departments have their own exclusive radio channels, and employees sometimes use walkie-talkie repeater systems.

Piggyback: Large piggyback facilities usually have at least one exclusive radio channel. The employees who move trailers to the flat cars use it to keep in contact with their office and the crane operators. In addition, employees on the ground use remote control radios to operate cranes.

Trucking: Several railroads have subsidiary trucking companies. They have their own dispatchers who keep in contact with truck drivers by radio. Sometimes the frequencies used are in the railroad band, sometimes in the trucking band.

Freight agent: The freight agent is the railroad employee responsible for writing waybills, written instructions for the movement of each car. Agents conduct most of their work by telephone from a central location. In some areas traveling agents call on shippers in person. Since they cover a large area, their vehicles are equipped with mobile telephones or special channels on the railroad band so shippers can contact them while they are out of their offices.

Commissary: The commissary is a storehouse for food and beverage supplies used on railroad dining cars. Amtrak commissaries at a few locations have their own radio channels, which are used to communicate with employees who haul supplies to the dining and lounge cars in the yard.

Wrecker: A wrecker is a heavy crane which lifts derailed cars and locomotives back onto the rails. Radio is often used to communicate instructions to the wrecker operator.

Car ferry: Barges or car ferries are used in some locations to move railroad cars across bodies of water. In North America, this activity occurs principally in New York City, on the Great Lakes, in British Columbia, and to and from Alaska. Radio is used to coordinate the loading and unloading of these barges and car ferries.

General operations: This is an all-encompassing category, usually only applicable to short lines where all communications occur on one channel.

Dispatcher: The dispatcher coordinates and directs all mainline train movements. The combination of channels used for communication between the dispatcher and the train crews varies from railroad to railroad.

On some roads, Southern Pacific and Union Pacific, for example, train crews and dispatchers transmit on the road channel. On others, such as Florida East Coast, two frequencies are used. The dispatcher transmits on the road frequency and crews transmit on a train-to-dispatcher frequency; the dispatcher monitors only that channel. A third system uses three frequencies for road, dispatcher to train, and train to dispatcher.

Dispatcher link: These channels receive transmissions from trains on the road channel and retransmit the information on the link channel. Monitoring the link channel makes it possible to hear trains at greater distances than would normally be possible.

PBX: Railroad mobile telephone service allows the radios in vehicles of supervisors and work crews to be connected to the railroad's telephone system, which is called a PBX (Private Branch eXchange).

Pairs of dedicated frequencies are used for PBX service. The base stations are located on tall radio or microwave towers along the railroad route. The radios operate as a repeater system with the base transmitting on one channel and the mobile transmitting on another. The base stations normally repeat what they receive from the mobile units and broadcast the base communications. Both sides of a conversation can be heard on the base station output frequency, making it unnecessary to monitor the mobile frequency. Some railroads use different repeater pairs for different geographical areas; others use only one system-wide.

Crew caller: When a departure time is established for a train, the crew dispatcher or crew caller determines who will operate it and notifies them when to report for work. When the crew reports to the office, it is transported to the train by a company vehicle which is sometimes equipped with its own radio channel to maintain contact with the crew caller.

Police: Large railroads usually have their own police departments. Railroad police, also called special agents, communicate with trains on the road channel and sometimes use a separate police channel. Police departments of various railroads in Chicago, St. Louis, Omaha, Pittsburgh, Houston, Kansas City, and Memphis, and along the Northeast Corridor coordinate their efforts on a mutual aid channel, 161.205 MHz. In Detroit the Conrail, CSX, Norfolk Southern, and Grand Trunk Western police departments now work together, and Grand Trunk Western dispatches calls to all these railroad police forces on 161.280 MHz. Chicago & North Western police in Chicago now use a 900-MHz trunked system; Illinois Central and Norfolk Southern police may be using a similar system.

Chicago Railroad Police Trunked System: 939.7625, 939.7750, 939.7875, 939.8000, 939.8125, 939.8250, 939.8375, 939.8500, 939.8625, 939.8750

Commuter: Commuter authorities often use a separate radio channel different from the road frequency of the host railroad.

AAR FREQUENCY ALLOCATION DEFINITIONS

End-to-end and point-to-train is a category that covers assignments for all radio communications with trains. These designations are assigned system-wide and carry the highest priority.

End-to-end (EE): Communication between the ends of a train.

Point-to-train (PT): Communication between wayside base stations and a train.

Right-of-way (RW): A category that covers assignments for radio communications primarily along the railroad right-of-way. This designation usually is for services which are not directly involved with train operations, such as maintenance, supervision, mobile telephone systems (PBX), police, and signal department.

General (G): Any frequency assigned to other than train or right-of-way service, and designated for such services as yard, switching, hump, hump cab signals, pull-down switching, car department, diesel shop, auto unloading site, van site, railroad trucking, stores department, crew dispatcher, remote data links, and car ferry or float operations.

Mobile relay (MR): Any frequency that is expected to be used for repeater service.

RAILROADS THAT DON'T USE RADIO

The following railroads were found with no licenses on file in the FCC Land Mobile database issue of January 1993. It is possible that these railroads could have radios licensed under some other corporate name, but it is likely they do not use radio in railroad operations.

Arcade & Attica
Baltimore & Annapolis
Black Hills Central
Branford Electric Railway Assoc
Champaign
Connecticut Trolley Museum
Delta Valley & Southern
East Jersey Railroad & Terminal
East Troy Municipal
El Dorado & Wesson
Middletown & New Jersey
Mount Rainier Scenic
Northwestern Oklahoma
Parr Terminal
Pearl River Valley
Prescott & Northwestern
Quincy Railroad
Rosedale-Bolivar County Port Commission (Great River Railroad)
Southern San Luis Valley
Stewartstown
Towanda-Monroeton
Virginia & Truckee
Wanamaker, Kempton & Southern

EXPLANATION OF LISTINGS

Listings in this compendium are arranged in alphabetical order by railroad name, and the names are alphabetized letter by letter, ignoring spaces and punctuation (& is alphabetized as *and*; St. as *Saint*). Mountain Laurel precedes Mount Hood; St. Louis precedes Salt Lake. Under each railroad heading, the first frequencies listed are those used system-wide. Below them are the listings for individual cities and yards.

The authors hope you find this publication of use. We are grateful for your continuing support and patronage. Your information, contributions, and corrections are appreciated. If you find errors or omissions, please send the corrections to THE COMPENDIUM OF AMERICAN RAILROAD RADIO FREQUENCIES, Kalmbach Publishing Co., P. O. Box 1612, Waukesha, WI 53187.

ADDITIONAL SOURCES OF INFORMATION

Radio Communications Monitoring Association
P. O. Box 4563, Anaheim, CA 92803
Monthly newsletter with a regular railroad radio column

Extra 2200 South
P. O. Box 8110-820, Blaine, WA 98230
Quarterly magazine with a regular railroad radio column

Railfan & Railroad
P. O. Box 700, Newton, NJ 07860
Monthly magazine; radio frequencies are listed with articles on specific railroads

TRAINS
Kalmbach Publishing Co.
21027 Crossroads Circle, P. O. Box 1612, Waukesha, WI 53187
Monthly magazine; radio frequencies are listed with articles on specific railroads

The Short Line
P. O. Box 607-T, Pleasant Grove, NC 27313
Bimonthly magazine covering shortline railroads

All Ohio Scanner Club
50 Villa Road, Springfield, OH 45503
Bimonthly newsletter with a regular railroad radio column covering Ohio and surrounding states

Canadian Trackside Guide
Bytown Railway Society, Inc.
P. O. Box 141, Station A, Ottawa, ON K1N 8V1, Canada
Annual book with rosters and radio frequencies

THE TRAIN-WATCHER'S GUIDE TO NORTH AMERICAN RAILROADS
Kalmbach Publishing Co.
21027 Crossroads Circle, P. O. Box 1612, Waukesha, WI 53187
Brief descriptions and statistics of North America's major railroads, commuter carriers, and regional railroads

AMERICAN SHORTLINE RAILWAY GUIDE
Kalmbach Publishing Co.
21027 Crossroads Circle, P. O. Box 1612, Waukesha, WI 53187
Brief descriptions and statistics of North America's short lines and regional railroads

AMATEUR RADIO FREQUENCIES FOR RAILFANS

A number of rail enthusiasts who hold Amateur Radio Service ("ham") licenses have found the two hobbies can complement each other during railfan events. The frequencies listed to the right have been used to establish QSOs (radio contacts) with other "railhams" during scheduled and impromptu meetings. You may want to add these frequencies to your selection of channels during rail events.

2 meter	146.490	Primary channel
2 meter	146.565	Secondary (backup) channel
1.25 meter	223.620	
70 cm	466.050	
23 cm	1294.425	

73! — Gary N9IJB

ABBREVIATIONS AND DEFINITIONS

Auto Site	Automobile unloading site
Base	Fixed radio locations
B&B	Bridges & Buildings Department; maintains bridges and buildings
C&S	Communications and signals
Car Dept.	Car men, car inspectors, car knockers
Car Ferry	Self-contained boat that carries freight cars
Car Float	Barge that carries freight cars and is pulled by a tug boat
Car Shop	Car repair facility
Cont.	Control
Disp.	Dispatcher
EE	End-to-end (From AAR Frequency Allocation Plan)
ET	Electric traction; includes maintenance of electrical distribution systems as well as the power dispatcher
FCC	Federal Communications Commission license issued on this frequency
FRT	Freight
G	General use (From AAR Frequency Allocation Plan)
Intermodal Facility	Trailer or container loading and unloading operation
Inter-Plant	Between industrial plants
Intra-Plant	Within an industrial plant

Jt. Ops.	Used in joint operations with another railroad
K	kilohertz
MDT	Mobile data terminal
MofE	Maintenance of equipment
MofW	Maintenance of way
MR	Mobile Repeater AAR Frequency Allocation
PBX	Mobile telephone
Police	Railroad police, special agents
Power Dispatcher	Person who controls the distribution of electric power to third rail and catenary supply systems.
PT	Point-to-train (from AAR Frequency Allocation Plan)
Talk-Around	Of the two channels used by a repeater, the one that is used for local conversation when the repeater is not activated or required. It is usually the repeater output channel.
TX	Transmit
Utility	Miscellaneous-use channel
USSB	Upper Single Sideband radio modulation
XXX.xxx/YYY.yyy	Repeater output/repeater input
•	Indicates new listing
Δ	Indicates frequencies used by Amtrak trains while operating on host railroad
~	Indicates unverified but possible channel use

RAILROADS OF THE UNITED STATES AND CANADA

A&G Railroad   Dothan, Alabama
160.545	Inter-plant switching

Aberdeen & Rockfish   Aberdeen, North Carolina
161.280		Ch 1 Road and repeater output
Raeford		
161.280	160 .530	Ch 2 Road repeater

Aberdeen, Carolina & Western   Charlotte, North Carolina
160.680	General operations

Adrian & Blissfield   Adrian, Michigan
160.650	General operations

Akron & Barberton Belt   Barberton, Ohio
160.650	General operations

Alabama & Florida   Opp, Alabama
461.150	466.150	General operations
160.380		FCC – Base and mobile

Alabama Railroad   Corduroy, Alabama
160.500	General operations
160.695	General operations

Alameda Belt Line   Alameda, California
160.935	General operations

Alaska Railroad   Anchorage, Alaska
160.305	Data Telemetry or Phone Patch (Proposed)
164.625	Ch 1 Road and dispatcher to train
161.355	Ch 1 Road (Proposed)
165.3375	Ch 2 Train to dispatcher
161.385	Ch 2 Dispatcher (Proposed)
165.2625	Ch 3 Yard and Police
161.415	Ch 3 Yard and Police (Proposed)
164.9875	Ch 4 Gravel train loading
161.445	Ch 4 Gravel train loading (Proposed)
161.475	Ch 5 MofW (Proposed) – Seward, Whittier, Willow, Gold Creek, Nenana, Fairbanks
161.505	Ch 6 MofW (Proposed) – Lawing, Rainbow, Wasilla, Hurricane
161.535	Ch 7 MofW (Proposed) – Moose Pass, Anchorage, Summit, Cantwell
161.565	Ch 8 MofW (Proposed) – Portage, Anchorage, Talkeetna, Garner
166.375	Ch 9 or 10 Phone Patch
171.725	Ch 11 Phone Patch

Albany Port District   Albany, New York
161.355	General operations

Alberta Resources Railway (operated by Canadian National)
160.485	161.295	Road and dispatcher
159.810	161.055	Road and dispatcher
161.415		Yard and CN Ch 1 Road

Alexander   Taylorsville, North Carolina
160.620   General operations

Algers, Winslow & Western   Oakland City, Indiana
160.575   General operations

Algoma Central   Sault Ste. Marie, Ontario
160.530   Ch 1 Road
160.575   Ch 2 Dispatcher – Hubert and Oba
160.605   Ch 3 Dispatcher – Northland and Helen
160.725   159.795 Ch 4 PBX – Northland and Helen
161.265   160.050 Ch 5 PBX – Hubert and Oba
160.995   Ch 6 Yard – A
161.355   Ch 7 Yard – B

Aliquippa & Southern   Aliquippa, Pennsylvania
161.010   Road and yard
161.490   Yard
161.100   MofW

Allegheny & Eastern   Warren, Pennsylvania
161.460   Road
160.290   161.460 Road repeater – Spartansburg and Ridgway
160.425   FCC – Base and mobile

Alma & Jonquiere   Alma, Quebec
160.020   Road
160.725   Dispatcher
160.650   Yard

Almanor   Chester, California
158.310   General operations

Alton & Southern   East St. Louis, Illinois
160.770   Ch 1 Road and dispatcher
160.335   Ch 2 Yard
160.560   Administration
160.905   North hump
161.445   South hump
161.145   Pulldown
161.175   Car Dept.

Amador Central   Martell, California
49.22   General operations

Amtrak   Washington, DC
452.900   Terminal services
160.305   On-board Manager – West of Chicago
160.440   On-board Manager – Portland to Klamath Falls,
                     Oregon; Oakland to Bakersfield, California; Oak-
                     land to Los Angeles
160.455   On-board Manager – Klamath Falls, Oregon, to
                     Oakland; Los Angeles to Kingman, Arizona
161.325   MofW
161.520   On-board Manager – Kingman, Arizona, to
                     La Junta, Colorado
New Orleans to Los Angeles
160.845   On-board Manager – Sunset Limited
160.440   On-board Manager – East of Alpine, Texas
160.650   On-board Manager – Alpine to Phoenix

160.740		On-board Manager – Alpine to Phoenix
160.455		On-board Manager – Phoenix to Los Angeles

Birmingham, Alabama
| 160.920 | | Switching |

Los Angeles, California
160.455		Terminal switching
452.900	457.900	Car Dept.
161.055	161.475	Police

Oakland, California
| 160.440 | | Car Dept. |

San Diego, California
| 161.055 | 161.475 | Police |

Denver, Colorado
| 161.550 | | Station Services |

Washington, D.C.
160.290	161.370	Ch 1 Road
160.350	161.145	Ch 2 Car Dept.
160.440	161.445	Ch 3 Administration and redcaps
160.800		Road – terminal area
160.365	161.295	Police

Bear, Delaware
| 161.445 | 160.425 | MofE |
| 161.280 | | Shop operations |

Wilmington, Delaware
| 161.445 | 160.425 | MofE |
| 452.900 | | Shop operations |

Sanford, Florida
| 160.845 | | Auto Train operations |
| 161.550 | | Switching |

Tampa, Florida
| 160.680 | | Tampa Union Station, MofE |

Atlanta, Georgia
| 160.920 | | Peachtree Station, Trains and Engine Crews |

Chicago, Illinois
160.305		Commissary and terminal road
160.740		Shop
161.265		Car Dept.
161.325	160.395	MofW and Signal Dept.
160.365	154.515	Amtrak/Union Station Police
161.205		Police-mutual aid

Indianapolis, Indiana
161.280		Beech Grove shop switcher
452.900		Beech Grove shop operations
457.900		Beech Grove shop operations
160.545		Police

Porter, Indiana, to Kalamazoo, Michigan
| 160.800 | | Road |

New Orleans, Louisiana
160.440		Clara Street Tower
161.055		MofW
160.335	161.415	Police

Boston, Massachusetts
| 160.635 | | South Station – Commissary and station services |
| 160.455 | | Southampton Yard – MofE |

(See Massachusetts Bay Transportation Authority for North Station)

Detroit, Michigan
| 161.505 | 160.245 | Police |

Minneapolis, Minnesota
| 160.380 | | Car Dept. |

Kansas City, Missouri
| 161.175 | | Car Dept. |

15

Amtrak

St Louis, Missouri
160.410   Car Dept.
452.900   Terminal services
Atlantic City, New Jersey
160.920   Road – Atlantic City Line
161.355   Stationmaster/station services
Newark, New Jersey
160.650   Station services
Trenton, New Jersey
160.650   Station services
Albany/Rensselaer, New York
160.635   Station services
457.900   Station administration
160.455   Turboliner shop – Yard
161.280   Turboliner shop – MofE
160.515 161.265 MofW
New York, New York – Penn Station
160.650   Station services
161.325 160.275 Car Dept.
452.900   Commissary and redcaps
New York, New York – West Side Line
160.920   Road
New York, New York – Sunnyside Yard
160.650   Yard
160.755 160.245 Car Dept.
Portland, Oregon
160.455   Yard
Philadelphia, Pennsylvania – 30th St Station
160.350   Road – SEPTA
160.350 161.265 Train Managers
160.455   Yard and work trains

160.650   Station services
452.900   Station administration
161.505 160.965 MofE
Dallas, Texas
160.440   Road and Car Dept.
160.500   Switching
San Antonio, Texas
160.440   Car Dept.
161.055   Yard
Salt Lake City, Utah
161.100   Station switching
Lorton, Virginia
160.845   Auto Train operations
Richmond, Virginia
457.900   Station services
Seattle, Washington
160.455   Yard
457.900   Station services
Washington to Boston
160.365 457.900 Police – Portable/Mobile repeater
160.455   Work trains and yard – except Sunnyside Yard
160.515 161.115 MofW
160.815   Ch 2 Police – Car to car
161.205   Ch 4 Police – Car to car
161.295 160.365 Ch 3 Police – Base to car
452.900 161.295 Police – Portable/Mobile repeater
New Haven to Boston
160.635   Station services
160.920   Road
New York to New Haven
161.160   Electric traction

161.280   Road – Metro-North
Washington to New York
160.650   Station services
160.920   Road

Angelina & Neches River   Lufkin, Texas

161.280   General operations

Ann Arbor   Toledo, Ohio

161.490   General operations
161.355   General operations
161.490   Road and Ottawa Yard, Toledo

Apache Railway   Snowflake, Arizona

452.900   457.900   Road and dispatcher
161.520   Yard and end-to-end
453.7375   Yard
Holbrook
452.825   457.825   Yard

Apalachicola Northern   Port St. Joe, Florida

160.380   160.980   Road
160.500   Port St. Joe Yard

Appanoose County Community Railroad   Centerville, Iowa

161.265   General operations

Arizona & California   Parker, Arizona

160.860   General operations
452.900   Dispatcher link

Arizona Central   Clarkdale, Arizona

160.560   General operations
461.450   466.450   FCC
462.100   467.100   FCC

Arizona Eastern   Claypool, Arizona

161.355   160.245   Ch 1 Road (Signal Peak, Globe)
160.215   161.475   Ch 2 Road (Moonshine Hill, Miami)
161.355   Ch 3 Talk-around
160.275   Ch 4
160.935   Ch 5
160.530   Ch 6

Arkansas & Missouri   Springdale, Arkansas

160.440   Ch 1 Road
160.785   Ch 2 Yard
161.160   Ch 3 BN Interchange
161.475   Ch 4 MofW
451.400   456.400   Dispatcher links – Springdale-Winslow-Fort Smith, Arkansas; Springdale to Exeter, Missouri

Arkansas Midland   Hot Springs, Arkansas

160.275   161.460   Road
160.905   Yard

Arkansas Louisiana & Mississippi   Monroe, Louisiana

160.980   General operations

Arnaud Railway   Pointe-Noire, Quebec

160.860   Road

160.980	Road	
160.050	Yard	
160.395	Yard	

Aroostook Valley — Presque Isle, Maine

464.950	General operations
160.890	Base and mobile

Asbestos & Danville — Asbestos, Quebec

160.605	Yard
160.995	Yard

Ashland Railway — Mansfield, Ohio

160.965	General operations
452.900	General operations

Ashley, Drew & Northern — Crossett, Arkansas

160.710	Road and yard
160.770	Road and yard
161.535	Yard and MofW
161.610	Yard

Atchison, Topeka & Santa Fe

160.650	Ch 1 Road
160.935	Ch 3 Road
161.190	Ch 4 Road
160.590	Ch 5 Road
161.010	MofW, except Kansas City
161.205	Police – mutual aid
457.9375	End-of-rain telemetry
160.560	MofW – Alternate

160.245	161.490	PBX P-1

Illinois: Lemont, Princeton
Missouri: Elkhorn,

160.245	161.535	PBX P-2

Arizona: Peach Springs
California: Cadiz, Hanford, Los Angeles, Mount Bullion, Richmond, Stockton
Colorado: Cheyenne Mtn. (Colorado Springs), Lamar
Kansas: Dodge City, Hutchinson, Manhattan, Topeka
Missouri: Marceline
New Mexico: Adamana, Clovis, Raton
Oklahoma: Moore, Tangier
Texas: Anton, Fluvanna, Haslet, Hitchcock

160.260	161 .490	PBX P-3

Arizona: Glendale, Sanders, Willams
California: Barstow, Goffs Mountain, Hanford
Illinois: Dallas City, Edelstein
Kansas: Arkansas City, Concordia, Hudson, Syracuse, Walton
New Mexico: Artesia, Yeso
Oklahoma: Davis
Texas: Amarillo, Copperas Cove, Lyons

160.335	161 .460	PBX P-4

Arizona: Kingman, Winslow, Yarnell
California: Bakersfield, Crestline, Ludlow Mountain, Oceanside
Colorado: Cheraw
Illinois: Dallas City, Gallup Hill
Kansas: Denton, Emporia, Garden City, Kansas

		City, Kiowa, Wichita
		New Mexico: Boaz, Las Vegas
		Texas: Buffalo Gap, Gainesville, Silsbee
160.425	161.295	PBX P-5
		California: Fresno
		Illinois: Galesburg
		Kansas: Argonia, Elmdale, Spearsville, Wellington
		Missouri: Carrollton, Laplata
		New Mexico: Krider, Socorro
		Oklahoma: Perry
		Texas: Cedar Hill, Houston, Miami, Spur Mountain, Sudan, Sweetwater, Temple
160.335	161.295	PBX P-6 – Ransom, Illinois
160.830	161.490	PBX P-7
		Illinois: Chicago
		Kansas: Princeton
160.425		PBX – Mount Diablo, California
161.085	161.280	PBX – Sierra Peak, California

Arizona
Glendale
| 161.370 | Yard |
| 161.190 | Intermodal facility |

California
Bakersfield
| 161.370 | Yard and car checkers |
| 161.190 | Intermodal facility |
Barstow – Barstow Yard
161.145	Main hump
160.305	Mini hump
452.925	Hump cab signals

161.250		West Yard #1
161.280		West Yard #2
161.445		West Yard #3
161.370		West Yard calling channel
160.530		East Yard #4
160.770		East Yard #5
160.275		East Yard #6
160.560		East Yard Calling channel
160.980		Hump maintenance and supervisory
160.440	161.565	Diesel service
161.340	160.215	Diesel shop
452.900	457.900	Car Dept.

Fresno
161.370	Yard
161.190	Trucking
452.900	Intermodal facility
Los Angeles
161.370		Yard
161.070	160.440	Car Dept.
161.190		Intermodal facility
161.205		Police
Richmond
161.370	Yard 1
161.145	Yard
160.365	Yard
160.590	Yard
160.905	Yard and Car Dept.
160.395	North Bay UPS
160.560	North Bay UPS
161.190	Intermodal facility
160.785	Emergency

19

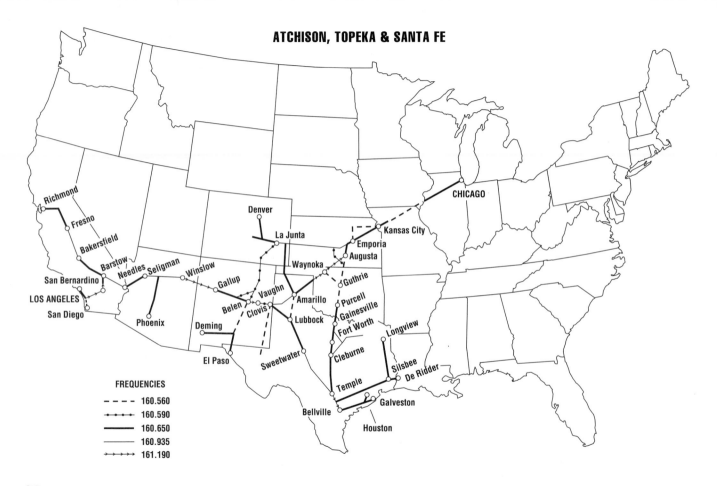

ATCHISON, TOPEKA & SANTA FE

FREQUENCIES

- – – – 160.560
- •••• 160.590
- ▬▬▬ 160.650
- ──── 160.935
- ►►►► 161.190

Richmond
Fresno
Bakersfield
Barstow
San Bernardino
Needles
Seligman
LOS ANGELES
San Diego
Phoenix
Winslow
Gallup
Vaughn
Belen
Clovis
Deming
El Paso
Sweetwater
Denver
La Junta
Waynoka
Amarillo
Lubbock
Cleburne
Temple
Bellville
Houston
Galveston
Kansas City
Emporia
Augusta
Guthrie
Purcell
Gainesville
Fort Worth
Longview
Silsbee
De Ridder
CHICAGO

20

San Bernardino
161.280	160.215	Diesel shop

Stockton
161.370	Yard 1
161.190	Yard

Summit
452.925	457.925	Locotrol repeater

Tehachapi
160.650	Ch 1 Road (Southern Pacific trackage rights)

Colorado
Denver – Big Lift Yard
160.110	ATSF Trucking
160.560	Intermodal facility

La Junta
161.370	Yard

Pueblo
160.560	Yard
161.100	MofW

Iowa
Fort Madison
161.370	Yard

Illinois
Chicago – Corwith Yard
160.995	Yard 3
160.785	Hump
159.705	ATSF Trucking
161.385	Intermodal facility
161.205	Police
220.8675	FCC
221.8675	FCC

Kansas
Kansas City
161-010		Traffic control
160.650		Tall Tower
160.845		Turner Tower
161.370		Yard
160.215		Eastbound hump
161.370		Westbound hump
160.905	161.535	Diesel shop
160.950	161.475	Eastbound Car Dept.
452.900	457.900	Westbound Car Dept.
159.555		ATSF Trucking
161.040		Intermodal facility
160.560		Crew cabs
161.205		Police
161.265		Police – mutual aid
220.8825		FCC
221.8825		FCC

Newton
161.370	160.440	Stores Dept.

Topeka
452.900	457.900	Diesel house
161.370	160.440	Car Dept.
159.495		ATSF Trucking
161.190		Building security
452.775	457.775	Building maintenance
452.875		Pagers

Wellington
161.190	160.485	Car Dept.
161.370		Yard

Atchison, Topeka & Santa Fe

Wichita
160.650		Yard
161.275		Yard

New Mexico
Albuquerque
161.370		Yard
160.560		Division Engineer
452.900	457.900	MofW equipment shop
160.110		ATSF Trucking

Belen
160.860		Terminal
161.370		Yard
161.250	160.440	Car Dept.

Clovis
160.290		Yard
161.250		Yard
161.370	160.440	Car Dept.
452.900		Pagers

Hanover
160.650	161.370	Crew cab to road repeater

Raton
452.925	457.925	Locotrol repeater

Oklahoma
Alliance
161.370		Yard 1
161.070		Yard
160.440		Yard
160.275		Intermodal facility

Oklahoma City
161.280		89th Street Yard – Hump
161.085		89th Street Yard – Switching Crew 1
161.175		89th Street Yard – Switching Crew 2
161.235		Flynn Yard
161.370		General Motors Yard
161.415		General Motors Yard – Switching Crew 1
161.505		General Motors Yard – Switching Crew 2
160.440		Mechanical Dept.
160.200		ATSF Trucking
160.215		Intermodal facility and ATSF Trucks

Tulsa
160.200		ATSF Trucking

Texas
Amarillo
160.770		Joint yard with Burlington Northern
161.370		Yard
160.440		Welded Rail Plant operation
160.935		Welded Rail Plant emergency train stop

Beaumont
161.415		Southern Pacific joint operation

Brownwood
161.280		Yard
161.370		Yard

Cleburne
160.275		Stores Dept.
160.875	161.505	Car Dept.

Dallas
161.370		Yard
161.190		Zacha Junction intermodal facility
159.585		ATSF Trucking

Fort Worth
161.370		Saginaw Yard
160.560		Saginaw Yard Yellow switcher – 2

159.585		ATSF Trucking

Houston

161.190		Yard
160.560		Pearland Yard 2
159.570		ATSF Trucking
161.475		Intermodal facility, trucks

Lubbock

161.370		Yard

Silsbee

161.370		Yard

Somerville

160.560		Tie treating plant operations

Temple

161.475		Yard
160.875	161.505	Car Dept.
452.900		Pagers

Dispatcher links

160.905	Cutler to Calwa, California
161.070	Yarnell to Hillside, Arizona
161.085	Garden City to Scott City, Kansas
161.190	Hanston to Dodge City, Kansas
161.235	Great Bend to Rush Center, Kansas
161.235	Webber to Concordia, Kansas
161.235	Fort Worth to Cresson, Texas
161.355	Lyons to McPherson, Kansas
161.355	Tiffany to Socorro, New Mexico
161.370	Carlsbad to Rustler, New Mexico (MP 212)
161.370	Rincon to Rincon Hill, New Mexico
161.370	Springer to Levy, New Mexico
161.370	Las Vegas to Blanchard, New Mexico
161.370	Longpoint to Stephenville, Texas
161.385	Copville to Temple, Texas
161.445	Enid to Jet, Oklahoma
161.445	Alva to Jet, Oklahoma
161.475	Springer to York Canyon, New Mexico
161.475	Carlsbad to Pecos Junction, New Mexico (MP 212)
161.475	La Junta to Delhi, Colorado
161.520	Ingalls to Satanta, Kansas
161.565	Newton to Hillsboro, Kansas
161.565	Las Vegas to Valmora, New Mexico
161.565	McPherson to Hillsboro, Kansas
452.825	Parnell to Midland, Kansas
452.900	Grand Summit to Arkansas City, Kansas
452.900	Comanche to Zephyr, Texas
452.900	Goldthwaite to Zephyr, Texas
452.900	Crescent to Guthrie, Oklahoma
452.900	Hope to Yarnell, Arizona
452.900	Olivet to Emporia, Kansas
452.900	Rice to Cadiz, California
452.900	Cassoday to Eldorado, Kansas
452.900	Cassoday to Walton, Kansas
452.900	Perry to Pawnee, Oklahoma
452.900	Domingo to Lamy, New Mexico
452.900	Frick to Hasty, Colorado
457.825	Midland to Parnell, Kansas
457.900	Chanute to Buxton, Kansas
457.900	Arkansas City to Grand Summit, Kansas
457.900	Zephyr to Comanche, Texas
457.900	Zephyr to Goldthwaite , Texas
457.900	Guthrie to Crescent, Oklahoma
457.900	Yarnell to Hope, Arizona

Atlanta – Batten

457.900		Emporia to Olivet, Kansas
457.900		Cadiz to Rice, California
457.900		Eldorado to Cassoday, Kansas
457.900		Walton to Cassoday, Kansas
457.900		Pawnee to Perry, Oklahoma
457.900		Lamy to Domingo, New Mexico
457.900		Hasty to Frick, Colorado
462.275	467.275	Richmond to Summit, California (160.650)
462.425	467.425	Richmond to Summit, California (161.190)

Atlanta & St. Andrews Bay Dothan, Alabama
160.770	Ch 1 Road
161.295	Ch 2 Road and yard
160.455	Yard
160.815	MofW

Atlanta, Stone Mountain & Lithonia Lithonia, Georgia
161.025	General operations (quarry switching)

Atlantic & Gulf Albany, Georgia
160.500	General operations
161.190	Alternate

Atlantic & Western Sanford, North Carolina
160.275	General operations

Austin & Northwestern Austin, Texas
161.520	General operations
160.305	General operations

Austin, Todd & Ladd Watonga, Oklahoma
160.785	Ch 1 General operations
160.590	Ch 2 Interchange with UP

AW&MP Houston, Texas
461.350	466.350	FCC

Bangor & Aroostook Bangor, Maine
160.440		Ch 1 Road
160.920	160.230	Ch 2 North end dispatcher – Presque Isle
160.740	160.320	Ch 3 South end dispatcher – Charleston
160.680		Ch 4 Yard
160.530		Wrecker

Dispatcher links
452.9125	(160.230 input) – Charleston to Northern Maine Junction
451.875	(160.740 output) – Northern Maine Junction to Charleston
451.925	(456.925 output) – Northern Maine Junction to Topsfield
451.925	(160.230 input) – Presque Isle to Topsfield
456.875	(160.230 input) – Charleston to Northern Maine Junction
456.925	(451.925 input) – Topsfield to Northern Maine Junction
456.925	(160.920 output) – Topsfield to Presque Isle

Batten Kill Greenwich, New York
160.905	General operations

Bauxite & Northern   Bauxite, Arkansas
   160.500   General operations

Bay Colony   Lexington, Massachusetts
   160.305△   Ch 1 Road
   160.305△ 161.355△ Ch 2 Dispatcher
   160.485   Spare channel
   161.265   Active

BC Rail   North Vancouver, British Columbia
   159.570   Ch 1 Road A – Squamish, Prince George, Fort
                             St. John, Talka, Fort Nelson, and Tumbler Sub-
                             divisions
   159.570   161.370   Ch 2 Dispatcher A – Same locations as Ch 1
   161.235   Ch 3 Terminal and road switcher
   160.395   Ch 4 MofW/Engineering PBX
   160.695   Ch 5 Road B – Electric territory – Lillooet,
                             Chetwynd, Dawson Creek, Port, and Stuart Sub-
                             divisions, and Mackenzie Spur
   160.695   161.520   Ch 6 Dispatcher B – Same locations as Ch 5
   160.245   Ch 7 Yard
   160.305   Ch 8 Yard
   160.815   Ch 9 MofW Gangs
   160.995   Mechanical Dept. – systemwide
   161.160   Priority Yard
   464.275   Locotrol data
   North Vancouver
   160.695   Ch 5 Yard and Roberts Bank
   160.245   Ch 7 Yard
   160.305   Ch 8 Yard

   160.575   Yard
   Prince George
   160.245   Ch 7 Yard
   160.305   Ch 8 Yard
   160.815   Ch 9 Yard

Beaufort & Morehead   Beaufort, North Carolina
   160.260   General operations

Beech Mountain   Alexander, West Virginia
   160.260   General operations

Belfast & Moosehead Lake   Belfast, Maine
   160.710   Road and repeater output
   161.385   Repeater input

Belt Railway of Chicago   Chicago, Ilinois
   160.500   Road and dispatcher
   160.380   West Yard
   161.445   East Yard
   160.965   Clearing Yard hump
   161.295   Car shop and diesel shop
   160.695   MofW
   161.205   Police – mutual aid

Belton   Belton, Texas
   160.335   General operations

Berlin Mills   Berlin, New Hampshire
   160.650   General operations

Bessemer & Lake Erie   Monroeville, Pennsylvania

160.830	Ch 1 Road
161.310	Ch 2 Yard
160.215	Ch 3 Car Dept. – Conneaut, Ohio
160.485	Ch 4 Car Dept. – elsewhere
161.220	Ch 5 MofW

Conneaut, Ohio – Pittsburgh & Conneaut Dock Railway

160.500	General operations
160.920	General operations
160.260	Remote control locomotives
72.40	Digital control of crane

Birmingham Southern   Fairfield, Alabama

160.290	Road and dispatcher
160.335	Koppers Coke Mill switcher
160.425	Switching
160.560	Switching
160.575	Switching
160.755	Switching
160.815	Switching
161.325	Switching
161.385	Switching
161.445	Switching
161.535	Switching
161.025	34th Street Yard – Ensley switcher
160.890	MofW and dispatcher

Black River & Western   Ringoes, New Jersey

161.085	General operations

Bloomer Line   Chatsworth, Illinois

161.355	160.365	General operations

Blue Mountain   Walla Walla, Washington

160.785	General operations

Blue Mountain & Reading   Hamburg, Pennsylvania

161.310	General operations

Boston & Maine (Guilford Transportation Industries)

161.160	Ch 1 Dispatcher to train
161.520	Ch 1 Train to dispatcher
161.400	Ch 2 Road and yard
161.370	Ch 3 MofW
161.250	Ch 4 Police

Boston, Massachusetts

160.440		Intermodal facility
161.250	160.230	Police

North Billerica, Massachusetts

160.440	Welded rail plant operations

Brandywine Valley   Coatesville, Pennsylvania

462.7625	467.7625	Ch A General operations
464.5625	469.5625	Ch B General operations

Brownsville & Rio Grande International   Brownsville, Texas

161.565	General operations

Buckingham Branch   Bremo, Virginia

160.470	General operations

Bucksgahuda & Western   Bucks County, Pennsylvania

154.570		FCC

Buffalo & Pittsburgh   Caledonia, New York

160.230		Road
160.320		Dispatcher
160.770	161.445	Dispatcher link – West Valley to Caledonia
160.530		Yard
160.785		MofW
161.160		Transportation

Buffalo Southern   Hamburg, New York

160.260		General operations

Burlington Junction   Burlington, Iowa

160.395		General operations

Burlington Northern

160.695		Ch 1 Road and dispatcher
160.920		Ch 2 Road and dispatcher
161.100		Ch 3 Road and dispatcher
161.160		Ch 4 Road and dispatcher
161.250		Ch 5 Road and dispatcher
160.280		Ch 6 Road and dispatcher
161.385		Ch 7 Road and dispatcher
161.415		Ch 8 Road and dispatcher
160.650		Yard
160.830		Yard
160.980		Yard
161.010		Yard
161.310		Yard
160.590		Car Dept.
160.590	161.460	Car Dept.
161.220		Wire Chief
161.205		Police
160.665	161.505	Ch 3 PBX (red)

Colorado: Denver, Trinidad, Wray
Idaho: Moyie Springs
Illinois: Savanna
Iowa: Creston, Ottumwa, Sioux City
Kansas: Troy
Minnesota: Carlton, Marshall, Morris, St. Cloud, St. Paul, Walker
Missouri: Aalberg, Palmyra
Montana: Benteen, East Portal, Forsyth, Harlem, Judith Gap, Pinnacle, Rapids, Shaw Butte, Spotted Robe, West Portal, Wiota
Nebraska: Angora, Hastings, Lincoln, Mason City, Seneca, Walt Hill
North Dakota: Fargo, Fryburg, Hettinger, Minot
Oregon: Bend, Green Mtn. (Portland), Klamath Falls
South Dakota: Chilson, Huron, Walker, Webster
Texas: Texline
Washington: Berne, Glenrose (Spokane), Richland, Wishram
Wisconsin: Prairie du Chien
Wyoming: Casper, Pine Ridge, Rocky Butte

160.620	161.565	Ch 4 PBX (blue)

Colorado: Pueblo, Walsenburg
Illinois: Barstow, Fandon, Galesburg, Mendota

Burlington Northern

Iowa: Glenwood, Sioux City
Minnesota: Bagley, Beauty Lake, Breckenridge, Hinckley, LaBoldt, Staples, Stockholm
Montana: Big Coulee, Blue Mountain, Cement Hill, Curry, Hinsdale, Pompey's Pillar, Raynesford, Snowslip, Wolf Point
Nebraska: Alliance, Arapahoe, Belmont, Culbertson, Dunning, Fairmont, Whitman
New Mexico: Des Moines
North Dakota: Antelope, Cleveland, Devils Lake, Epping, Grand Forks
Oregon: Albany, Beal, Madras
South Dakota: Bowdle, Garretson, Mitchell
Texas: Channing, Clarendon, Corsicana, Dallas, Decatur, North Zulch, Vernon
Washington: Cunningham, Hill, Kettle Falls, Mission Ridge, Roosevelt, Stevenson, Tiger Mtn. (Seattle)
Wisconsin: Nelson
Wyoming: Basin, Cherry Creek, Cheyenne, Robertson Flats, Sheridan

161.130	160.545	Ch 5 PBX (green)

Alabama: Birmingham, Jasper
Arkansas: Jonesboro
Colorado: Akron, Wiggins, Peetz
Iowa: Burlington, Griswold, Williamson
Idaho: Little Blacktail
Illinois: Galva, Jacksonville, Rochelle
Kansas: Fort Scott
Montana: Buelow, Big Mountain, Blossburg, Culbertson, Dodson, Ethridge, Miles City, Plev-

na, Rimrock
Missouri: Cabool, Cape Girardeau, Elsberry, Hayti, Joplin, Kansas City, Lebanon, Macon, Otto, Rosati, St. Louis, Springfield, Thayer
Mississippi: Amory, Holly Springs
North Dakota: Lincoln, Orrin, Park River, Peak
Nebraska: Abbott, Lakeside, Minden, Tecumseh, Winslow
Oklahoma: Ada, Catale, Dustin, Madill, Oklahoma City, Tulsa
Minnesota: Holland, McGregor, Minneapolis, Richdale
Oregon: Maupin
South Dakota: Aberdeen, Viborg, Watertown
Tennessee: Memphis
Texas: Amarillo, Childress, Fort Worth, Houston, Sherman, Shiro, Teague, Tomball, Wichita Falls
Washington: Chehalis, Lind, Magnason Butte, Omak, Plymouth, Skykomish
Wisconsin: Superior
Wyoming: Arminto, Douglas, Lariat, New Castle

161.310	160.290	Ch 6 PBX (orange)
161.490	160.245	Ch 7 PBX (yellow)

Minnesota: Wolverton
Montana: Shelby Jct., Havre, Meyers, Fallon
North Dakota: Angora, McHenry, Marmarth, Tagus
South Dakota: Mobridge, Thunder Hawk
Wisconsin: Allouez

160.425	160.935	Ch 8 PBX (white)

Illinois: Downers Grove

	Montana: Fort Benton	
	North Dakota: Bowman	
	Wisconsin: Potosi, La Crosse	
160.320	PBX Link 160.545/161.130 – Everett to Index (Skykomish)	
161.505	MofW	
160.620	Supervisory – Frisco territory	
160.920	Police – Frisco territory	
161.205	Police mutual aid	
161.430	MofW – Frisco territory	
Dispatcher links		
160.260	Pasco to Sunset, Washington	
160.260	Pasco to Wishram, Washington	
160.260	Spokane, Washington, to Moscow, Idaho	
160.290	Forsyth to Pompeys Pillar, Montana	
160.320	Kettle Falls to Hillyard (Spokane), Washington	
160.320	Great Falls, Montana	
160.365	Wenatchee to Merritt, Washington	
160.380	Cascade Tunnel, Washington	
160.380	Cut Bank to Red Eagle, Montana	
160.380	Merritt to Index, Washington	
160.380	Klamath Falls, Oregon, to Bieber, California	
160.380	Whitefish, Montana	
160.410	Havre to Whitlash, Montana	
160.410	Helena, Montana	
160.455	Davenport to Hanson, Washington	
160.470	Broadview, to Billings, Montana	
160.470	Cutbank to Red Eagle, Montana	
160.500	Berne to Wenatchee, Washington	
160.500	Hanson to Coulee City, Washington	
160.500	Hanson to Wenatchee, Washington	

160.500		Quincy to Wenatchee, Washington
Alabama		
Birmingham – East Thomas Yard		
160.530		Yard
160.635		Yard
160.710		Yard
160.875		Yard
161.235		Yard
161.430		Yard
160.965	160.485	Car Dept.
160.995		Intermodal facility – Dixie Hub
161.205		Police
Colorado		
Denver – Renick Yard		
161.295		Yard
161.100		Yard
161.160		Ch 2 Yard
160.575		Mechanical Dept.
160.590	161.460	Car Dept.
160.995		Intermodal facility
855.1625	810.1625	Mobile data terminals
Fort Collins		
161.100		Yard
Roggen		
161.355	160.215	Traveling freight agents
Illinois		
Chicago		
452.9375	457.9375	Car Dept.
160 .335		Cicero Yard Car Dept., Police, and hump
452 .900	457.900	Union Station Diesel Shop
851.0625	806.0625	Mobile data terminals

Burlington Northern

Galesburg
160.365		Hump
160.395		Yard
161.385		Yard
161.475		Yard
161.505		Yard
452.900	457.900	Yard
160.905		Yard control
160.845	161.445	Car Dept. and hostler
855.1125	810.1125	Mobile data terminals

Iowa
Des Moines
452.900	457.900	Car Dept.

Glenwood
161.355	160.215	Traveling freight agents

Kansas
Fort Scott
462.050	467.050	FCC

Minnesota
Dilworth
854.8875	Mobile data terminals

Fridley
452.950	Administration

Minneapolis and St. Paul
160.500	Signal Dept.
160.830	Engineering Dept.
160.335	OCS calling channel
161.010	Telemetry
161.250	Police and administration
452.900	Administration

855.1875	810.1875	Mobile data terminals

St. Paul – Northtown Yard
161.160		Yard
160.365		Hump
160.410		Pulldown
160.590		Car Dept.
160.290	160.875	Machine Shop
160.710		Fuel truck
452.950	457.950	Hump cab signals

St. Paul – Midway Yard
161.550	Intermodal facility

Union Yard and Others
160.650	Yard and industrial

Mississippi
Amory
160.800	Yard

Missouri
Kansas City
161.100	Ch 1 Yard
160.275	10th Street Yard
160.800	19th Street Yard
160.935	Crew cab
160.695	Intermodal facility
161.265	Police – mutual aid
161.415	Active – use undetermined
952.2375	Microwave data

Kansas City – Murray Yard
160.485	Hump
160.995	Pulldown
161.235	Pulldown

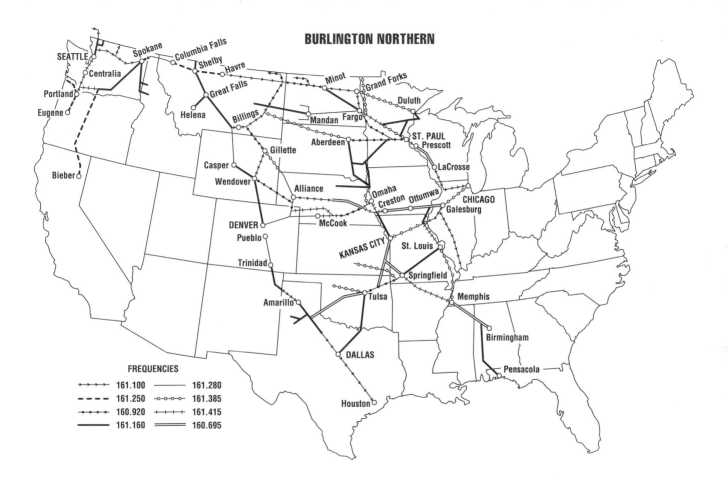

BURLINGTON NORTHERN

SEATTLE
Spokane
Columbia Falls
Shelby
Havre
Centralia
Minot
Grand Forks
Portland
Great Falls
Duluth
Eugene
Helena
Billings
Mandan
Fargo
Bieber
Gillette
Aberdeen
ST. PAUL
Prescott
Casper
LaCrosse
Wendover
Alliance
Omaha
CHICAGO
Creston
Ottumwa
Galesburg
DENVER
McCook
Pueblo
KANSAS CITY
St. Louis
Trinidad
Springfield
Amarillo
Tulsa
Memphis
Birmingham
DALLAS
Pensacola
Houston

FREQUENCIES

+—+—+	161.100	——	161.280
- - - -	161.250	-o-o-o-	161.385
·····•·····	160.920	+++++	161.415
▬▬▬▬	161.160	══════	160.695

31

Burlington Northern

161.355		Pulldown
160.725		Diesel Shop
161.385	160.710	Car Dept.

St. Louis – Lindenwood Yard

160.695		Yard
160.785		Yard
161.415		Yard
160.665		Car Dept.
161.295		Intermodal facility
854.8875	809.8875	Mobile data terminals

Springfield

160.620		Ch 3 Supervisory and Police
160.620	161.505	Ch 4 Supervisory and Police
452.900	457.900	Diesel Shop – inactive
462.050	467.050	FCC

Springfield – Springfield Yard

160.800		East end switcher
161.310		East end switcher
160.830		West end switcher
160.920		West end switcher
161.070		Diesel shop
160.230		Diesel shop hostler
160.500		Maintenance facility
160.710	161.400	Car Dept.
161.400		Car Dept. – Talk-around
160.725		Stores Dept.
160.905		Hub Center

Tarkio

161.355	160.215	Traveling freight agents

Montana

Billings

854.8625	809.8625	Mobile data terminals

Libby

160.590	161.460	Car Dept.

Miner

160.590	161.460	Car Dept.

Somers

160.590	161.460	Car Dept.

Nebraska

Alliance

160.995		Diesel shop
160.650		Stores and diesel pit
161.250		Mechanical
160.845		Car Dept.

Lincoln

160.710		Hump
160.770		Hump
161.280		Havelock Shop
161.355		MofW
161.205		Police

Omaha

854.9375	809.9375	Mobile data terminals

Oklahoma

Clinton

161.460		Traveling freight agents

Cordele

161.460	160.860	Traveling freight agents

Enid

160.920		Switch Crew 2 and Police
160.530		Switch Crew 3

Helena
160.500   160.980   Traveling freight agents
Madill
462.050   467.050   FCC
Oklahoma City
160.530   Ch 2 Switching and wrecker
Perry
160.800   161.325   Traveling freight agents
Tulsa
161.100   Ch 1 End to end
160.920   Ch 3 Police
160.620   Ch 8 Supervisory
Tulsa – Cherokee Yard
160.500   A2 Hump
160.800   A3 Switching
160.980   A4 Switching
160.950   B1 Switching
160.830   B3 Hump
160.860   B4 Switching
160.380   Eastbound arrival indicator tone from Mannford
160.530   Wrecker
161.250   160.710   Car Dept.
Tulsa – DX Refinery
160.890   B2 Plant switching
Oregon
Klamath Falls
160.380   Yard
Portland
160.725   Willbridge Yard
161.250   Willbridge Yard
160.965   Portland Hub

Tennessee
Memphis
160.965   160.485   Police – PBX
160.995   C&S – Simplex PBX
161.430   MofW – Simplex PBX
160.230   Hump
Memphis – Tennessee Yard
160.515   Yard
160.560   Yard
161.160   Ch A1 Road and yard
161.385   Ch A2 Intermodal facility
160.800   Ch A3 Yard
161.040   Ch A4 Yard
160.725   Ch B2 Yard
160.845   Ch B4 Yard
160.470   UP Interchange
160.905   Police
Texas
Amarillo
854.8875 809.8875 Mobile data terminals
Dallas
161.355   Yard
Irving
160.530   Intermodal facility
464.775   FCC – Base and mobile
853.2625 808.2625 Mobile data terminals
Fort Worth
160.485   Yard
161.520   Yard
160.725   Data
161.460   Data

Burlington Northern

Washington

Everett

161.010	Delta Yard switcher
161.160	Delta Yard switcher 1
161.250	Car Dept.

Index

160.650	161.220	Active

Mount St. Helens

160.590	161.460	Land Management Dept.

Pasco

160.650	Yard
161.310	Yard

Seattle

161.550	International Gateway Yard
161.220	Interbay loco shop Stores Dept. and Wire Chief
160.590	Administration
161.250	Car Dept.
161.550	South Seattle Yard intermodal facility

Seattle – Balmer Yard

160.650	West end switcher and yardmaster
161.310	East end switcher and Hump

Seattle – Stacy Street Yard

161.265	Yard
160.830	North End switcher
161.010	West Seattle switcher
161.160	South End switcher
161.250	Harbor Island switcher
160.980	South Seattle intermodal facility

Spokane

160.830	Yardley Yard and Police
160.905	Yardley Yard

160.965	Spokane Hub

Tacoma – Tacoma Yard

161.010	West end switcher
161.160	East end switcher
160.650	Smelter switcher
161.310	Continental switcher
161.250	Car Dept.
160.440	Intermodal facility

Vancouver

160.575	Yard
160.830	Yard
161.010	Yard
161.310	Yard
161.370	Yard

West Portal

452.950	457.950	Remote control locomotive repeater

Wisconsin

Allouez

160.410		Ch 1 Ore dock
160.710		Ch 2 Ore dock
160.515		Ch 3 Ore dock
160.590	161.565	PBX

Superior

161.010	Yard
160.590	Shop

Wyoming

Casper and Greybull

161.100	Yard

British Columbia

Vancouver

161.100	Yard

Burlington Northern (Manitoba) Ltd.　　Winnipeg, Manitoba
　160.650　　　General operations
　161.415　　　CN trackage rights

Burlington River Terminal　　Burlington, Iowa
　464.475　　　General operations

Cairo Terminal　　Cairo, Illinois
　161.070　　　General operations
　462.125　467.125　Station-to-station link, Cairo to Jackson, Missouri (Jackson & Southern)

California Northern　　Napa, California
　161.385　　　Road
　160.635　　　Switching

California Western　　Fort Bragg, California
　160.650　　　General operations

Camas Prairie　　Lewiston, Idaho
　160.515　　　Road, west of Lewiston
　161.250　　　Road, east of Lewiston
　161.250　160.500　Road repeater
　161.100　　　Lewiston yard switcher

Cambria & Indiana　　Colver, Pennsylvania
　161.490　160.440　Road
　161.415　160.395　MofW

Canada & Gulf Terminal　　Mont Joli, Quebec
　161.415　　　CN Ch 1
　160.665　　　CN Ch 4
　160.935　　　CN Ch 3
　161.205　　　CN Ch 2

Canadian National　　Montreal, Quebec
Primary channels in use are 1-8 and 20. For track line-ups monitor channels 2, 3, 8, and 20 0700-0815, 1201-1315, and 1600-1630 hrs.
　161.415△　　Ch 1 Road
　161.205△　　Ch 2 Dispatcher
　160.935△　　Ch 3 Dispatcher
　160.665　　　Ch 4 Switch tenders, Yard
　160.365　　　Ch 5 General terminal
　160.485　161.295　Ch 6 Dispatcher (Western Area)
　159.810　161.055　Ch 7 Dispatcher (Western Area)
　161.025△　　Ch 8 Dispatcher
　160.575　　　Ch 13 Police
　160.605　　　Ch 14 Yard, Intermodal facility
　160.635　　　Ch 15
　160.215　　　Ch 16 Yard and MofW
　160.695　　　Ch 17 Road and yard
　160.725　　　Ch 18 Yard and car ferry
　160.755　　　Ch 19 Yard
　160.785　　　Ch 20 MofW
　160.815　　　Ch 21 Yard
　160.245　　　Ch 22
　160.875　　　Ch 23 Hump
　160.905　　　Ch 24 C&S/Police /Ferry

Canadian National

160.275		Ch 25 Yard
160.965		Ch 26 Police/Yard/Car Shop
160.995		Ch 27 Police
160.305		Ch 28 Yard Hump Car Shop
161.055		Ch 29 Yard and terminal
161.085		Ch 30 Yard and hump
160.395		Ch 31 Car Shop and Police
160.455		Ch 32 Hump
160.485		Ch 33 Yard
160.515		Ch 34 Yard
161.235		Ch 35 Hump/Police
160.545		Ch 36 Road commuter/Police mutual aid
161.295		Ch 37 Yard and terminal
161.115		Ch 38
161.355		Ch 39 CP Rail interchange
161.385		Ch 40 Yard
161.265		Ch 41
161.445		Ch 42 Yard and intermodal facility
161.475		Ch 43 Road – CP Rail
161.505		Ch 44 Yard – Moncton, New Brunswick
159.810		Ch 47 Yard and terminal
159.930		Ch 48
160.050		Ch 49 Yard
160.785	160.215	Ch 50 MofW
160.905	160.215	Ch 51
160.215	160.965	Ch 52
160.215	161.085	Ch 53
160.215	161.295	Ch 54
160.995	161.505	Ch 55 Yard
161.085	160.215	Ch 56
161.085	160.305	Ch 57
160.965	160.395	Ch 58 Car Shop
161.355	160.605	Ch 59
160.305	161.085	Ch 60
161.235	160.305	Ch 61 Yard and terminal
161.445	160.305	Ch 62
160.395	160.965	Ch 63
160.395	161.055	Ch 64
160.395	161.445	Ch 65
161.475	160.425	Ch 66 to contact CP Rail
161.475	161.115	Ch 67 to contact CP Rail
161.475	161.535	Ch 68 to contact CP Rail
160.395	160.695	Ch 69
160.485	161.085	Ch 70
159.810	160.695	Ch 71
159.810	160.965	Ch 72
159.810	161.085	Ch 73
159.810	161.295	Ch 74
161.085	159.810	Ch 75 Yard, terminal, and hump
160.965	160.305	Ch 76
160.245	161.055	Ch 77
160.050	160.965	Ch 78
161.085		Ch 79
161.115	160.395	Ch 80
160.455	161.085	Ch 81 MofW
160.215	160.905	Ch 82 MofW – PBX
160.515	161.505	Ch 83 MofW
160.275	161.145	Ch 84 MofW
160.395	161.235	Ch 85 MofW
160.575	161.235	Ch 90 Police
150.160		Ch 100 Ch 1 Former CN Express trucks
150.460		Ch 101 Ch 2 Former CN Express trucks

150.610		Ch 107 Ch 3 Former CN Express trucks
140.970		Ch 108
141.060		Ch 109
170.310		Ch 110
173.040		Ch 121 Intermodal facility
167.010	172.020	Ch 122 CN-CP Telecommunications link between Saskatoon, Conquest, and Rosetown, Saskatchewan
172.530		Ch 123 – Link – Sterling and Rogersville to Lutes Mountain, New Brunswick
165.090	154.540	Ch 125 Point-to-point link between Churchill and Souris, Prince Edward Island
154.540	165.120	Ch 126 Point-to-point link between Churchill and O'Leary, Prince Edward Island
142.695	138.225	Ch 127 Point-to-point link between Pass Creek, and House Mountain, Alberta
142.665	138.255	Ch 128 Point-to-point link between Whitecourt and House Mountain, Alberta
162.480	152.660	Ch 129 Point-to-point link between Leyland Mountain and Edson, Alberta
138.105	142.095	Ch 130 Point-to-point link between Chapmans and Yale, British Columbia
138.465	142.455	Ch 131 Point-to-point link between Chapmans and Yale, British Columbia
138.735	142.725	Ch 132 Point-to-point link between Jarvis and Hope, British Columbia
148.255	143.595	Ch 133 Point-to-point link between Yale and Hope, British Columbia
161.700		Ch 134 Point-to-point link
453.4750		Ch 400 Yard and terminal

453.8625	Ch 401 Yard and terminal
419.4375	Ch 402 Yard and terminal
469.0125	Ch 403 Yard and terminal
469.3500	Ch 404 Yard and terminal
469.6500	Ch 405 Yard and terminal
469.2125	Ch 406 Yard and terminal
469.0875	Ch 407 Yard and terminal
464.0875	Ch 408 Yard and terminal
456.8625	Ch 409 Yard and terminal
469.6625	Ch 410 Yard and terminal
464.8625	Ch 411
464.8625	Ch 411 – 1 base and 20 mobiles
457.6625	Ch 412
453.4375	Ch 413
453.8375	Ch 414
469.8375	Ch 415
453.0375	Ch 416
469.4000	Ch 417 Link – MP 42 to Marble Mountain, Nova Scotia
469.4000	Ch 417 Link – MP 77 to Barochos, Nova Scotia
459.2250~	Ch 418
460.9500	Ch 419
467.6500	Ch 420
469.7500	Ch 421
439.5000	Ch 422
453.7375	Ch 423
464.2750	Ch 424 Yard
464.0500	Ch 425 Yard
469.3625	Ch 426
469.3875	Ch 427

Canadian National

469.9875		Ch 428
458.0375		Ch 429
453.5125		Ch 430
464.2875		Ch 431
451.8500	456.8625	Ch 500
452.0750	457.0875	Ch 501
452.6500	457.6625	Ch 502
460.2750	465.2875	Ch 503
460.6000	465.6125	Ch 504
460.9000	465.9125	Ch 505
461.1250	466.1375	Ch 506
461.9500	466.9625	Ch 507
451.2750	456.2875	Ch 508
464.2000	469.7000	Ch 509
451.0750	456.0875	Ch 510
451.6000	456.6125	Ch 511
460.0875	465.0875	Ch 513 – 1 base and 1 mobile
452.0125	457.0125	Ch 514
460.4125	465.4125	Ch 515 Point-to-point link between Cochrane and Norembega, Ontario
414.0125	419.0000	Ch 516 Point-to-point link between Copper Mountain and Terrace, British Columbia
414.5875	419.5750	Ch 517 Point-to-point link between Copper Mountain and Devils Island, British Columbia
452.7125	457.7125	Ch 518
414.9375	419.9375	Ch 519 Point-to-point link between Kitchener and Moorefield, Ontario
414.3375	419.3375	Ch 520 Point-to-point link between Kedgewick and South Alexis, New Brunswick
462.7500	467.7625	Ch 521 Yard
463.0500	468.0625	Ch 522 Yard
463.2250	468.2375	Ch 523 Yard
463.8750	468.8875	Ch 524 Yard
414.0375	419.0375	Ch 525 Point-to-point link between Paisley and Moorefield, Ontario
414.5625	419.5500	Ch 526 Point-to-point link between Joannes and Noranda, Quebec
451.0000		Link – Mount Hayes to Skeena, British Columbia
453.0000		Link – Terrace to Salvus, British Columbia
456.0000		Link – Skeena to Mount Hayes, British Columbia
458.0000		Link – Salvus to Terrace, British Columbia
142.515		Link – Moth to Minaki, Ontario
138.525		Link – Minaki to Moth, Ontario
171.750		Link – Mount St. Joseph, Quebec
171.750		Link – Campbellton to Mount Carlton, New Brunswick
171.930		Link – Lutes Mountain to Sterling and Rogersville, New Brunswick
172.350		Link – Mount Carlton to Campbellton, New Brunswick
172.350		Link – Mount St. Joseph, Quebec
172.530		Former CN Express trucks
172.590		Former CN Express trucks

Alberta

Calgary

453.1625		Ch 414 – 1 base and 12 mobiles

Edmonton

160.575	161.235	Ch 90 Police
170.310		Ch 110 – 1 base
451.8500~	456.8625~	Ch 500 – 1 base and mobiles

452.0750~ 457.0875~ Ch 501 – 1 base and mobiles
453.1625 — Ch 414 – 1 base and 17 mobiles
453.4375 — Ch 400 – 1 base and 7 mobiles
453.5125 — Ch 430 – 1 base and 20 mobiles
469.2125~ — Ch 406 – 6 mobiles
469.6500 — Ch 405 – 1 base and 3 mobiles
Pyramid
172.020 — Ch 122 CN-CP Telecommunications
British Columbia
Barnaby Mountain
172.590 — Ch 124 – 1 base
173.040 — Ch 121 – 1 base
Blackpole, Canoe, Iron, and Jarvis
172.020   166.560   Ch 122 CN-CP Telecommunications
Kamloops
159.930   160.995   Switching
160.305   161.235   Car Dept.
Vancouver
159.810   161.055   Ch 7 Yard
160.215   160.905   Ch 82 PBX MofW/Police
160.305 — Ch 28 Yard
160.485 — Ch 33 Yard
160.785 — Ch 20 MofW
160.935 — Ch 3 Terminal
161.295 — Ch 37 Yard
161.385 — Ch 40 Yard
161.445 — Ch 42 Yard
173.040 — Ch 121 Intermodal facility dispatcher
856.4625 811.4625 Police
857.4625 812.4625 Corporate couriers

Vancouver – Lake City Yard
160.965 — Ch 26 Yard
Vancouver – Lulu Island
160.965 — Ch 32 Yard
Vancouver – Lynn Creek Yard
160.365 — Ch 5 Yard
160.455 — Ch 32 Yard
Vancouver – Thornton Yard
160.665 — Ch 4 Yard
161.025 — Ch 8 BN trackage rights
451.8625 456.8625 Ch 500 Car Dept.
452.6625 457.6625 Ch 502 Locomotive hostler
453.4750 — Ch 400 Car Dept.
469.0875 — Ch 407 Yard
469.650 — Ch 405 Yard
473.250 — Car checkers
Manitoba
Winnipeg
160.365 — Ch 5 Terminal switching
160.485   161.295   Ch 6 Yard
160.695 — Ch 17 Yard
160.965 — Ch 26 Yard
160.395 — Ch 31 Yard
160.545 — Ch 36 Yard
161.385 — Ch 40 Yard
161.445 — Ch 42 Yard
140.970 — Ch 108 – 1 base and 50 mobiles
141.060 — Ch 109 – 1 base and 50 mobiles
469.6500 — Ch 405 – 1 base and 14 mobiles
469.3125 — Ch 407 – 1 base and 14 mobiles

Canadian National

469.8375		Ch 415 – 1 base and 15 mobiles
453.0375		Ch 416 – 1 base and 19 mobiles
469.3625		Ch 426 – 1 base and 11 mobiles
469.3875		Ch 427 – 1 base and 11 mobiles
469.7375		1 base and 3 mobiles
451.6625	456.6625	1 base and 3 mobiles
451.8500	456.8625	Ch 500 – 1 base and 49 mobiles
452.6500	457.6625	Ch 502 Active

New Brunswick

Cape Tormentine

160.725		Ch 18 Marine operations
160.905		Ch 24 Marine operations

Lutes Mountain

469.9875		Ch 428 -1 base to Moncton

Moncton

160.545		Ch 36 Police – mutual aid
160.575	161.235	Ch 90 Police
469.6500		Ch 405 – 1 base and 4 mobiles
469.9875		Ch 428 – 20 mobiles, from Lutes Mountain
451.850	456.8625	Ch 500 – 1 base and 20 mobiles

Moncton – Franklin Yard

161.025		Ch 8 Yard transfer
160.815		Ch 21 Yard and new shop
160.995	161.505	Ch 55 Switching

Moncton – Gordon Yard

160.485	161.295	Ch 6 East Class
159.810	161.055	Ch 7 General terminal
160.875		Ch 23 Hump
160.395		Ch 31 Car shop
161.355		Ch 39 Car Dept.
160.050	160.965	Ch 78 West Class

Moncton – Lower Yard

160.365		Ch 5 Switching

Moncton – V.I.C.

160.665		Ch 4

Moncton – Wharf Branch

160.815		Ch 21 Branch switching

Saint John

160.365		Ch 5
160.725		Ch 18 Marine operations
160.815		Ch 21 Yard
160.905		Ch 24 Marine operations
451.8625	456.8625	Ch 500 – 1 base and 4 mobiles
452.0125	457.0125	Ch 514 – 1 base and 4 mobiles

Nova Scotia

Digby

160.725		Ch 18 Marine operations
160.905		Ch 24 Marine operations

Geiser Hill

172.530		Ch 123 – 1 base

Halifax

160.275		Ch 25 Signal maintainers
160.575	161.235	Ch 90 Police
452.0125	457.0125	Ch 514 – 1 base and 8 mobiles

Halifax – Dartmouth Yard

160.725		Ch 18 East switcher
160.050		Ch 49 West switcher

Halifax – Fairview Roundhouse

160.545		Ch 36 Engine hostler

Halifax – Ocean Terminal

161.205		Ch 2 Yard 3 elevator area
160.485	161.295	Ch 6 Yard 2 intermodal facility

161.025   Ch 8 Yard 1 coach yard
Halifax – Rockingham Yard
160.665   Ch 4 Switch Crew 1
160.365   Ch 5 Switch Crew
159.810   161.055   Ch 7 Switch Crew 2
Ontario
Belleville
469.6625   Ch 410 – 1 base and 6 mobiles
469.6875~   15 mobiles
Brampton
160.365   Ch 5 Intermodal facility – secondary
160.665   Ch 4 Intermodal facility – primary
459.225   Ch 418 Yard
469.9875   Ch 428 Intermodal facility
Hamilton
172.530   Ch 123 CN Express trucks
London
160.665   Ch 4 Shop
160.905   Ch 24 Signal Dept.
160.965   Ch 26 Police
160.995   Ch 27 Police
Midland
460.0875 465.0875 Ch 513 – 1 base and 6 mobiles
Oshawa
454.3750 459.3750 1 base and 100 mobiles
Ottawa
160.365   Ch 5 Terminal switching
Talbotville
160.485   Ch 33 Yard
Toronto
160.215   Ch 16 Yard

160.695   Ch 17 Road and yard
160.905   Ch 24 C&S
160.305   Ch 28 Yard
161.055   Ch 29 Yard
161.235   Ch 35 Police
464.8625   Ch 411 – 1 base and 20 mobiles
459.2250~   Ch 418 – 1 base and mobiles
469.9875   Ch 428 Yard
458.0375   Ch 429 – 1 base and mobiles
464.2000 469.7000 Ch 509 – 1 base and 20 mobiles
460.0875 465.0875 Ch 513 – 1 base and 1 mobile
Toronto – MacMillan Yard
160.665   Ch 4 Switch tenders
160.605   Ch 14 intermodal facility
160.395   160.965   Ch 63 Car Dept
460.2750 465.2875 Ch 503 Hump – Yellow/Red
460.6000 465.6125 Ch 504 Eastbound departure yard – Blue
460.9000 465.9125 Ch 505 Inspection and South Control – White
461.1250 466.1375 Ch 506 Train make-up – Express Yard
461.950   466.9625 Ch 507 Westbound departure yard – Green
Toronto – Malport Yard
160.665   Ch 4 Yard
160.365   Ch 5 Yard – alternate
Windsor
160.215   Ch 16 Yard and MofW
160.695   Ch 17 Yard
Quebec
Montreal
160.215   160.905   Ch 82 MofW
160.275   161.145   Ch 84 MofW
160.395   161.235   Ch 85 MofW

Canadian National

160.455	161.085	Ch 81 MofW
160.515		Ch 34 General terminal
160.515	161.505	Ch 83 MofW
160.545		Ch 36 Road – Commuter trains – Montfort and St. Laurent Subdivisions
160.575		Ch 13 Police
414.3375	419.3375	Ch 520 Point-to-point
451.0750	456.0875	Ch 510 1 base
451.2750	456.2875	Ch 508 – 1 base and 10 mobiles
451.8500~	456.8625~	Ch 500 – 1 base and mobiles
452.6500	457.6625	Ch 502 – 1 base and 30 mobiles
453.7375		Ch 423 – 1 base and 12 mobiles
454.0750	459.0750	1 base and 18 mobiles
456.8625~		Ch 409 – 75 mobiles

Montreal – Point St. Charles Yard

160.725		Ch 18 Diesel shop
160.245		Ch 22 Coach yard
160.275		Ch 25 Coach yard
419.4375		Ch 402 Pager and shop forces
453.475		Ch 400 Pager and shop forces
453.8625		Ch 401 Pager and shop forces

Montreal – St. Lambert Yard

160.665	Ch 4 Yard
160.365	Ch 5 Yard

Montreal – Taschereau Yard

160.665		Ch 4 Yardmaster and local yard
160.365		Ch 5 Yardmaster and Car Dept.
161.235		Ch 35 Hump
161.085	159.810	Ch 75 East Class
464.275		Ch 424 Yard
464.0500		Ch 425 Yard

469.0125		Ch 403 Pager and shop forces
469.3500		Ch 404 Pager and shop forces
469.6500		Ch 405 Pager and shop forces
462.7500	467.7625	Ch 521 Hump Tower
463.0500	468.0625	Ch 522 Car Dept.
463.2250	468.2375	Ch 523 Retarder tower
463.8750	468.8875	Ch 524 Yardmaster

Montreal – Turcot Yard

160.665	Ch 4 Yard
160.365	Ch 5 Yard

Montreal – Val Royal Yard

160.665	Ch 4 Yard

Quebec City

451.8500	456.8625	Ch 500 – 1 base and 20 mobiles
451.2750	456.2875	Ch 508 – 1 base and 20 mobiles
451.0750	456.0875	Ch 510 – 1 base and 20 mobiles
451.6000	456.6125	Ch 511 – 1 base and 20 mobiles

Saskatchewan

Melville

160.665		Ch 4 Yard
160.365		Ch 5 Terminal switching
160.485	161.295	Ch 6 Yard
159.810	161.055	Ch 7 Yard
161.025		Ch 8 Yard

Saskatoon

160.665		Ch 4 Yard
160.365		Ch 5 Switchmen
160.485	161.295	Ch 6 Yard
159.810	161.055	Ch 7 Yard
161.025		Ch 8 Switchmen
160.305		Ch 28 Yard workers

161.055		Ch 29 Yard
160.515		Ch 34 Yard workers
161.385		Ch 40 Yardmaster
161.445		Ch 42 Yard
160.965	160.395	Ch 58 Car Dept.
172.530		Ch 123 CN Express trucks
49.16		CN Express trucks

Caney Fork & Western   McMinnville, Tennessee

160.545   General operations

Canton Railroad   Baltimore, Maryland

160.980   General operations

Cape Breton & Central Nova Scotia   Sydney, Nova Scotia

161.310   Road
160.050   Yard

Cape Fear   Fort Bragg, North Carolina

160.860   General operations

Carbon & Schuylkill   Jim Thorpe, Pennsylvania

161.310   General operations

Carolina & Northwestern   Varina, North Carolina

160.950   Joint operations with Norfolk Southern
160.650   Joint operations with Norfolk Southern
469.550   General operations – See also Rail Link Inc.

Carolina Coastal   Pinetown, North Carolina

469.550   General operations – See also Rail Link Inc.

Carolina Piedmont   Laurens, South Carolina

161.085   General operations
160.770   General operations

Carrollton   Carrollton, Kentucky

161.175   General operations

Cartier Railway   Port Cartier, Quebec

161.130   Ch 1 South end dispatcher
160.800   Ch 2 North end dispatcher
160.980   Ch 3 Road
160.740   Ch 4 MofW – Local
161.070   Ch 5 Yard
160.920   Ch 6 Yard – Lac Jeanine
160.860   Ch 7 Yard
160.680   Ch 8 MofW – Off-track

Cedar Rapids & Iowa City   Cedar Rapids, Iowa

160.500   Ch 1 Road
161.055   Ch 2 MofW/MofE/Administration
160.860   Ch 3 Yard
160.635   Ch 4 Yard

Central California Traction   Stockton, California

160.305		Ch 1 Road and repeater output
160.305	161.415	Ch 2 Repeater
160.320		Ch 3 SP interchange

Central Indiana & Western   Lapel, Indiana

160.335   General operations

Central – Chesapeake

Central Kansas   Wichita, Kansas
161.085   General operations

Central Michigan   Tawas City, Michigan
161.280   Ch 1 General operations
161.310   Ch 2 Yard and joint with Lake States at Bay City
160.350   Ch 3 Limited use
160.530   Ch 4 GTW interchange, Durand
160.230   Ch 5 CSX interchange, Muskegon

Central Montana   Denton, MT
160.800   General operations

Central of Tennessee   Nashville, Tennessee
160.635   General operations

Central Railroad of Indianapolis   Kokomo, Indiana
160.455   Ch. 1 Road
161.295   Ch. 2 Yards at Kokomo and Marion

Central Railroad of Indiana   Lawrenceburg, Indiana
160.545   Road
161.415   Switching

Central Vermont   St. Albans, Vermont
161.415   Ch 1 Road and dispatcher
161.205   Ch 2 Yard and MofW
160.935   Ch 3 Yard
161.040 160.545 Ch 4 PBX

Central Western   Stettler, Alberta
160.590 161.445 Road
160.590   Yard

Champagne Switching   Independence, Missouri
452.475~ 457.475~ FCC
161.505~   FCC

Chattahoochee Industrial   Cedar Springs, Georgia
160.860   Ch 1 switching
160.620   Ch 2 switching
161.235   Ch 3 Shop and MofW

Chattooga & Chickamauga   Lafayette, Georgia
160.455   Ch. 1 General operations – primary
160.695   Ch. 2 General operations – secondary
160.500   Coordinated operations with Norfolk Southern

Chehalis Western   Longview, Washington
160.245 160.995 Road and MofW
160.635   Switching

Chesapeake & Albemarle   Elizabeth City, North Carolina
160.755   General operations

Chesapeake Western   Harrisonburg, Virginia
161.250   Road and dispatcher
160.440   Switching – Shenandoah to Harrisonburg
161.190   Switching – Harrisonburg to Mount Jackson
161.490   Switching – Harrisonburg

Chestnut Ridge   Palmerton, Pennsylvania
   154.515   General operations

Chicago & Chemung   Woodstock, Illinois
   153.830   General operations

Chicago & Illinois Midland   Springfield, Illinois
   160.950   Road
   160.290   Yard
   160.830   MofW and Administration

Chicago & North Western
   160.890   Ch 1 Road
   160.455   Ch 2 MofW and road
   161.040   Ch 3 Road
   161.175   Ch 4 Branch lines and yard
   161.205   Ch 4 Police
   160.575   Ch 5 Yard 1
   160.485   Ch 6 Police
   161.220   General use
   161.475   Yard 2
   452.900   457.900   Dispatcher link – southwest Minnesota
   Iowa
   Boone
   160.320   Yard
   Clinton
   161.040   Ch 3 Police
   Des Moines – Short Line Yard
   160.455   Ch 2 Yard
   160.320   Yard

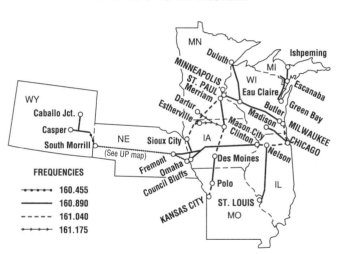

CHICAGO & NORTH WESTERN

FREQUENCIES
- •••• 160.455
- —— 160.890
- ---- 161.040
- +++ 161.175

Chicago – City

Illinois
Chicago
160.980	IHB interchange
452.9125	Global One intermodal facility

Chicago – Proviso Yard
161.175	Ch 4 Yard 1 – intermodal facility
160.575	Ch 5 Yard 2 – pulldown
160.815	Ch 5 Yard 2 – pulldown
161.475	Ch 6 Hump – mobiles only

Minnesota
Minneapolis – Valley Park Yard
161.220	Yard

Wisconsin
Janesville
160.455	Ch 2 Yard
161.040	Ch 3 Yard
161.220	Yard

Milwaukee
161.040	Ch 3 Police
161.205	Ch 4 Police

Butler
161.175	Ch 4 Yard

Chicago Central & Pacific   Waterloo, Iowa
160.755		Road – East of Freeport, Illinois
161.190		Ch 1 Road – West of Freeport, Illinois
160.410		Ch 2 Yard – All locations except Cedar Rapids, Iowa
161.460		Ch 3 Yard – Cedar Rapids, Iowa
161.535	160.605	Road – Cedar Valley Railroad

Chicago Rail Link   Chicago, Illinois
160.635	Road – Off Metra
161.340	Road – On Metra
160.035	Canal Street Yard intermodal facility

Chicago Short Line   Chicago, Illinois
160.335	General operations

Chicago SouthShore & South Bend   Michigan City, Indiana
161.355		Ch 1 Road and repeater output
161.355	161.010	Ch 2 Road repeater, east of Hillside, Indiana, and west of Gary, Indiana
161.025		Ch 3 IC Trackage rights, Chicago to Kensington, Illinois
161.100		Ch 4 MofW

Chicago Union Station   Chicago, Illinois
154.515	Police

Chicago, West Pullman & Southern   Chicago, Illinois
160.215	General operations

Cimarron River Valley   Cushing, Oklahoma
26.965 – 27.405	Variable – CB channels in use

Cincinnati Terminal   Cincinnati, Ohio
161.385	General operations

City of Prineville Railway   Prineville, Oregon
161.190	General operations

Claremont Concord   Claremont, New Hampshire
160.950   General operations

Coe Rail   Walled Lake, Michigan
161.025   General operations

Colonel's Island   Brunswick, Georgia
808.4650   Switching
852.4375   Switching

Colorado & Wyoming   Pueblo, Colorado
161.250   Road
Allen Mine
160.305   Switching
160.380   Switching
160.425   Switching
160.515   Switching
160.545   Switching
160.575   Switching
160.665   Switching
160.785   Switching
160.875   Switching
160.950   MofW
161.055   Switching
161.250 160.710 Road repeater
161.385   Switching
161.505   Switching

Columbia & Cowlitz   Curtis, Washington
160.425 161.385 Ch 1 Road and MofW
161.115   Ch 2 Yard

Columbia & Silver Creek   Shelbyville, Mississippi
160.770   FCC – mobiles

Columbus & Greenville   Columbus, Mississippi
160.230   Ch 1 Switching
160.245   Ch 2 Road
160.260   Ch 3 Station to station
160.605   Ch 4 Administration

Columbus & Ohio River   Sugarcreek, Ohio
160.845   General operations

Commonwealth Railway   Suffolk, Virginia
469.550   General operations – See also Rail Link Inc

Conemaugh & Black Lick   Johnstown, Pennsylvania
161.250   General operations
161.100   FCC – Base and mobile

Connecticut Central   Middletown, Connecticut
160.695   General operations
160.290   FCC – Base only
160.650   FCC – Base and mobile

Consolidated Rail Corporation (Conrail)
160.800Δ   Ch 1 Road
161.070Δ   Ch 2 Road and yard
160.860Δ   Ch 3 Yard and road
160.980   Ch 4 Yard and road
161.055   Commuter trains (NJ Transit)

Conrail

161.400		Commuter trains (NJ Transit)
161.055		MofW – Special projects
161.130		Ch 3 MofW
161.130	160.710	Ch 4 PBX and MofW
457.9375		End-of-train telemetry
160.680		Ch 3 Police – Car to car, systemwide except Buffalo, Chicago, Michigan, and Youngstown to Cincinnati
160.680		Ch 3 Police – Base to car, Buffalo
160.545		Ch 4 Police – Base to car, Cleveland to Chicago
160.560		Ch 4 Police – Car to car, Youngstown, Ohio, to Cincinnati; Chicago; Buffalo
160.560		Ch 4 Police – Base to Car, systemwide except Cleveland to Elkhart, Indiana

District of Columbia
Washington – Benning Yard

160.980	Ch 4 Yard

Illinois
Chicago

160.860		Ch 3 – 51st Street Yard
160.545	161.535	Ch 3 Police – Base to car
161.055		Intermodal facility

Rose Lake

161.325	160.275	Yard

Indiana
Anderson

161.445	160.485	Ch A PBX – Administration

Burns Harbor

160.860	Ch 3 Yard

Elkhart – Elkhart Yard

160.980	Hump

160.305		Pulldown 1
161.295		Pulldown
160.995		Pulldown
161.385		Pulldown
161.445		Pulldown
161.340	160.470	Car Dept.
160.740		Intermodal facility – PTL Trucking

Indianapolis

161.445	160.485	Ch A PBX – Administration
161.445		Administration – Simplex

Indianapolis – Avon Yard

160.350		Hump 1
160.410		Hump 2
160.425		Pulldown 1
160.365		Pulldown 2
161.340		Pulldown 3
160.860		Ch 3 Crew cab
160.980		Ch 4 switching
160.920		Diesel Shop
160.650	161.505	Car Dept.
160.740		Car Dept. to Tower 1

Indianapolis Union

161.220	Terminal Belt 1
161.400	Terminal Belt 2
161.010	Terminal Belt 3
160.965	Terminal Belt 4

Massachusetts
Boston

161.550	160.680	Police repeater
161.550	160.560	Police repeater

48

Maryland
Baltimore – Bayside Yard
160.860   Ch 3 Yard
160.980   Ch 4 Yard
161.325 160.275 Car Dept. and car shop
Michigan
Detroit
160.500   PBX – Administration
160.860   Towers south and west of West Detroit
160.980   Towers north and east of West Detroit
161.055   MofW – Special projects
161.100   Yard
161.280   Police mutual aid
161.325   Crew cabs
161.430   MofW
161.535   Police – Car to car
Detroit – River Rouge Bridge
156.600   Bridge to river traffic
Grand Rapids
160.860   Ch 3 Hughart Yard
160.980   Ch 4 Hughart Yard
Jackson
160.860   Ch 3 Yard
160.275 161.520 Car Dept.
Kalamazoo
160.860   Ch 3 Botsford Yard
160.980   Ch 4 Botsford Yard
Missouri
St. Louis
160.710   Yard
160.995   Yard

161.055   Yard
161.085   Yard
160.485   Brooklyn Yard
New Jersey
Elizabethport – Elizabeth Yard (E'port)
160.770   Yard
161.430   Train Movement Desk and taxi
161.340 160.680 Police – PBX
Newark – Oak Island yard
160.245   Hump
North Bergen
160.665   Intermodal facility
160.740   Yard
Perth Amboy
161.355   Former Raritan River yard
New York
Buffalo – Frontier Yard
160.650 161.370 Hump
160.245   Pulldown 1
160.410   Pulldown 2
160.995   Pulldown 3
161.055   Pulldown 4
160.350 161.310 Car Dept.
Buffalo – Kenmore Yard
160.980   Ch 4 Yard
Buffalo – Seneca Yard
160.980   Ch 4 Yard
New York
160.950   Ch 1 Road – Metro-North
160.560   Yardmaster, Oak Point Yard

Conrail

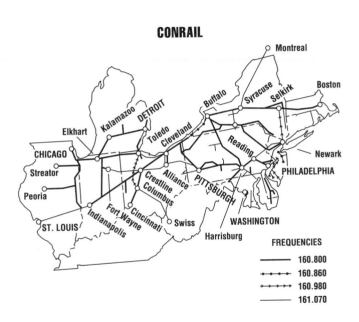

CONRAIL

FREQUENCIES

——————	**160.800**
•–•–•–•	**160.860**
›–›–›–›	**160.980**
——————	**161.070**

Niagara Falls – Niagara Yard
160.350   161.310   Car Dept.
160.980   Ch 4 Yard
Rochester – Goodman Street Yard
160.980   Ch 4 Yard
Selkirk – Selkirk Yard
160.920   Hump
160.335   Pulldown 1
160.245   Pulldown 2
160.440   Pulldown 3
161.430   Pulldown 4
161.325   160.275   Car Dept.
161.460   160.380   Diesel Shop
160.860   Ch 3 intermodal facility and auto site
161.565   160.740   Administration PBX
Syracuse – DeWitt Yard
160.860   Ch 3 Hump
160.245   Pulldown
160.410   Pulldown
160.350   Car Dept.

Ohio
Cincinnati – Sharonville Yard
160.980   Ch 4 Industrial switching
160.410   161.565   Pulldown
Cleveland – Collinwood Yard
160.860   Ch 3 North Yard pulldown
160.980   Ch 4 Yardmaster and taxi
161.460   160.470   Car Dept.
Columbus
161.445   160.485   Ch A PBX – Administration
160.980   Ch 4 Local industrial switching

Conrail

Columbus – Buckeye Yard
160.860		Ch 3 Intermodal Yard
160.775		Ch 5 Hump 1
160.350		Ch 6 Hump 2
160.995		Ch 7 Crew cabs
161.505	160.890	Pulldown 1
161.400	160.650	Pulldown 2
161.325	160.305	Pulldown 3
160.740		Intermodal facility – PTL Trucking
161.460	160.275	Car Dept.
160.920		Stores Dept.
160.905		C&S Shop

Dayton – Moraine Yard
160.980	Ch 3 GM Yard

Lordstown
160.545	Auto Parts Dock
160.860	Ch 3 Industrial switching
160.980	Ch 4 Industrial switching

Springfield
160.860	Ch 3 Yard
160.980	Ch 4 Yard

Toledo – Stanley Yard
160.485	161.445	Ch A PBX – Administration
160.860		Ch 3 Hump – 2
161.325	160.305	Ch 3 Pulldown and crew cab
160.350	161.310	Ch 4 Pulldown
160.980		Ch 4 Industrial switching
160.245		Ch 5 Hump – 1
161.460	160.470	Ch 16 Car Dept.
160.740	161.340	Intermodal facility – PTL Trucking

Pennsylvania

Altoona
160.350	Pager

Altoona – Juniata Shop
160.410		Car shop
160.740	161.340	Locomotive shop
160.980		Shop hostler

Enola – Enola Yard
161.055		East hump
160.980		West hump
160.410		West end pulldown
161.475		Eastbound receiving yard
160.395		Westbound class yard
160.305		Diesel house
161.520	160.830	Car Dept.
160.995		Crew cab

Erie
160.860	Ch 3 Yard

Harrisburg
161.010	PBX – Administration
160.860	Ch 4 Yard

Lancaster
160.860	Ch 3 Yard
160.980	Ch 4 Yard

Philadelphia
161.010	Active – PBX Administration
161.205	Police – Conrail and Amtrak

Philadelphia – Coal Pier
160.830	Yard
161.220	Yard

Copper – CP Rail

Philadelphia – Race Street Yard
161.520	160.275	Car Dept.

Philadelphia – Reading Division
160.350	SEPTA commuter trains

Philadelphia – South Philadelphia Yard
160.860	Ch 3 Yard
160.590	Active – use unknown
160.995	Active – use unknown
161.190	Active – use unknown
161.340	Active – use unknown
160.260	Crew Bus
161.430	Crew Bus

Philadelphia – Wayne Junction
161.400	Signal Dept. Trouble Desk

Pittsburgh – Conway Yard
161.460		Hump – east
160.470		Hump – west
160.860		Ch 3 Hump 2
160.215		Pulldown
160.365		Pulldown
160.755		Pulldown
161.190		Pulldown
161.280		Pulldown
161.565		Pulldown
160.980		Ch 4 Industrial switching
161.445	160.485	Ch A PBX – Administration
160.275	161.325	Car Dept.

Copper Basin — Hayden, Arizona
160.545	General operations
161.505	General operations

Corbin Railway Service — Erwin, Tennessee
160.695	General operations

Corinth & Counce — see TennRail

CP Rail — Montreal, Quebec
161.475		CP 1 Road and dispatcher
161.475	161.535	CP 2 Train to dispatcher
161.475	160.425	CP 3 Train to dispatcher
161.115		CP 4 Road and dispatcher
161.325		CP 5 Road and dispatcher
161.325	160.425	CP 6 Train to dispatcher
161.535		CP 7 Road and dispatcher
161.535	160.425	CP 8 Train to dispatcher
161.115	160.425	CP 9 Train to dispatcher
160.725	160.425	CP 10 Train to dispatcher
160.845		CP 11 MofW – 2
160.845	160.335	CP 12 Utility PBX – 1
161.175		CP 13 MofW – 1
161.175	160.335	CP 14 Utility PBX – 2
160.845	160.245	CP 15 Utility PBX – 3
161.265		CP 16 MofW – 3
161.265	160.245	CP 17 Utility PBX – 4
161.175	160.635	CP 18 Utility PBX – 5
161.505		CP 19 MofW – 4
161.505	160.635	CP 20 Utility PBX – 6
161.265	160.605	CP 21 Utility PBX – 7
161.505	160.605	CP 22 Utility PBX – 8
160.425		CP 33
160.245		CP 34
160.335		CP 35

160.605		CP 36
160.635		CP 37
159.810		CP 50
159.885		CP 51 Police
159.930		CP 52 Hump cab signals
160.050		CP 53 Yard and terminal
160.070		CP 54
160.145		CP 55
160.185		CP 56 Yard and intermodal facility
160.215		CP 57 Canadian National Ch 16
160.245		CP 58 Yard and intermodal facility
160.275		CP 59 Yard and shop
160.290		CP 60 Yard – Winnipeg
160.305		CP 61 Canadian National Ch 28
160.335		CP 62 Diesel shop and yard
160.365		CP 63 Canadian National Ch 5
160.395		CP 64 Ogden Wheel Shop
160.425		CP 65 Yard and terminal
160.440		CP 66 Bangor & Aroostook Ch 1 Road
160.455		CP 67 Canadian National Ch 32
160.485		CP 68 Canadian National Ch 33 Yard
160.515		CP 69 Yard and terminal
160.545		CP 70 Police Mutual Aid
160.575		CP 71 Canadian National Ch 13 Police
160.590		CP 72
160.605		CP 73 Yard and hump
160.620		CP 74 Maine Central Ch 1 Road
160.635		CP 75 Yard
160.665		CP 76 Canadian National Ch 4 Yard
160.695		CP 77 Canadian National Ch 17
160.725		CP 78 Road and dispatcher
160.755		CP 79 Yard and terminal

160.755		CP 80 Car Dept.
160.785		CP 81 Canadian National Ch 20 MofW
160.815		CP 82 Yard and terminal
160.875		CP 83 Intermodal facility and yard
160.905		CP 84 Canadian National Ch 24
160.935		CP 85 Canadian National Ch 3
160.965		CP 86 Canadian National Ch 26
160.995		CP 87 Yard
161.025		CP 88 Canadian National Ch 8
161.055		CP 89 Canadian National Ch 29
161.070		CP 90 Conrail Ch 2
161.085		CP 91
161.100		CP 92 Burlington Northern Ch 1 and Delaware & Hudson dispatcher and road
161.145		CP 93 Yard and terminal
161.160		CP 94
161.205		CP 95 Canadian National Ch 2 Dispatcher
161.235		CP 96
161.295		CP 97
161.325		CP 98
161.355		CP 99 Yard and branchline
161.385		CP 100
161.415		CP 101 Canadian National Ch 1 Road
161.445		CP 102
160.545	159.865	CP 110
159.930	160.725	CP 111 Car Dept.
159.930	160.755	CP 112 Car Dept.
160.035		CP 113 Road (Esquimault & Nanaimo)
160.050	160.755	CP 114 Car Dept.
160.245	160.050	CP 115
160.050	161.175	CP 116 Dispatcher link – Sparwood to Greenhills, British Columbia

CP Rail

161.265	160.050	CP 117
161.355	160.050	CP 118
161.505	160.050	CP 119
160.335	160.185	CP 120
160.425	160.185	CP 121
160.845	160.185	CP 122
160.875	160.185	CP 123
161.115	160.185	CP 124
160.185		CP 125 Dispatcher link
161.505	160.185	CP 126
161.325	160.245	CP 127
161.475	160.335	CP 128
160.845	160.245	CP 129
160.875	160.425	CP 130
160.425	161.175	CP 131 Montreal 1 and 18
161.475	160.440	CP 132
160.755	161.505	CP 133
161.325	160.635	CP 134
159.960	160.725	CP 135
160.635	160.725	CP 136
160.815	160.755	CP 137
160.755	161.505	CP 138 Car Dept.
159.930	160.785	CP 139
159.930	160.815	CP 140
161.355	160.815	CP 141
160.845	161.535	CP 142 MofW
161.505	161.115	CP 143
161.535	161.115	CP 144
160.875	161.145	CP 145 MofW – PBX
161.175	161.355	CP 146
161.535	161.475	CP 147
161.505		CP 148
161.175	160.635	CP 149
161.265	160.635	CP 150
161.755		CP 151
161.535	160.845	CP 152
160.755	160.185	CP 153
161.370		CP 154 Soo Line Ch 1
161.520		CP 155 Soo Line Ch 2
159.810	161.055	CP 156 Canadian National Ch 7
160.485	161.295	CP 157 Canadian National Ch 6
159.930	161.520	CP 161 Car Dept.
160.230		CP 164 CSX Ch 1
160.320		CP 166 CSX Ch 2
160.530		CP 170 Delaware & Hudson Yard
160.800		CP 176 Conrail Ch 1
160.980		CP 177 Conrail Ch 4
159.885	160.725	CP 178
159.885	161.145	CP 193
160.275	161.235	CP 196
160.425	161.475	CP 203
160.425	161.325	CP 206
160.425	161.535	CP 208
160.425	161.115	CP 209
160.545	159.885	CP 210 Police Mutual Aid
159.930	160.755	CP 211
160.335	160.845	CP 212
160.335	161.175	CP 214
160.245	160.845	CP 215
161.175	160.050	CP 216 Point-to-point Link
160.245	161.265	CP 217
160.635	161.175	CP 218
161.505	160.050	CP 219
160.635	161.505	CP 220

160.605	161.265	CP 221
160.605	161.505	CP 222
161.115	160.185	CP 224
161.145		CP 225 Dispatcher link
161.505	160.185	CP 226 Hump – Calgary
161.325	160.245	CP 227 Hump – Calgary
160.425	160.845	CP 229
160.425	161.175	CP 231
160.050	160.755	CP 233
160.635	161.325	CP 234
160.755	161.505	CP 238
160.815	161.355	CP 241
160.845	161.535	CP 242
161.505	161.115	CP 243
161.115	161.535	CP 244
160.635	161.535	CP 260 Link
160.725	159.885	CP 278
161.145	159.885	CP 293
161.235	160.275	CP 296
161.355	160.050	CP 299 Diesel shop
161.475		CP 300
161.475		CP 301
161.115		CP 304
161.325		CP 305
161.535		CP 307
161.115		CP 309
160.845		CP 311
161.175		CP 313
161.175		CP 314
161.505		CP 319
159.930		CP 352
160.050		CP 353

160.185		CP 356
160.515		CP 369
160.605		CP 373
160.725		CP 378
160.815		CP 382
160.875		CP 383
160.995		CP 387
161.145		CP 393
161.355		CP 399
411.5625	416.5625	CP 401
414.1125	419.1125	CP 402
414.1375		CP 403 Dispatcher link – Bamoos to Horn, Ontario
414.1875		CP 404 Dispatcher link – Winnipeg to and from Rosser, Manitoba
414.4625		CP 405 Dispatcher link – Mont Tremblant to Mount Sir Wilford, Quebec
414.4625	419.4750	CP 406
414.4625	452.4125	CP 407
414.4875		CP 408 Montreal
414.4875		CP 409 Dispatcher link – Cote St. Luc (Montreal) to Mont Sauvage, Quebec
414.5375		CP 410
414.5625		CP 411
419.4500	414.5625	CP 412 Point-to-point link
414.5625		CP 413 Dispatcher link – Mont Tremblant to Mont Sauvage, Quebec
411.5625	416.5625	CP 414 Point-to-point link
414.1875	417.1025	CP 415 Point-to-point link
418.5750		CP 416
419.1375		CP 418 Dispatcher link – Horn to Bamoos, Ontario

CP Rail

419.4500		CP 419 Dispatcher link – Mount Sir Wilford to Mont Tremblant, Quebec
419.4500		CP 420
419.4750		CP 423
419.5375		CP 424
419.5500		CP 425 Dispatcher link – Mont Sauvage to Mont Tremblant, Quebec
419.5500		CP 427
451.1500		CP 429 Toronto
451.1750	456.1875	CP 430 Montreal
451.1750		CP 431 Montreal
451.1750	462.1250	CP 432 Longueuil, Quebec
451.2250		CP 434 Agincourt, Ontario
451.2250	451.2375	CP 435 Agincourt, Ontario
451.7375		CP 436
451.7375	456.7375	CP 437
452.4000	457.4125	CP 438 Agincourt, Ontario
452.4125		CP 439
452.7000		CP 440
452.7000	457.7125	CP 441 Agincourt, Ontario
452.9250		CP 442
452.9250	457.9250	CP 443
452.9000		CP 444
452.9500	457.9500	CP 445
452.9500	457.9625	CP 446
456.1875		CP 447
456.1875	467.1375	CP 449 Montreal
456.2375		CP 451
456.5625	456.5625	CP 452 Marathon Realty
457.4125		CP 457
457.5125		CP 458
457.6000		CP 459
457.7000		CP 460
457.7125		CP 462
458.1850		CP 467
458.1875		CP 468 Vancouver
459.2000		CP 469 Toronto/Agincourt
460.550		CP 470
460.9500		CP 471 All Canada mobile
460.9625		CP 472
460.9625	465.9625	CP 473
462.1250	451.1750	CP 474 Montreal
462.1250		CP 475 Longueuil, Quebec
462.1250	467.1375	CP 476 Longueuil, Quebec
464.0750		CP 477 Montreal and Robertsonville
464.2375		CP 478
464.3750		CP 479 Tring Junction, Quebec
464.4500		CP 480 Outremont, Quebec
464.5500		CP 481 Toronto Montreal
464.700		CP 483 MofW – Calgary
464.8250		CP 484
464.8450		CP 485 All-Canada mobile
464.8750		CP 486 All-Canada mobile
467.1375	456.1875	CP 488 Longueuil, Quebec
469.2250		CP 491 Montreal
469.375		CP 492 Yard – Calgary
469.4625		CP 493 Link – Winnipeg
469.4625		CP 494
469.6000		CP 495 Montreal
469.9625		CP 496 Link – Winnipeg
457.9375		CP 497
469.2375		CP 500
469.6875		CP 501
469.8625		CP 502

469.9875		CP 503
414.0500	419.0500	CP 504
457.9375		CP 507 End-of-train telemetry
452.9375		CP 508 Head-of-train telemetry
27.56		CP 602
140.160	142.815	CP 612 Remote control locomotive repeater
140.700		CP 613 Remote control locomotive
140.700	142.815	CP 614 Remote control locomotive repeater
142.815	140.160	CP 615 Remote control locomotive repeater
142.815	140.700	CP 616 Remote control locomotive repeater
151.145		CP 621 Coquitlam, British Columbia
153.230		CP 622
153.320		CP 623
153.350		CP 624
159.540		CP 680 Montreal – Smith Transport
162.300		CP 681 Winnipeg
166.800		CP 683 Hump cab signal
172.380		CP 685 1 base and 8 mobiles
462.4500		Montreal, Quebec City
469.2500		Montreal
469.7000		Montreal
469.8250		Montreal
464.4000		Toronto
469.3875		Calgary, Lethbridge
469.4000		Montreal
160.695		Lake Erie & Northern interchange

Lake Erie & Northern Railway

160.695	Road

Grand River Railway and Lake Erie & Northern Railway

160.335	CP 62 Dispatcher
161.145	CP 93 Road

TH&B Sub-Division

160.815	Ch 1 Yard
161.355	Ch 2 Road and dispatcher
160.845	Ch 3 Car Dept. and MofW

Alberta

Calgary

161.115		CP 4 Yard
160.845		CP 11 Pulldown
160.050		CP 53 Hump
160.515		CP 69 Pulldown
160.635		CP 75 Pulldown
160.815		CP 82 Industrial yard
160.875		CP 83 Yard
160.995		CP 87 Yard
159.930	160.725	CP 111 Car Dept.
161.505	160.185	CP 226 Hump – Orange
161.325	160.245	CP 227 Hump – White
161.355	160.050	CP 299 Diesel shop
464.700		CP 483 Pettibone crane
469.375		CP 492 Intermodal facility
166.800		CP 683 Hump cab signal

Calgary – Alyth Shops

160.335	CP 62 Diesel shop
161.145	CP 93 Diesel shop

Calgary – Ogden Shop

160.395	CP 64 Wheel shop
160.755	CP 79 Car shop

Edmonton

160.845	CP 11 Yard
160.815	CP 82 Yard
160.875	CP 83 Intermodal facility

CP Rail

160.995		CP 87 Yard
161.355		CP 99 Yard
Lethbridge		
161.355		CP 99 Yard
Medicine Hat		
160.815		CP 82 Yard
161.355		CP 99 Yard
British Columbia		
Aldergrove		
160.845	161.535	CP 142
Canyon Division		
160.845	160.335	CP 212 UT-1
Cranbrook		
160.635		CP 75 1 base and 1 mobile
Golden		
160.725	159.930	Car shop
160.875		CP 83 Car shop switching
Hope		
160.845	161.535	CP 142
Nelson		
160.635		CP 75 Yard
North Bend		
160.845	161.535	CP 142 1 base/repeater
Revelstoke		
161.355		CP 99 Yard
Sparwood		
161.325		CP 5 Yard
Vancouver		
161.115		CP 4 Terminal
160.845	160.335	CP 12 MofW
160.175		CP 13 MofW
159.885		CP 51 Police

161.520		CP 155 Auxiliary crane
458.1875		CP 468 – 1 base and 5 mobiles
469.375		CP 492 3 mobiles
160.275		Southern Railway of British Columbia trackage rights
160.935		Canadian National Ch 5
161.100		Burlington Northern Ch 1
Vancouver – Roberts Bank Port		
160.245		CP 58 Coal port operations
160.695		BC Rail – Hotbox talker
Vancouver – Coquitlam Yard		
160.050		CP 53 Loco shop
160.185		CP 56 Car shop
160.695		CP 77 Yard
160.725		CP 78 Transfer 1
160.755		CP 79 Yard 2
160.815		CP 82 Production control
160.875		CP 83 Transfer 2
160.995		CP 87 Yard 4
161.145		CP 93 Yard 3
161.355		CP 99 Yard 1
159.930	161.520	CP 161 Car Dept.
Vancouver – Waterfront		
161.355		CP 99 Switcher
Vancouver Island – See Esquimault & Nanaimo Railway		
Manitoba		
Winnipeg		
161.325		CP 5 Yard
161.265		CP 16 Yard
160.185		CP 56 Intermodal facility
160.290		CP 60 Yard
160.335		CP 62 1 base and 5 mobiles

160.605		CP 73 Yard
160.725		CP 78 Yard
160.815		CP 82 Diesel shop
160.875		CP 83 Intermodal facility
160.995		CP 87 Yard
161.145		CP 93 Yard
161.355		CP 99 Yard
159.930	160.755	CP 139 Car Dept.
469.4625		CP 494 1 base-6 watts
469.9625		CP 496 1 base-6 watts
162.300		CP 681 1 base and 11 mobiles

Winnipeg – Transcona Yard

160.845	CP 11 Welded Rail Plant
160.050	CP 53 Crane

Winnipeg – Weston Yard

161.505	CP 19 Weston car shop
160.275	CP 59 Weston car shop

Maine

Brownville Junction

160.440	Interchange with Bangor & Aroostook
160.875	CP 83 Yard

Mattawamkeag

160.875	CP 83 Yard

Vanceboro

160.875	CP 83 Yard

New Brunswick

Saint John

160.185	CP 56 1 base and 9 mobiles
160.245	CP 58 1 base and 8 mobiles
161.355	CP 99 3 Base and 20 mobiles

Nova Scotia

Digby

160.185	CP 56 1 base and 19 mobiles

Ontario

London

161.175	CP 13 Radio Shop
161.505	CP 19 MofW
161.145	CP 93 Yard

Oshawa

160.185	CP 56 1 base and mobiles

Smith Falls

160.755	CP 79 1 base and 10 mobiles

Sudbury

161.355	CP 99 1 base and 4 mobiles

Thunder Bay

161.115	CP 4 Yard
160.050	CP 53 Car planner/crane
160.185	CP 56 Diesel shop
160.335	CP 62 MofW
160.515	CP 69 Yard
160.515	CP 69 Harbor Commission
160.605	CP 73 Hump
160.635	CP 75 Yard
160.815	CP 82 Yard
160.875	CP 83 Yard
160.995	CP 87 Yard
161.145	CP 93 Car planner
161.355	CP 99 Yard

159.930	160.725	CP 111 Car Dept.

Toronto

161.265	CP 16 Yard
159.885	CP 51 Police
160.245	CP 58 Intermodal facility
160.545	CP 70 Police mutual aid

CP Rail

161.235		CP 96 Police
161.355		CP 99 Industrial yard
159.930	160.755	CP 112 Car Dept.
452.700		CP 440 Yard
456.2375		CP 451 Yard
457.4125		CP 457 Yard
464.550		CP 481 Yard

Toronto – Agincourt Yard

161.325		CP 5 Yard
159.930		CP 52 Yard
160.050		CP 53 Loco shop/car planner
160.185		CP 56 Industrial yard
160.275		CP 59 Yard
160.335		CP 62 Diesel shop
160.725		CP 78 Yard
160.755		CP 79 Yard
160.875		CP 83 Hump
160.050	160.755	CP 114 Car Dept.
451.150		CP 429 1 base and 3 mobiles
451.2250	456.2375	CP 435 1 base and 5 mobiles
452.4000	457.4125	CP 438 1 base and 5 mobiles
452.7000	457.7125	CP 441 1 base and 5 mobiles
459.2000		CP 469 1 base and 19 mobiles

Toronto – Cambridge Yard

160.815	CP 82 Yard

Toronto – Obico Yard

161.145	CP 93 Yard

Toronto – Oshawa Yard

160.995	CP 87 Yard

Windsor

161.115	CP 4 Yard
161.265	CP 16 Yard

160.185		CP 56 Yard and intermodal facility
160.755		CP 79 Car Dept.
161.355		CP 99 Yard

Quebec

Montreal

160.845		CP 11 MofW – 2
161.175		CP 13 – MofW – 1
161.265		CP 16 – MofW – 3
159.885		CP 51 Police
160.050		CP 53 Smith Transport
160.515		CP 69 Harbor Commission
160.545		CP 70 Police mutual aid
160.875	161.145	CP 145 Utility PBX – Montreal terminal zone
451.1750	456.1875	CP 430 1 base and 25 mobiles
469.225		CP 491 1 base and 11 mobiles
159.540		CP 680 Smith Transport

Montreal – Angus Shops

469.600	CP 495 Trackmobiles

Montreal – Glen Yard

161.115	CP 4 Coach yard and Car Dept.

Montreal – Hochelaga Yard

161.115	CP 4 Yard
160.725	CP 78 Yard

Montreal – La Salle Yard

464.0750	CP 477 1 base and 18 mobiles
464.5500	CP 481 1 base and 24 mobiles

Montreal – Lachine Yard

160.830	Intermodal facility
161.115	CP 4 Intermodal facility

Montreal – Longueuil Yard

160.050	CP 53 1 base and 92 mobiles
462.1250 467.1375	CP 476 1 base and 12 mobiles

Montreal – Outremont Yard
160.815	CP 82 Yard
464.450	CP 480 2 Base and 5 mobiles

Montreal – Seaway Tower
161.115	CP 4 Tower operator

Montreal – St. Luc Yard
161.325	CP 5 Yard
159.930	CP 52 Hump cab signals
160.245	CP 58 1 base and 20 mobiles
160.995	CP 87 Hump
161.145	CP 93 Van and auto site
161.355	CP 99 Pulldown
160.755 161.505	CP 138 Car Dept.
161.490	Diesel Shop
161.520	CP 155 Diesel shop
27.56	CP 602 1 base-5 Watts

Montreal – Ste. Therese Yard
161.355	CP 99 Yard

Montreal – Vankleek Yard
160.845 160.335	CP 212 Car Dept.

Montreal – Windsor Station
161.115	CP 4 Tower operator

Quebec City
160.755	CP 79 1 base and 5 mobiles
160.815	CP 82 3 Base and 9 mobiles

Robertsonville
464.0750	CP 477 1 base and 3 mobiles
464.5500	CP 481 1 base and 3 mobiles

Tring Junction
464.375	CP 479 1 base and 21 mobiles

Trois Rivieres
160.755	CP 79 1 base and 3 mobiles

160.815	CP 82 3 Base and 16 mobiles

Saskatchewan
Moose Jaw
160.755	CP 79 2 Base and 4 mobiles

Saskatoon – Sutherland yard
161.115	CP 4 Yard
160.515	CP 69 Yard
160.725	CP 78 Yard workers
160.755	CP 79 Car Shop
160.815	CP 82 Yardmaster
161.355	CP 99 Yard

Crab Orchard & Egyptian   Marion, Illinois
160.350	General operations

CSX Transportation   Jacksonville, Florida
160.230Δ	Road – Former Chessie
161.370Δ	Road – Former L&N
160.590Δ	Road – Former SCL
161.100Δ	Road – Former SCL
160.995	Road – Former P&LE
160.320Δ	Dispatcher – Former Chessie
161.520Δ	Dispatcher – Former L&N and SCL
160.290	Yard – Former Chessie
160.410	Yard – Former Chessie
160.470	Yard – Former Chessie
160.530	Yard – Former Chessie
160.890	Yard – Former Chessie
161.160	Yard – Former Chessie
160.440	Yard – Former L&N
160.620	Yard – Former L&N
161.280	Yard – Former L&N

CSX

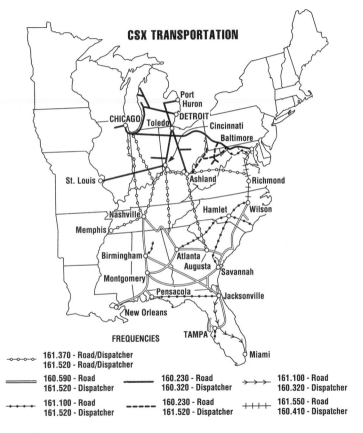

CSX TRANSPORTATION

FREQUENCIES

○-○-○-○-○ 161.370 - Road/Dispatcher
161.520 - Road/Dispatcher

━━━━━ 160.590 - Road
161.520 - Dispatcher

●-●-●-● 161.100 - Road
161.520 - Dispatcher

━━━━━ 160.230 - Road
160.320 - Dispatcher

- - - - - 160.230 - Road
161.520 - Dispatcher

➤➤➤ 161.100 - Road
160.320 - Dispatcher

+++++ 161.550 - Road
160.410 - Dispatcher

160.290		Yard – Former SCL
161.400		Yard – Former SCL
161.460	160.440	Car Dept. – Former SCL
160.380		MofW – Southern areas
160.785		MofW – Systemwide
160.305		MofW/C&S – Former L&N
161.175		MofW/C&S – Southern areas
161.310		MofW – Former SCL
160.875		Police – Systemwide
161.040		Police – Former SCL
161.205		Police mutual aid
161.265	160.395	PBX 1

Alabama: Birmingham
Florida: Bushnell, Hialeah, Jacksonville, Orlando, St. Petersburg, Tampa
Georgia: Atlanta, Augusta, Dooling, Fitzgerald, Hatley, Manchester, Race Pond, Savannah, Senioa, Sessoms, Union City, Waycross
Kentucky: Elizabethtown, Louisville
North Carolina: Benson, Cary, Charlotte, Hamlet, Henderson, Raleigh, Rocky Mount
South Carolina: Charleston, Columbia, Florence
Tennessee: Chattanooga, Erwin, Memphis, Nashville
Virginia: Petersburg

161.430	161.350	PBX 2
160.890	161.415	PBX 3

Alabama

Birmingham

161.205	Police

Birmingham – Boyles Yard

160.305	Signal Dept.

160.860		Hump
160.985		MofW
161.010		Pulldown
161.055		Retarder tower
161.310	160.620	Car Dept.
452.950		Hump cab signals

Birmingham – Tote Yard

160 .440	Yard

Mobile

160.230	G – 1 base
160.260	G – 1 control base
160.305	RW – 1 base
160.320	MR – 1 base
160.380	Yard
160.620	G – FCC
161.175	RW – FCC
161.265	EE – FCC
161.280	Yard

Montgomery

160.380	Yard
160.260	Car Dept.

Ragland

161.460	160.440	Car Dept.

Delaware

Wilmington – Wilsmere Yard

160 .530	161.415	Ch 3 Yard

Florida

Hialeah

160.800	G-1 base
160.890	G-1 base
161.220	G-1 base
161.460	G-1 base

Jacksonville – Moncrief Yard

160.350	G-1 base
160.485	G-1 base
160.710	G-1 base
160.800	G-1 base
160.995	G-1 base
161.070	G-1 base
161.220	G-1 base

161.460	160.440	Car Dept.

Pensacola

160.380	Yard

Tampa

161.220	Stores Dept.
161.220	Rockport Yard – portables only
161.340	Rockport Yard

161.460	160.440	Car Dept., Uceta and Yoeman Yards

Georgia

Athens

160.890	G-1 base
161.220	G-1 base

Atlanta

161.100	Terminal road
160.230	Terminal dispatcher
161.040	Police

Atlanta – Howells Yard

160.770	Hump
160.230	Pulldown

Atlanta – Hulsey Yard

161.310	Yard – Former Georgia Railroad

Atlanta – Tilford Yard

161.610	Hump
160.440	Pulldown

CSX

160.860		Yard
160.770		Yard
161.010	160.620	Car Dept.
452.950		Hump cab signals

Augusta

160.485	Yard Clerks

Cartersville

160.440	Yard

Savannah

160.920	160.410	Yard
161.460	160.440	Car Dept.

Waycross

160.290		Active
160.710		Active
161.070		Active
161.310		Active
160.380	161.250	Diesel shop
161.460	160.440	Car Dept.
452.925		Hump cab signals

Illinois

Chicago – 48th Street Yard

160.290	Ch 5 Yard

Chicago – Ashland Avenue Yard

161.415	Yard Clerks

Chicago – Barr Yard

160.275	Car Dept. and intermodal facility
160.740	Ch 7 Yard

Chicago – Dolton Yard

161.145	Yard

Chicago – Halsted Street Yard

161.310	Clerks and crew van

Danville

160.290	Brewer Yard
160.590	Administration
160.905	Traveling freight agent
161.175	Communications Dept.

East St. Louis

161.280	Yard
160.530	Ch 3 Intermodal facility
160.605	Remote control locomotives
160.875	Car Dept.
161.205	Police – mutual aid

Indiana

Evansville

161.025	Radio Communications Dept.
161.175	Radio Communications Dept.
161.205	Police

Evansville – Howell Yard

160.440	Yard 1
160.770	Yard 2

160.380	161.220	Car Dept.

Lafayette

160.470	Yard

Kentucky

Ashland

160.290	Ch 5 Yard

Corbin

160.260	Car Shop
160.305	Signal Dept.
160.380	Car inspectors
160.440	West Yard
160.770	East Yard

Lebanon
161.010	Yard

Louisville
160.260	Yard
161.280	Yard
160.620	Car Dept.

Louisville – East Louisville Yard
161.550	Yard

Louisville – Mapother Yard
161.130	Yard

Louisville – Osborne Yard
160.380	Yard
160.440	Hump and pulldown
160.890	Hump

Russell
160.290	Ashland Refining Yard
160.530	Russell Yard eastbound hump
160.890	Russell Yard westbound hump
161.370 160.770	Russell Yard coal hump

Louisiana

New Orleans
161.205	Police – Car to car
161.370	Gentilly Tower
160.380	Yard
160.875	Gentilly yardmaster and bridgemaster
160.305	Intermodal
160.575	Active

Maryland

Baltimore
160.740	Active
161.250	Active
161.535	Active

160.530	Ch 3 Bay View Yard
160.470	Locust Point Yard

Baltimore – Curtis Bay Yard
160.890	Yard
161.370	Coal dock

Brunswick
160.530	Ch 3 Yard

Cumberland
160.530	Ch 3 West hump
161.160	Ch 4 East hump
160.785	Ch 8 MofW and Signal Dept.
160.650	Locomotive shop and ready track
161.220	Locomotive shop and ready track
160.470	East end Car Dept.
160.290 161.040	West end Car Dept.
160.305	Signal Dept.

Frederick
161.040	Car Dept.

Hagerstown
160.530	Ch 3 Yard
160.530	Ch 3 Pitt Yard
161.160 160.380	Ch 4 Yard – Portables
160.290	Ch 5 Switching
160.785	Ch 8 MofW and Signal Dept.
160.770	Pagers
160.935	Active

Michigan

Detroit
161.160	Ch 4 Yard
160.410	Yard
160.665	Yard
160.695	Yard

CSX

160.725		Yard
161.280		Police mutual aid

Flint – Buick Yard

160.410		Ch 6 Yard

Flint – Fisher Body Yard

160.290		Ch 5 Yard

Grand Rapids – Wyoming Yard

160.290		Ch 5 Yard westbound
160.635		Yard and rip track
160.410		Ch 6 Yard
160.500		Stores Dept.
160.740		Ch 7 Diesel house hostler
160.785		Ch 8 MofW and Signal Dept.
160.875		Ch 9 Police
160.905		Yard
161.160		Ch 4 Yard
161.460		Car Dept.

Plymouth

160.905		Ch Y1 Yard

Port Huron

160.290		St. Clair River car float

Saginaw

160.485		Yard
160.410		Ch 6 Norman Street Yard
160.290		Ch 5 Wadsworth Yard

Missouri

St. Louis

160.260		Yard
160.935		Yard
160.365		Cone Yard

Mississippi

Gulfport

160.305		Signal Dept.
160.320		Active
160.545		Active

North Carolina

Charlotte

160.905		Active
161.100		Pinoca Yard

Fayetteville

161.220		G-1 base

Hamlet, NC

161.070		G-1 base
161.340		Yard
161.400		Hump
161.460	160.440	Car Dept.
160.485		FCC – 2 BM
160.710		FCC – 2 BM
160.785		FCC – 2 BM
160.890		FCC – 1 BM
160.920		FCC – 1 BM

Monroe

161.370		Yard
161.100		Yard

Rocky Mount

161.460	160.440	Car Dept.
160.215		FCC – 1 BM
160.290		FCC – 2 BM
160.860		FCC – 2 BM
161.355		FCC – 1 BM

Ohio

Cincinnati – Queensgate Yard

160.530		Ch 3 Yard
161.160		Ch 4 Yard and industrial switching
160.290		Ch 5 Pulldown
160.410	161.340	Ch 6 Car Dept.
160.785		Ch 8 MofW and Signal Dept.
160.875		Ch 9 Police – Ch 1
160.605		Hump
160.425		Pulldown 1
160.635		Pulldown 3
160.455		Car Dept.
160.695		Car Dept. (may be unused)
161.295		Police – Ch 2 Portables
452.950	457.950	Hump speed control

Cleveland

160.890	Switching, former Newburgh & South Shore

Columbus – Parsons Yard

160.530		Ch 3 Yard
161.160		Ch 4 Yard
160.410		Ch 6 Switching
160.785		Ch 8 MofW and Signal Dept.
160.455		Clerks
160.470		Y Yard
160.890		Y1 Yard
160.590	161.370	Car Dept.
160.725		C&O mobiles

Dayton – Needmoore Yard

160.530	Ch 3 Yard

Lima

160.530	Ch 3 Yard

Middletown

160.530	Ch 3 Yard

Oregon – Presque Isle Docks

160.470	Switching
161.100	Ore dock operations
161.310	Hump

Toledo

160.785	Ch 8 MofW and Signal Dept.
160.485	Ch 9 Police
160.875	Ch 9 Police
160.650	Active
161.340	Active
161.370	Active

Toledo – Plymouth Yard

160.410	Ch 6 Yard

Toledo – Rossford Yard

160.410	Ch 6 Yard

Toledo – Toledo Terminal

160.590	Dispatcher

Toledo – Walbridge Yard

161.160		Ch 4 Yard
160.290		Ch 5 Hump
160.410		Ch 6 Switching
161.025		Ch 10 Car Dept.
161.400	160.215	Ch 10 Car Dept.

Willard

160.530	Ch 3 Westbound hump
161.160	Ch 4 Eastbound yard
160.290	Ch 5 Yard switching
160.785	Ch 8 MofW and Signal Dept.

Youngstown

160.530	Ch 3 Yard

CSX

Pennsylvania

Connellsville
160.530	Ch 3 Yard

Demmler
160.530	Ch 3 Yard

Glenwood
160.530	Ch 3 Yard

Philadelphia
160.380	Yard
160.410	Ch 6 MofW locomotive service
160.725	Police

Philadelphia – Waterfront area
160.470	Ch Y Yard
160.890	Ch Y1 Yard

Riker
160.530	Ch 3 Yard

South Carolina

Charleston
160.215	FCC – 2 BM
160.290	Yard
160.485	FCC – 2 BM
160.355	FCC – 3 BM
161.100	Yard
161.520	Yard
161.400	Yard

Dillon
160.290	G-1 base

Florence
161.460	160.440	Car Dept.
160.290		FCC – 2 BM
160.485		FCC – 1 BM

Greenwood
160.530	Stores Dept.

Tennessee

Chattanooga
160.440	Yard
160.890	Active

Erwin
160.680	Yard

Johnson City
161.550	Yard

Knoxville
160.440	Yard
160.305	Signal Dept.
160.785	Signal Dept.

Memphis
160.305	MofW
161.175	MofW
161.205	Police

Memphis – Leewood Yard
160.440	Yard – Primary
160.335	IC interchange
160.920	IC interchange

Nashville
161.175	C&S

Nashville – Radnor Yard
160.230		Crew caller
160.260		Pulldown
160.380	161.220	Hump
160.440		Pulldown
160.710		Yard
160.770		Terminal

68

160.845		Active
161.130		Locomotive maintenance
161.550		Yard
452.950		Hump speed control

Virginia
Clifton Forge

160.485		Yard
160.560	161.550	Car Dept.
160.890		Yard

Jarratt

161.460	160.440	Car Dept.

Lynchburg

160.530	Ch 3 Lower Basin Yard
160.290	Ch 5 Switching
160.410	Ch 6 Switching

Newport News

160.410	G-3 Bases
160.650	Car Dept.
160.680	G-3 Bases
160.725	G-2 Bases
160.815	G-2 Bases
160.890	G-9 Bases
161.010	G-3 Bases
161.355	MR – G-3 Bases
161.370	G-2 Bases
161.415	G-2 Bases
161.550	G-4 Bases

Petersburg

161.460	160.440	Car Dept.

Richmond

160.215	161.430	Yardmaster
160.485		Yardmaster

West Virginia
Charleston

160.485	Ch 3 Yard

Hancock

160.530	Ch 3 Yard

Huntington

160.650	Yard
161.310	Yard
161.460	Yard
452.900	Yard
452.9125	457.9125 Yard

Kenova – Coal Yard

160.890	Yard

Former Atlanta & West Point territory

161.370	Ch 1 Road and dispatcher to train
161.520	Ch 2 Train to dispatcher
160.785	Yard
161.310	Old Ch 1 Road
161.430	Old Ch 2 Yard

Former Chesapeake & Ohio/Baltimore & Ohio/Western Maryland territory

160.230Δ		Ch 1 Road
160.320Δ		Ch 2 Dispatcher
160.530		Ch 3 Yard (B&O)
161.160		Ch 4 Yard (C&O)
160.290		Ch 5 Switching (B&O)
160.410		Ch 6 Switching (C&O)
160.740		Ch 7 Mechanical Dept.
160.785		Ch 8 MofW and Signal Dept.
160.875		Ch 9 Police
161.400	160.215	Ch 10 Car Dept.
160.470		Ch Y Yard and pulldown

CSX – Dakota

160.890	Ch Y1 Yard and pulldown	
161.415	G – Chessie Except Detroit, Cleveland, Toledo, and state of Virginia	

Former Durham and Southern territory
160.650 General operations

Former Gainesville Midland territory
160.590 Road

Former Georgia Railroad territory
160.590 Road
161.310 Ch 1 Yard
161.430 Ch 2 Yard

Former Louisville & Nashville territory
161.370△ Ch 1 Road
161.520△ Ch 2 Dispatcher
161.175 Ch 3 Wrecker, Signal Dept.
161.205 Ch 3 Police
160.305 Signal Dept. and radio shop
160.380 Yard
160.440 Yard
160.620 Yard
161.280 Yard

Former Seaboard Coast Line territory
160.590△ Ch 1 Road
161.100△ Ch 2 Road
161.400 Ch 3 Yard
160.290 Ch 4 Yard
161.520 Dispatcher
160.710 Ch 1 Wrecker
160.920 Ch 2 Wrecker
161.310 MofW
161.040 Police

Former Western Railway of Alabama territory
161.310 Old Ch 1 Road
161.370 Road
161.430 Old Ch 2 Yard
161.520 Dispatcher

Cuyahoga Valley　　　　Cleveland, Ohio
160.290 Road and yard
160.260 MofW
160.380 Dispatcher
160.950 Active

D & I Railroad　　　　Sioux Falls, South Dakota
161.190 General operations

Dakota, Minnesota & Eastern　Brookings, South Dakota
160.395 Road
160.965 Yard

Dakota, Missouri Valley & Western　Bismarck, North Dakota
160.305 Road

Dakota Rail　　　　Milbank, South Dakota
160.275 161.055 General operations, Milbank
160.275 General operations, Wayzata, Minnesota

Dakota Southern　　　　Wagner, South Dakota
161.535 General operations

Dallas, Garland & Northwestern   Garland, Texas
161.085 160.455 General operations
160.410   Union Pacific interchange

Danbury Terminal – operated by Housatonic Railroad

Dardanelle & Russellville   Dardanelle, Arkansas
160.365   Ch 1 General operations
161.280   Ch 2 General operations
160.410   Ch 3 UP Interchange

Davenport, Rock Island & Northwestern   Davenport, Iowa
160.710   General operations
161.100   Burlington Northern Interchange
160.770   CP Rail Interchange

De Queen & Eastern   De Queen, Arkansas
160.230 161.445 Ch 1 Repeater Input
160.230   Ch 2 Road and repeater output
160.605   Ch 3 Yard
160.785   Ch 4 Yard

Decatur Junction   Chillicothe, Illinois
160.380   General operations

Delaware & Hudson (CP Rail)   Albany, New York
160.320   Police
161.100△   Road and dispatcher north of Central Bridge, New York
161.475   Road and dispatcher south of Central Bridge
160.425   Tone access to dispatcher, all areas
160.530   Yard
160.590   Future PBX

Buffalo
160.590   SK Yard
East Binghamton
160.500 161.490 Car Dept.

Delaware Coast Line   Lincoln, Delaware
160.455   General operations

Delaware Lackawanna   Scranton, Pennsylvania
161.460   General operations

Delaware Valley   Kennett Square, Pennsylvania
160.545   General operations
160.605   FCC – Base and mobile

Delray Connecting   Detroit, Michigan
153.080   Plant switching
153.050   Mill operations

Delta Valley Southern   Wilson, Arkansas
160.335~   G – FCC
161.220~   G – FCC

Denver & Rio Grande Western (Southern Pacific Lines)
Denver, Colorado
160.920△   Ch 1 Road – Denver to Arvada; Moffat Tunnel to Dotsero; Denver to Alamosa and Trinidad; Grand Junction to Helper, Utah; Orestod to Phippsburg
160.455△   Ch 4 Road – Arvada to Moffat Tunnel; Pueblo to Grand Junction; Helper to Ogden, Utah
160.725   Ch 5 MofW, systemwide
160.485   Yard portables

Denver – Des Moines

160.635		Yard portables
160.695		Yard portables
160.755		Yard portables
160.905		Yard Portables
161.175	160.365	PBX – Cheyenne Mountain (Colorado Springs)
161.175	160.275	PBX – Glenwood Springs, Pueblo, and Winter Park, Colo.; Mounds and Salt Lake City, Utah
161.190		Police
161.235	160.365	PBX – Denver, Grand Junction; Salt Lake City
161.310	160.830	Car Dept.
161.415		Yard Portables
161.460		DRGW Trucking
161.490		Ch 2 Yard and Portables
161.565△	160.395△	Ch 3 Road – Moffat Tunnel; Phippsburg to Craig; Paonia Branch
457.9375		End-of-train telemetry

Colorado
Denver – North Yard

160 .275~		FCC – MR
160 .335~		FCC – MR
160 .485~		G – FCC
160 .755~		FCC
160 .890~		FCC
160 .905~		FCC
160 .950~		FCC
160 .980		Intermodal facility
161 .220		Yardmaster
161 .265~		G – FCC
161 .340~		FCC

Grand Junction

160.740	Yard
161.130	Hump

161.310	160.830	Car Dept. and roundhouse

Pueblo

160.500		Yard
160.755		Yard
161.310	160.830	Car Dept. and Clerks
161.415		Yard

Utah
Helper

160.335	Car Dept.

Salt Lake City

160.335	Car Dept.

Dispatcher links

161.415	(160.920)	– Hot Sulphur Springs to Ephraim
452.900	(160.920)	– Denver to Mount Thorodin
452.900	(160.920)	– Moab, Utah
457.900	(160.920)	– Pueblo to Alamosa
457.900	(160.920)	– Bond to Grand Junction
457.900	(160.455)	– Helper, Utah, to Salt Lake City

Map: See Southern Pacific, page 110

Denver Terminal   Denver, Colorado

160.845	General operations

Depew, Lancaster & Western   Depew, New York

160.920	General operations

Des Moines Union   **Des Moines, Iowa**

161.100	Road
161.070	General operations
160.440	Yard and MofW
160.770	Joint Operations with CP Rail
161.250	Switching

Devco   Sydney, Nova Scotia
160.305   General operations

Duluth & Northeastern   Cloquet, Minnesota
161.490   General operations

Duluth, Missabe & Iron Range   Duluth, Minnesota
160.800   Ch 1 Road and dispatcher – north
160.350   Ch 2 Road and dispatcher – south
160.230   Ch 3 Ore dock operations
161.340   160.320   Ch 4 MofW
161.280   Ch 5 Ore docks and MofW
160.620   Ch 6 Maintenance
Two Harbors
161.235   Ch 6 Maintenance

Duluth, Winnipeg & Pacific   Duluth, Minnesota
161.415   Ch 1 Road
161.205   Ch 2 Dispatcher
160.935   Ch 3 MofW
161.550   Pokegama Yard

Dunn-Erwin Railway   Aberdeen, North Carolina
161.280   160.530   General operations

East Camden & Highland   East Camden, Arkansas
160.380   General operations

East Cooper & Berkeley   Charleston, South Carolina
160.980   General operations

East Erie Commercial   Erie, Pennsylvania
160.590   General operations
161.100   General operations

East Portland Traction   Portland, Oregon
160.575   Ch 1 General operations and MofW
160.575   161.190   Ch 2 – PBX, Mount Scott
161.340   Ch 3 MofW
161.550   Ch 4 – Southern Pacific interchange
160.575   160.335   Ch 5 – Dispatcher
462.275   Switching
160.050   Remote control crossing signals

East Tennessee   Johnson City, Tennessee
160.425   General operations

Eastern Alabama   Sylacauga, Alabama
161.070   General operations

Eastern Idaho   Idaho Falls, Idaho
161.370   Road
160.845   Yard

Eastern Illinois   Charleston, Illinois
160.815   General operations

Eastern Shore   Cape Charles, Virginia
161.445   General operations
160.695   General operations
160.800   Ch 1 Road – Conrail

Elgin – Florida

161.070	Ch 2 Road – Conrail
160.980	Ch 4 Interchange-Conrail

Elgin, Joliet & Eastern — Joliet, Illinois

160.350	Road and dispatcher
160.260	Yard
160.725	Steel Mill switcher
161.475	Car Dept. – Kirk Yard
161.550	MofW and Police
159.675	Intermodal

Ellis & Eastern — Sioux Falls, South Dakota

161.385	General operations

Escanaba & Lake Superior — Wells, Michigan

160.320	161.550	Ch 1 Road
161.310	160.290	Ch 2 Road

Esquimalt & Nanaimo (CP Rail) — Victoria, British Columbia

160.035		CP 113 Road – Lineup on CP 4 at 0800 Hrs.
160.035	161.535	Road repeater
160.185		CP Ch 56 Yard
161.175		CP Ch 13 MofW
928.0125		Link – Victoria to Mount McDonald
928.0125		Link – Mount Horne to Mount Wesley
952.0125		Link – Mount McDonald to Victoria
952.0125		Link – Mount Wesley to Mount Horne

Essex Terminal — Windsor, Ontario

160.905	Road and dispatcher
160.605	Yard

Eureka Springs & North Arkansas — Eureka Springs, Arkansas

160.275	General operations

Everett Railroad — Everett, Pennsylvania

160.365	General operations

Farmrail — Elk City, Oklahoma

161.100	General operations

Florida Central — Plymouth, Florida

160.545	Ch 1 Road
161.475	Ch 2 Switching

Florida East Coast — St. Augustine, Florida

160.530	Road and dispatcher to train
160.770	Train to dispatcher

Belle Glade, Fort Lauderdale, Fort Pierce, and West Palm Beach

161.190	Trucks

Jacksonville

160.380	Trucks
161.190	Trucks
161.370	Bowden Yard car shop
469.950	FCC

Miami

161.370	Hialeah Yard car shop
469.950	FCC

Florida Midland — Plymouth, Florida

160.545	Ch 1 Road
161.475	Ch 2 Switching

Florida Northern   Ocala, Florida
    160.545   Ch 1 Road
    161.475   Ch 2 Switching

Florida West Coast   Trenton, Florida
    160.980   General operations
    161.190   Spare cChannel

Fordyce & Princeton   Fordyce, Arkansas
    160.770   Ch 1 Road
    161.535   Ch 2 Yard

Fore River – see Quincy Bay Terminal

Fort Smith   Fort Smith, Arkansas
    160.380   General operations

Fort Worth & Western   Fort Worth, Texas
    160.215   General operations
    160.785   General operations

Fort Worth Belt   Fort Worth, Texas
    160.410   General operations

Fox Valley & Western – see Wisconsin Central

Franklin County   Franklinton, North Carolina
    160.980   General operations

Fremont, West Point & Pacific   Fremont, Nebraska
    160.245   General operations
    161.265   General operations

Galveston Railway   Galveston, Texas
    161.355   General operations
    160.830 161.520 Dock administration

Garden City Western   Garden City, Kansas
    152.990   General operations
    154.600   FCC – BM

Gateway Eastern – Subsidiary of Gateway Western. Same frequencies probably used.

Gateway Western   Fairview, Illinois
    161.280   Ch 1 Road (SPCSL)
    161.460   Ch 2 Road (GWWR)
    161.025   Ch 3 East St. Louis Mechanical Dept.
    Venice, Illinois
    161.010   Ch 4 Intermodal facility
    East St. Louis, Illinois
    160.725   Ch 5 Yard
    161.295   Ch 6 Yard
    St. Louis, Missouri
    161.025   Intermodal facility
    160.860   Intermodal facility

Genesee & Mohawk Valley   Batavia, New York
    160.920   General operations

Genesee – Grand

Genesee & Wyoming   Retsof, New York

160.770	161.445	Road and repeater (Rochester & Southern)
160.500		Road (Genesee & Wyoming)
160.590		Shop and MofW
161.100		Yard

Georgetown   Georgetown, Texas

160.995	General operations

Georgia & Alabama   Dawson, Georgia

161.085	General operations

Georgia Central   Vidalia, Georgia

451.675	456.675	FCC – Link/Repeater, Dublin to Vidalia
159.585		FCC – BM
Vidalia		
160.800		Ch 1 Road
Macon		
160.680		Ch 2 Yard

Georgia Eastern   South Washington, Georgia

160.815	Road
160.965	Administration and MofW

Georgia Northeastern   Jasper, Georgia

461.250	466.250	General operations

Georgia Ports Authority   Savannah, Georgia

160.590	Joint Switching with CSX

Georgia Southwestern   Americus, Georgia

160.335	161.325	General operations
161.085		Yard and Joint operations with Georgia & Alabama

Gettysburg   Gettysburg, Pennsylvania

160.800	General operations
161.235	FCC – Base and mobiles

Gloster Southern   Gloster, Mississippi

160.770	General operations

Goderich-Exeter   Goderich, Ontario

161.310	General operations

Golden Triangle   Columbus, Mississippi

160.455	General operations
160.680	G – Base and mobiles

Grafton & Upton   Hopedale, Massachusetts

160.245	General operations

Grainbelt   Clinton, Oklahoma

161.520	Repeater input
161.100	Joint operations with Grainrail

Grand Canyon Railway   Williams, Arizona

160.350		Ch 1 Road
160.350	161.565	Ch 2 Road Repeater
160.485		Ch 3 Yard
160.830		Ch 4 Yard

Grand Rapids & Eastern   Grand Rapids, Michigan
161.235   General operations

Grand Trunk Western   Battle Creek, Michigan
160.470   Police, except Chicago
160.590△   Ch 1 Road and dispatcher
160.530△   Ch 2 Road and dispatcher
160.845   Ch 3 Chicago Yard and East Michigan Dispatcher
160.815   Ch 4 Orion Yard
161.220   Ch 5 Road – former DT&I
160.800   Ch 6 Road – Conrail
160.920 160.260   PBX – Battle Creek, Detroit, Durand, and Edwardsburg, Michigan
160.950 160.845   PBX – Ainsworth, Indiana
161.010 160.260   PBX – Grand Rapids, Pontiac, and Saginaw, Michigan
160.455   PBX – Flat Rock, Michigan
160.950   MofW
Illinois
Chicago
160.905   Police
161.205   Police mutual aid
Michigan
Battle Creek
160.350   Diesel shop
161.040   Yard
161.550 160.740   Car Dept.
Detroit
161.280   Police mutual aid
161.550 160.740   Chevrolet Plant Yard
Durand
161.040   Yard
Ferndale
160.350   Yard
Flint
160.350   Yard
161.550 160.740   Car Dept.
Lake Orion
160.815   Chevy Plant switching
Lansing
161.430   Car Dept.
Pontiac – Motor Plant
160.350   Car shop
160.845   Yardmaster
161.550   Ch 4 Yard
Pontiac – Stamping Plant
161.205   Ch 3 Yard
Pontiac – Johnson Avenue Yard
160.740   Ch 1 Yard
Port Huron
160.350   Yard
160.980~ 160.260~ G-1 base and 10 mobiles
161.040   Yard
Ohio
Toledo – Lang Yard
160.845   Ch 3 Yard
161.040   Car shop
161.520   Car shop
Detroit, Toledo & Ironton Subdivision
161.220   Ch 5 Road

77

Michigan
Flat Rock
161.340   Hump
161.430   Yard
161.490   Yard
Ohio
Lima, Napoleon, and Springfield
161.430   Yard
Shore Line Subdivision
160.530   Ch 2 Road
160.890   MofW

Great Miami & Scioto   Cincinnati, Ohio

160.905   General operations

Great Slave Lake (CN)   Peace River, Alberta

161.415   Ch 1 Yard
160.665   Ch 4 Yard
160.485   161.295   Ch 6 Road
159.810   161.055   Ch 7 Dispatcher
160.725   Yard
160.215   MofW
160.785   MofW
160.275   CN interchange at Roma Junction, Alberta

Great Smoky Mountains   Murphy, North Carolina

464.1625   General operations

Great Southwest   Grand Prairie, Texas

160.860   General operations
160.830   General operations

Great Walton Rail   Monroe, Georgia

160.815   General operations
160.995   General operations

Great Western   Loveland, Colorado

Colorado Division
160.875   160.260   General operations
California-Oregon Division
160.875   General operations

Greater Winnipeg Water District   Winnipeg, Manitoba

167.670   169.590   Dispatcher
158.190   Yard at Hadashville

Green Bay & Western – see Wisconsin Central

Green Mountain   Bellows Falls, Vermont

160.605   161.445   Ch 1 Road repeater
160.605   Ch 2 Road and repeater output
161.355   Ch 3 Yard

Greenville & Northern   Greenville, South Carolina

160.425   General operations

Guilford Transportation Industries
– See Boston & Maine, Maine Central, Springfield Terminal

Gulf & Ohio   Lula, Mississippi

160.500   General operations

Hampton & Branchville   Hampton, South Carolina
49.26   General operations
48.80   FCC – Mobiles only

H&S   Knoxville, Tennessee
160.500   General operations

Harbor Belt Line   Los Angeles, California
160.980   General operations

Hardin Southern   Hardin, Kentucky
161.505   General operations

Hartwell   Hartwell, Georgia
158.240   General operations

High Point, Thomasville & Denton High Point, North Carolina
160.590   Ch 1 Road – CSXT
161.250   Interchange with NS

Hillsdale County – see Indiana Northeastern

Housatonic Railroad   Canaan, Connecticut
160.395   161.505   General operations
160.395   Talk-around

Houston Belt & Terminal   Houston, Texas
160.530   160.770   Road
160.380   Yard
160.575   Congress Yard

161.220   New South Yard
161.505   161.340   Settegast Yard
160.215   Diesel shop
161.325   Diesel shop
161.175   Car Dept.
160.800   Basin Yard Car Dept.
160.920   160.275   South Yard Car Dept.
160.680   Signal Dept.
160.995   160.260   PBX
161.055   Car placement notification
160.455   Police 1
160.350   Police 2
161.205   Police – mutual aid

Huron & Eastern   Bad Axe, Michigan
160.440   Road and yard
161.355   Dispatcher
161.400   FCC – Base and mobile

Hutchinson & Northern   Hutchinson, Kansas
160.380   General operations

Idaho Northern & Pacific   Island City, Oregon
Nampa, Idaho
161.265   Road
161.190   Yard
160.890   Switching
LaGrande, Oregon
161.295   Road
160.890   Yard and switching

79

Illinois – Indiana

Illinois Central
Chicago, Illinois

161.190△	Ch 1 Road
160.920△	Ch 2 Road
161.010	Ch 4 Yard
161.205	Police
161.280	Yard
161.460	Ch 3 Yard

Illinois
Chicago – Markham Yard

161.280	Yard
161.505	Yard
160.815	Woodcrest locomotive shop
160.920	Car Dept.

Louisiana
Baton Rouge

161.010	Yard
161.280	Yard
161.460	Yard

New Orleans

160.920	Mays Tower
161.280	Yard
161.460	Yard
161.085	Local switching
160.590	Car Dept. and engine service
161.100	Active
160.980	Active
160.935	Active

Tennessee
Memphis

160.920	Road – terminal area
161.205	Police

Memphis – Johnston Yard

160.620		Yard
160.785		Yard
161.460		Ch 3 Yard
161.010		Ch 4 Yard
161.250		Active – "S5"
160.650		Active – use undetermined
160.740		Active
161.280		Active
161.400		Locomotive service
160.590	161.280	Car Dept.

Indian Creek
Frankton, Indiana

151.625~	FCC – Mobiles

Indiana & Ohio
Brookville, Indiana

161.385	160.575	General operations

Indiana & Ohio Central
Logan, Ohio

161.295	160.695	General operations

Indiana & Ohio Eastern
Wellston, Ohio

161.295	160.695	General operations
160.335		General operations
452.875		FCC – Link

Indiana Harbor Belt   Hammond, Indiana

160.980		Ch 1 Road
161.070		Ch 2 Road
161.400		MofW
160.545		Police
160.545	463.4625	Police portable mobile repeater

Chicago – East Blue Island yard

161.565		Hump
161.565	161.535	Car Dept.

East Chicago – Gibson Yard

160.665		Yard

Indiana Hi-Rail   Connersville, Indiana

160.590	Ch 1 Road and dispatcher – Connersville, Indiana; Evansville, Indiana
160.845	Ch 2 Yard – Connersville; Evansville
160.695	Ch 3 Road and dispatcher – Delphos, Ohio; Tiffin, Ohio; Rochester, Indiana
161.505	Ch 4 Yard – Delphos; Tiffin; Rochester

Ohio City to Glenmore, Ohio

160.965	Ex-Spencerville & Elgin

Tiffin, Ohio

160.230	Joint operations with CSX
160.320	Joint operations with CSX

Indiana Northeastern   Reading, Michigan

161.100	Ch 1 Road and yard
161.400	Ch 2 MofW

Indiana Railroad   Indianapolis, Indiana

161.100	Road and yard
160.260	Dispatcher

Indiana Southern   Petersburg, Indiana

160.995	General operations

Iowa Interstate   Iowa City, Iowa

161.220	Ch 1 Road and dispatcher – Bureau, Illinois, to Iowa City, Iowa, and Peoria Branch
160.305	Ch 2 Road – Iowa City to Council Bluffs, Iowa
160.305	Ch 2 Yard – Chicago to Joliet
161.205	Police – mutual aid
160.230	CSX trackage rights – Joliet to Bureau, Illinois
161.340	Metra trackage rights

Iowa City, Iowa

160.305	Ch 2 Yard

Rock Island, Illinois

160.305	Ch 2 Yard

Iowa Northern   Greene, Iowa

161.385	Road
161.175	Interchange with Chicago & North Western

Iowa Traction   Mason City, Iowa

161.475	General operations

Itel Rail Corp   Dothan, Alabama

464.925~	FCC

J – Kiamichi

J&J Railroad – see Hardin Southern, page 79

Jaxport Terminal Railway Jacksonville, Florida
160.815   FCC – BM

Jefferson Warrior Railroad Birmingham, Alabama
153.260   General operations

JK Lines Monterrey, Indiana
153.245   General operations

Kankakee, Beaverville & Southern Beaverville, Illinois
160.215   General operations

Kansas City Public Service Freight Operations
Kansas City, Missouri
161.055   General operations

Kansas City Southern Kansas City, Missouri
160.260   Ch 1 Road and dispatcher to train; line-ups at 0630 and 1230 hrs.
160.350   Ch 2 Train to dispatcher
161.250   Ch 3 Mobiles
160.890   Ch 4 Supervisory – mobiles
161.565   Remote control locomotives
160.085   Intermodal facility
160.305   KCS Trucks and yard
160.860   KCS Trucks
New Orleans, Louisiana
160.305   Yard

160.890   Active
Shreveport, Louisiana
452.900 457.900   Deramus Yard Car Dept.
Kansas City, Missouri – Knoche Yard
161.055   Yard
160.305   Intermodal facility
Dallas, Texas
161.055   Local switching

Kansas City Terminal Kansas City, Missouri
Now operated by Gateway Western
161.310   Ch 1 Road and yard
160.500   Ch 2 Engineering Dept
161.010   Ch 3 Dispatcher/Police

Kansas Southwestern Wichita, Kansas
160.995   General operations

Kentucky & Tennessee Stearns, Kentucky
160.800   General operations

Keokuk Junction Keokuk, Iowa
160.395   Ch 1 General operations
160.845   Ch 2 General operations

Kiamichi Railroad Hugo, Oklahoma
160.920   General operations
161.160   General operations
160.425   FCC – Link/repeater, Nashville and Ashdown, Arkansas
161.415   FCC – Link/repeater, Nashville and Ashdown

Klamath Northern   Gilchrist, Oregon
160.545   General operations

Knox & Kane   Kane, Pennsylvania
160.800   General operations
161.235   FCC – Base and mobiles

KWT Railway   Paris, Tennessee
161.145   General operations
462.300   467.300   FCC – Link/repeater at Paris, Tennessee

Kyle Railroad   Phillipsburg, Kansas
160.440   161.325   Road – Repeater
160.440   Road
160.275   Switching
160.530   Shop
160.320   FCC – Base and mobile

Lackawanna Valley – see Delaware Lackawanna

Lake Erie, Franklin & Clarion   Clarion, Pennsylvania
160.650   Ch 1 Road and yard
160.335   Ch 2 Road, administration, and MofW

Lake States   Tawas City, Michigan
161.310   Ch 1 General operations
161.280   Ch 2 Administration
160.350   Ch 3 Limited use

Lake Superior & Ishpeming   Marquette, Michigan
160.230   Road and repeater output
160.230   161.490   Road repeater
160.950   MofW
156.800   Ore Docks – Ship to shore

Lake Superior Terminal & Transfer   Superior, Wisconsin
160.740   General operations

Lake Terminal   Lorain, Ohio
160.590   Switching
160.755   Switching
160.905   Switching
161.040   Switching
160.365   MofW
161.505   Assistant Trainmaster

Lakeside Transportation   Panama City Beach, Florida
160.395   General operations

Lamoille Valley   Morrisville, Vermont
160.230   Road and repeater output
160.230   161.340   Road repeater

Lancaster & Chester   Lancaster, South Carolina
161.130   General operations

Landisville Railroad   Landisville, Pennsylvania
160.485   General operations

Laurinburg & Southern   Laurinburg, North Carolina

160.980	Ch 1 MofW
160.605	Ch 2 Road

Lewis & Clark   Battle Ground, Washington

160.785	General operations
160.440	Alternate

Liberty Railway Services   Pueblo, Colorado

464.675	469.675	Switching

Little Rock & Western   Perry, Arkansas

160.965	Road

Little Rock Port Railroad   Little Rock, Arkansas

453.750	General operations

Livonia, Avon & Lakeville   Lakeville, New York

160.830	General operations

Long Island   Jamaica, New York

160.380	Ch 1 Road and towers
161.445	Ch 2 Dispatcher
161.265	Ch 3 Yard; Road on Port Jefferson branch and main line east of Hicksville
160.335	Jamaica stationmaster
161.385	Ch 1 Signal Dept and ET
160.785	Ch 2 Signal Dept.
160.725	Ch 3 MofW – B&B Dept.
160.395	MofW – Mobiles
161.535	Ch 4 Car Dept and end to end
161.535	Ch 4 Car Dept and MofE
160.455	Ch 1 Police – Base to car
160.605	Ch 2 Police – Car to car
160.620	Police link at Easthampton, Holbrook, Mastic-Shirley, Speonk, and Westhampton
452.6375 457.6375	Low power use
452.6875 457.6875	Low power use
452.7625 457.7625	Low power use
452.8125 457.8125	Low power use
452.8625 457.8625	Low power use
452.9125 457.9125	Police – Mobile/portable repeater
75.44	Point-to-point link
75.60	Point-to-point link

Brooklyn – Flatbush Avenue

161.490	160.320	Ch 4 Police

Hollis

464.525	469.525	FCC

New York

160.320	161.490	Ch 3 Penn Station Police

Longview, Portland & Northern   Gardiner, Oregon

160.500	General operations

Los Angeles Junction   Los Angeles, California

161.130	General operations

Louisiana & Delta   New Iberia, Louisiana

161.445	Ch 1 General operations
161.550	Ch 2 Southern Pacific trackage rights

Louisiana & North West   Homer, Louisiana
    160.530   Ch 1 Road
    160.650   Ch 2 Yard
    161.010   Mobile repeater

Louisiana Southern   Lake Charles, Louisiana
    464.375   FCC – BM

Louisville & Indiana   Jeffersonville, Indiana
    160.860   General operations
    161.070   Jeffersonville and Louisville terminal areas

Louisville, New Albany & Corydon   Corydon, Indiana
    160.275   General operations

Lowville & Beaver River   Lowville, New York
    161.460   160.470 General operations

Luzerne & Susquehanna   Wilkes-Barre, Pennsylvania
    161.310   General operations

Madison Railroad   Madison, Indiana
    160.605   General operations

Magma Arizona   Superior, Arizona
    452.900   457.900 General operations
    153.020   Plant operations

Mahoning Valley   Campbell, Ohio
    160.965   Road
    160.245   Switching

    160.515   Switching
    160.605   Switching
    160.635   Switching
    160.695   Switching
    160.815   Switching
    161.115   Switching
    161.355   Switching
    161.445   Switching
    161.475   Switching
    161.295   Switching at Youngstown

Maine Central (Guilford Transportation Industries)
                                           Portland, Maine
    160.620   Ch 1 Road
    160.380   Ch 2 Yard
    161.250   Ch 3 – Rigby Yard, South Portland
    161.400   Ch 4 – Rigby Yard, South Portland

Maine Coast   Rockland, Maine
    161.190   160.425 Road
    467.225   Dispatcher link, Bath and Thomaston
    161.280   Engineering and spare

Manufacturers Railway   St. Louis, Missouri
    160.740   Road and yard
    160.515   Administration
    161.385   River Yard – Car Dept
    464.675   FCC

Manufacturers' Junction   Chicago, Illinois
    161.475   General operations

Maryland – Midland

Maryland & Delaware Federalsburg, Maryland
161.385 General operations
160.695 FCC – Base and mobile

Maryland & Pennsylvania York, Pennsylvania
160.335 Road and MofW
160.695 Yard and MofW

Maryland Midland Union Bridge, Maryland
160.545 Ch 1 MofW and administration
160.965 Ch 2 Road and yard
160.425 FCC – Base and mobile

Massachusetts Central Palmer, Massachusetts
160.470 General operations

Massena Terminal Massena, New York
160.500 General operations

Mattagami Railroad Smooth Rock Falls, Ontario
165.000 General operations

McCloud Railway McCloud, California
160.695 Road and repeater output
160.695 161.205 Road repeater
160.860 Switching
161.025 Switching

McCormick, Ashland City & Nashville
– see Central of Tennessee, page 44

McKeesport Connecting Monroeville, Pennsylvania
160.440 General operations

Meridian & Bigbee Meridian, Mississippi
160.350 General operations

MG Rail Jeffersonville, Indiana
452.900 457.900 General operations

Michigan Shore Muskegon, Michigan
161.235 General operations

Michigan Southern White Pigeon, Michigan
152.915 Current channel
160.755 Future channel

Michigan Wisconsin Transportion Co. Ludington, Michigan
160.470 FCC
160.500 Ship-to-shore – Lake Michigan auto ferry

Mid-Atlantic Railroad Tabor City, North Carolina
161.505 Road
160.470 Switching

Middletown & Hummelstown Hummelstown, Pennsylvania
161.505 General operations

Midland Terminal Midland, Pennsylvania
160.245 General operations
160.515 General operations

160.695	General operations
160.815	General operations
160.965	General operations
161.115	General operations
161.220	Road
161.475	Road
466.1625	Switching
466.2125	Switching
466.2625	Switching
466.3125	Switching
466.3625	Switching
466.4125	Switching
466.4625	Switching
466.5125	Switching
466.5625	Switching
466.6125	Switching
466.6625	Switching

MidLouisiana Rail Corp. – see Kansas City Southern

Mid-Michigan Railroad   Greenville, Michigan

161.235	General operations
161.145	General operations
160.815	MofW
154.600	FCC – Mobiles
161.235	FCC – Base and mobiles
154.570	FCC – Mobiles

MidSouth Rail Corp.   Jackson, Mississippi

| 160.545 | Road |
| 161.010 | Yard and MofW |

160.215	Yard and MofW – joint operations with MidLouisiana
161.130	Base agents to train
161.190	Illinois Central interchange
160.590	IC interchange, Jackson, Mississippi
161.370	IC interchange, Jackson, Mississippi

Midwest Coal Handling Co.   Madisonville, Kentucky

| 161.295 | General operations |

Minnesota Commercial Railway   Minneapolis, Minnesota

| 160.560 | Ch 1 Road |
| 160.740 | Ch 2 Yard |

Minnesota, Dakota & Western   International Falls, Minnesota

160.530	General operations
160.410	General operations
160.680	General operations

MNVA Railroad   Morton, Minnesota

161.265 160.305 General operations

Mississippi & Skuna Valley   Bruce, Mississippi

| 160.845 | General operations |

Mississippian Railway   Amory, Mississippi

| 160.770 | General operations |

Mississippi Central   Holly Springs, Mississippi

161.220 160.635 General operations

Mississippi – Montana

Mississippi Delta   Clarksdale, Mississippi

160.500   General operations

Mississippi Export   Moss Point, Mississippi

160.500   Road and repeater output
160.500   161.490   Road rRepeater
161.220   Yard 1
161.400   Yard 2

Missouri & North Arkansas   Carthage, Missouri

160.635   Road
160.980   Yard

Modesto & Empire Traction Co.   Modesto, California

161.325   Ch 1 Road
160.965   Ch 2 Switching
161.175   Ch 3 Switching
161.505   Ch 4 MofW

Mohawk, Adirondack & Northern   Lowville, New York

161.460   160.470   Road and dispatcher
161.460   Yard and Talk-around

Molalla Western   Liberal, Oregon

160.575   Ch 1 General operations and MofW
160.575   161.190   Ch 2 PBX, Mount Scott
161.340   Ch 3 Switching
161.550   Ch 4 Southern Pacific trackage
160.575   160.335   Ch 5 Dispatcher

Monessen Southwestern   Monessen, Pennsylvania

160.620   General operations

Monongahela Connecting   Pittsburgh, Pennsylvania

161.400   Road
161.220   MofW and yard

Monongahela Railway – see Conrail

Montana Rail Link   Missoula, Montana

160.355   MRL Ch 1 Road – Helena to Huntley, Montana
160.950   MRL Ch 2 Road – Helena to Kootenai, Idaho
160.665   161.505   MRL Ch 3 – BN Ch 3 PBX
                         Idaho: Tuscor
160.620   161.565   MRL Ch 4 – BN Ch 4 PBX
                         Montana: Blossburg, St. Regis, Shadoan
161.130   160.545   MRL Ch 5 – BN Ch 5 PBX
                         Idaho: Tuscor
161.490   160 .245   MRL Ch 6 – BN Ch 7 PBX
                         Montana: Big Timber, Lombard, Rimrock,
                         TV Mountain
161.340   MRL Ch 7 Maintenance
160.395   MRL Ch 8 Yard – Billings, Helena, Laurel, Liv-
                         ingston, Helena
160.815   161.385   MRL Ch 9 PBX
                         Idaho: Clark Fork
                         Montana: Cyr, Drummond, Plains, Rapids,
                         Three Forks
160.950   160.380   MRL Ch 10 Blossburg Tunnel

Bozeman
160.590 161.460 Car Dept.
161.010 Yard
Missoula
160.590 161.460 Car Dept.
161.190 Car shop
161.220 Car shop
161.310 Hump

Montana Western   Butte, Montana
161.190 Road and yard
161.430 MofW

Morristown & Erie   Morristown, New Jersey
160.230 161.310 Ch 1 Road repeater
160.230 Ch 2 Road
161.100 Ch 3 Yard
158.385 MofW

Moscow, Camden & San Augustine   Camden, Texas
161.205 General operations

Mountain Laurel   Lawsonham, Pennsylvania
161.160 General operations
160.740 General operations

Mount Hood   Hood River, Oregon
160.365 161.055 Ch 1 General operations
160.365 Ch 2 General operations

Mount Vernon Terminal   Mount Vernon, Washington
160.875 General operations

Muncie & Western   Muncie, Indiana
160.950 General operations

Napa Valley   Napa, California
160.575 161.475 F1 General operations
160.575 F2 Talk-around
161.085 F3 Simplex
161.175 F4 Simplex
452.9125 457.9125~ FCC

Napierville Junction (CP Rail)   Rouses Point, New York
161.325 CP 5 Road and dispatcher
161.325 160.425 CP 6 Train to dispatcher
160.845 Ch 11 MofW
160.845 160.335 Ch 12 Utility PBX

Nash County   Rocky Mount, North Carolina
160.980 General operations

Nashville & Eastern   Lebanon, Tennessee
160.365 Road
160.560 Yard
161.070 Yard
161.475 Yard

Natchez Trace – see Mississippi Central

National Harbours Board   Montreal, Quebec
159.630 Dispatcher
159.990 Road and yard
167.610 1 base and 29 mobiles

Nebraska Central   Columbus, Nebraska

161.265	Ch 1 General operations
161.190	Ch 2 General operations

New England Southern   Concord, New Hampshire

161.025	General operations
160.395	Signal Dept.
161.520	FCC – Mobile

New Hampshire North Coast   Wakefield, New Hampshire

160.275	161.385	General operations

New Hope & Ivyland   Penndel, Pennsylvania

152.960		General operations
161.475	160.425	General operations

New Orleans & Lower Coast   Belle Chase, Louisiana

160.635	Ch 1 Road
160.995	Ch 2 Road
160.470	UP trackage rights

New Orleans Public Belt   New Orleans, Louisiana

160.320	Road and yard
160.530	MofW and shop

New Orleans Terminal   New Orleans, Lousiana

161.490	General operations

New Orleans Union Passenger Terminal
New Orleans, Louisiana

160.440	Switching

New York & Lake Erie   Gowanda, New York

160.365	161.355	General operations

New York Cross Harbor   Brooklyn, New York

160.590	General operations
156.650	Marine operations – Ch 13

New York, Susquehanna & Western   Cooperstown, New York

161.295		Ch 1 Road and yard – New York Division
160.620	161.295	Ch 2 Road repeater – New York Division
160.485		Ch 3 Road and dispatcher – New Jersey Div.

Nicolet Badger Northern   Cavour, Wisconsin

160.215	General operations

Nimishillen & Tuscarawas   Canton, Ohio

160.425		Local switching
160.695		Local switching
160.815		Local switching
160.965		Local switching
161.355		Local switching
Canton		
161.445	160.635	Operations
161.445		Talk-around
Massillon		
161.295	160.605	Operations
161.295		Talk-around

Nittany & Bald Eagle   Bellefonte, Pennsylvania

160.590	General operations

Nobles Rock   Morton, Minnesota

160.800	FCC

Norfolk & Portsmouth Belt   Norfolk, Virginia

160.980	Ch 1 Road and yard – Berkley to Portsmouth
160.905	Ch 2 Road and yard – Berkley to Sewells Point

Norfolk Southern   Norfolk, Virginia

Illinois Terminal Subdivision, St. Louis, Missouri

160.335	IT-1
160.695	IT-2 MofW
160.350	Trainmasters and WR Tower

Former Norfolk & Western Territory

161.190	Ch 1 Road – Norfolk, Virginia, to Cincinnati and Bellevue, Ohio; Norton to Bluefield, Virginia; Roanoke, Virginia, to Winston-Salem, North Carolina
161.250	Ch 2 Road – Buffalo to Chicago; Cincinnati to Fort Wayne; Frankfort, Indiana, to Arcadia, Ohio, via Muncie; Peru, Indiana, to Indianapolis; and New Jersey, Indiana & Illinois Railroad
160.440	Ch 3 Road – Chicago to St. Louis; Roanoke, Virginia, to Hagerstown, Maryland; Detroit to Kansas City; Moberly, Missouri, to Des Moines, Iowa; and Illinois Terminal Subdivision
161.490	Ch 9 MofW

Former Southern Railway Territory

160.245Δ	Dispatcher to train
160.365	Car Dept. (without repeater)

160.365	161.295	Car Dept. (with repeater)
160.500		Traveling freight agents and wrecker
160.650		Yard clerks
160.830Δ		Ch 2 Train to dispatcher
160.950Δ		Ch 5 Road
161.490		Ch 9 Yard
161.250		Yard and NS trains
161.505		Wrecker
161.535		C&S mobile to mobile
161.475		Digital remote control of locomotives – eastbound
161.565		Digital remote control of locomotives – westbound

Systemwide

161.115		End-of-train telemetry
161.205		Police
160.275	161.145	PBX8

Alabama: Anniston, Mobile, Selma, Sheffield
Georgia: Macon, Rome, Valdosta
Illinois: Baylis
Kentucky: Louisville, Somerset
Missouri: Moberly
Mississippi: Richburg
New York: Westfield
North Carolina: Asheville, Salisbury
Ohio: Portsmouth
Tennessee: Memphis, Morristown, Oakdale
Virginia: Abington, Danville, Front Royal, Monroe, Roanoke, Waverly, Waynesboro
West Virginia: Beckley, Williamson

Norfolk Southern

160.515	161.235	PBX 9
		Georgia: Atlanta, Columbus, Toccoa
		Illinois: Decatur, Tilton
		Indiana: Fort Wayne, Lafayette, Muncie, Wabash
		Michigan: Detroit
		North Carolina: Charlotte, Greensboro
		New York: Buffalo
		Ohio: Bellevue, Cincinnati, Cleveland, Columbus, Conneaut, Monnette, Montpelier, Painesville, Portsmouth
		South Carolina: Charleston
		Tennessee: Knoxville
		Virginia: Crewe, Norfolk
		West Virginia: Bluefield, Crum, Norton
160.275	161.235	PBX 10
		Alabama: Birmingham, Brookside, Huntsville
		Georgia: Ashburn, Augusta, Midville, Savannah, Smithville
		Louisiana: New Orleans
		South Carolina: Coumbia, Greenville
160.380	161.235	PBX 11 – St Louis
160.785	161.415	PBX 12 – Kansas City
160.365	161.445	PBX 13 – Chicago
160.215	161.145	PBX 14 – Danville, Kentucky
160.635	161.250	PBX 15 – Manassas, Virginia
160.775	161.490	PBX 16 – Jacksonville, Florida
161.535		Ch 4 Signal Dept.
161.205		Police
161.115		End-of-train devices

Alabama

Anniston

855.4125	810.4125	Mobile data terminals

Birmingham – Norris Yard

161.250		Hump
160.320	160.740	Pulldown 1
161.145	160.770	Pulldown 2
161.430		Yard
160.665	161.085	Local yard
161.490		Ch 3 Yard
160.650		Yard clerks
160.365	161.295	Car Dept.
161.535		C&S Dept.

Mobile

161.250	Yard
161.490	Yard

Sheffield – Claytor Yard

161.250		Hump
160.665	161.355	Pulldown
160.875		Pulldown
160.365	161.295	Car Dept.

Florida

Jacksonville

161.190	Intermodal facility

Georgia

Atlanta

161.010	Technical Training Center
161.190	Signal maintainers and radio shop
161.490	Ch 3 Local switching
161.535	Signal Dept. mobiles

Norfolk Southern

Atlanta – Inman Yard
160.875 160.320 Hump
160.335 161.325 Pulldown
160.530 160.470 Pulldown
160.740 161.160 Pulldown
161.250   Yard
160.365 161.295 Car Dept.
160.635   Intermodal facility
Macon
160.650   Traveling freight agents
161.205   Police
161.490   Ch 3 Industrial Switching
161.535   MofW
Macon – Brosnan Yard
161.250   Hump
160.635 160.230 Pulldown 1
160.755 160.470 Pulldown 2
161.190   Yard
161.445 160.320 Car Dept.
Macon – Savannah Yard
161.010   Yard
Savannah
161.010   Yard
Illinois
Chicago
160.440   Cummins Drawbridge
160.620   Police – Car to car
160.950   MofW
Chicago – Calumet Yard (ex-Nickel Plate)
160.485 161.115 Car Dept.
160.515   Intermodal facility

Chicago – Landers Yard
161.415   Car Dept.
Decatur
160.650   Car Inspectors
160.740   Active – use undetermined
160.845   Active – use undetermined
160.965   G-1 Base
161.040 160.380 Car Dept.
161.490   Active
160.350   Former Illinois Terminal yard
161.250   Former Wabash yard
East St. Louis
160.620   Yard clerks
Indiana
Fort Wayne
161.190   Ch 1 East Wayne Yard
160.440   Ch 3 East Wayne Yard
161.205   Police
Kentucky
Danville
161.490   Yard
Erlanger
854.3625 809.3625 Mobile data terminals
Lexington
161.085   Yard
Louisville – Youngtown Yard
160.665   Louisville operator and yard
Louisville – Kentucky & Indiana Terminal Yard
161.355   Yard
Portsmouth
851.0125 806.0125 Mobile data terminals

93

Norfolk Southern

Louisiana
New Orleans

161.490		Yard
160.500		Intermodal
161.535		C&S
160.365	161.295	Car Dept.
161.205		Police

Michigan
Detroit

160.305	Police – Car to car
161.205	Police – Car to car
161.280	Police – Mutual aid

Detroit – Melvindale Yard

160.380	Car Dept.
160.620	Car Dept.

Detroit – Oakwood Yard

161.250	Yard

Mississippi
Laurel

160.740	Ch 3 Yard

Missouri
Kansas City

161.190		Ch 1 Yard
160.380		Claycomo Yard Switching
161.445	160.575	Car Dept.
161.265		Police – Mutual aid

Moberly

160.935	Wrecker

St. Louis

161.250	A. O. Smith Yard
160.350	Luther Yard

160.695	IT-2 MofW
160.575	Police
161.205	Police

New York
Buffalo

161.205	Police – Car to car
161.490	MofW

Buffalo – Bison Yard

161.190		Ch 1 Road-Railer/auto site
160.440		Police – Car to car
852.6125	807.6125	Mobile data terminals

North Carolina
Asheville

160.590	160.470	East end switcher
161.250	160.740	West end switcher
161.490		Ch 3 Yard
160.365		Car Dept.

Badin, Belmont, and Bryson City

160.650	Yard clerks

Charlotte – Charlotte Yard

160.290	North end yard locomotive
161.490	South end yard locomotive
160.365	Car Dept.
160.650	Yard clerks
161.205	Police

East Durham, Elizabeth City, Elkin, Goldsboro, Graham, High Point, Lenoir, and Liberty

160.650	Yard clerks

Linwood – Spencer Yard

160.755	160.470	Hump 1
160.875	161.310	Hump 2

NORFOLK SOUTHERN

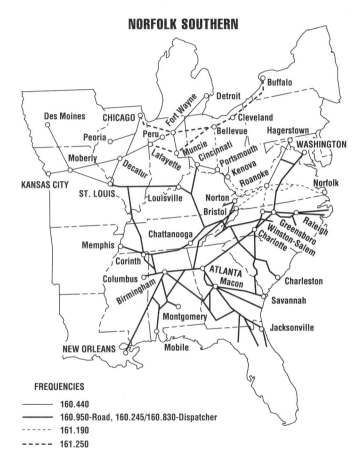

FREQUENCIES

———	160.440
▬▬▬	160.950-Road, 160.245/160.830-Dispatcher
- - - -	161.190
▬ ▬ ▬	161.250

160.320		Pulldown
161.325		Pulldown
161.430		Pulldown
160.365	161.295	Car Dept.
161.490		Air bleeders
452.950		Hump speed control
161.010		Maintainers

Mocksville, Newton, and Star

160.650	Yard clerks

Ohio

Bellevue

161.490	MofW

Bellevue – Bellevue Yard

161.340	Hump
161.565	Pulldown
161.190	Yardmaster
160.665	Loco shop
160.485	Car Dept.
160.575	Active
160.770	Active

452.925	457.925	Hump speed control

Cleveland

160.440	Yard
161.250	Cuyahoga River drawbridge
161.490	MofW

Columbus

160.380	Signal Dept.

Columbus – Joyce Avenue Yard

161.250	Ch 2 Yard
161.280	Yard

161.385	160.440	Yard

Norfolk Southern

Lima – South Lima Yard
161.250		Yard and road

Marion
161.100		Yard

Maumee
160.440		Yard
161.250		Yard

Oregon
161.145		Active

Portsmouth – Starr Yard
161.250		Ch 2 Yard
160.485		Car Dept.
161.280	160.380	Car Dept.
161.490		Car Dept.
161.385		Car shop
160.470		Crew bus

Sandusky
161.100		Yard
452.925	457.925	Remote control locomotives
452.950	457.950	Remote control locomotives

Summit Hill
452.900		Yard clerks
852.0375	807.0375	Mobile data terminals

Toledo – Homestead Yard
160.620		Car Dept.
161.250		Ch 2 Yard
160.515		Intermodal facility
452.900		Shops

South Carolina
Columbia
161.505		Wrecker

Dorchester
153.095		FCC
153.215		FCC

Tennessee
Chattanooga – De Butts Yard
161.250		Hump
160.905	160.215	Pulldown
161.085	160.335	Pulldown
161.325	160.260	Pulldown
160.500		Receiving and departure yards
160.365	161.295	Car Dept.

Knoxville
160.470		Yard
160.590		Yard
161.250		Yard
161.535		Signal Dept.
161.205		Police

Knoxville – Sevier Yard
160.290	160.755	Pulldown
161.490		Ch 3 Yard
160.365	161.295	Car Dept.
160.740		Active
160.920		Active

Memphis
161.535		C&S

Memphis – Forest Yard
160.365		Car Dept. – Simplex
160.470		Union Pacific interchange
161.490		Yard
161.550		Southern Pacific interchange

Virginia
Altavista
160.500   Traveling freight agents
Carbo
161.250   Yard
Chesapeake
160.500   Traveling freight agents
Clinchfield
161.250   Yard
Council
854.9375 809.9375 Mobile data terminals
Crewe
161.250   160.470   Car Dept.
Culpepper
160.500   Traveling freight agents
160.650   Yard clerks
Duty
161.250   Yard
Harrisonburg, Keysville
160.500   Traveling freight agents
Lynchburg
161.250   Yard
161.490   Yard
Manassas, Monroe
160.500   Traveling freight agents
Norfolk – Lamberts Point Yard
161.250   Ch 2 Yard
161.070   Pier 5
160.305   Pier 6 – Ch A
161.490   Pier 6 – Ch B
Norfolk – Norfolk Yard

161.025   Ch 3 Hump
452.900   Hump cab signals
160.260   161.385   Car Dept.
Norfolk – Portlock Yard
160.950   Ch 4 Yard and road
161.280   160.470   Car Dept.
Norton
160.245   160.950   Road – not dispatcher
160.365   Andover Yard Car Dept.
Roanoke
161.250   Yard and Police
160.740   Active
160.935   Active
161.490   Active
161.505   Active
452.900   457.900   Active
452.9125 457.9125 Active
Roanoke – Roanoke Shops
160.965   Paint shop
161.040   160.305   Diesel shop hostler
161.070   160.605   Diesel shop
Roanoke – Shaffers Crossing
160.695   MofW
161.040   160.440   Car Dept.
161.340   160.470   Yard
161.385   160.335   Pulldown
161.430   Hump
Tiller Fork Junction, Wilcoe, and Williamson
161.250   Yard
Woodstock
160.500   Traveling freight agents

North – Old

West Virginia
Arista
854.8875 809.8875 Mobile data terminals
Bluefield
161.250   Yard
161.280 160.440 Car Dept.
Huntington
161.295   Yard

North Carolina & Virginia   Ahoskie, North Carolina
161.310   Traveling freight agents

North Carolina State Ports Authority
                    Wilmington and Morehead City, North Carolina
160.320   General operations

North Coast   Eureka, California
161.520 160.755 Road and repeater output

North Shore   Northumberland, Pennsylvania
160.455   General operations
160.725   FCC – Base and mobile

Northeast Kansas & Missouri   Hiawatha, Kansas
160.815   General operations

Northern Alberta (CN)   Edmonton, Alberta
160.275   Ch 1 Yard
160.515   Ch 2 Road and dispatcher

Northwestern Pacific – see California Northern

Oakland Terminal   Oakland, California
160.935   General operations

Octoraro Railway – see Delaware Valley

Ogeechee Railway   Dover, Georgia
160.320~   General operations
161.280~   G – FCC

Ohio Central   Baltic, Ohio
160.215   General operations
160.845 160.215 Dispatcher and road repeater output
161.025   W&LE interchange
160.455   R. J. Corman interchange
160.230   CSXT interchange
161.070   CR interchange

Ohio Southern   Sugar Creek, Ohio
160.845   General operations

Oil Creek & Titusville   Titusville, Pennsylvania
160.920   General operations

Old Augusta   New Augusta, Mississippi
160.425   G-FCC
160.815   G-FCC

Omaha, Lincoln & Beatrice Lincoln, Nebraska
160.740 Switching – Mobiles only

Ontario Central Canandaigua, New York
161.370 General operations

Ontario Midland Sodus, New York
161.370 General operations

Ontario Northland North Bay, Ontario
160.545 161.265 Road and dispatcher
160.995 Yard

Oregon, Pacific & Eastern Cottage Grove, Oregon
160.980 General operations

Otter Tail Valley Fergus Falls, Minnesota
160.425 General operations

Ouachita Railroad El Dorado, Arkansas
161.295 General operations – Primary
161.175 General operations – Secondary

Owego & Harford Owego, New York
161.310 General operations

Paducah & Louisville Paducah, Kentucky
160.740 Road
160.695 Yard 1
161.325 Yard 2
160.455 MofW/MofE – Mobiles

161.205 Police
160.290 161.505 PBX
160.830 FCC – Mobile
160.335 FCC – 27 base and mobiles

Palouse River Colfax, Washington
160.785 General operations

Panhandle Northern Bolger, Texas
161.085 General operations
160.650 AT&SF trackage

Panther Valley Jim Thorpe, Pennsylvania
161.310 General operations

Parr Terminal Richmond, California
462.8125 General operations (possibly no longer in use)
469.525~ FCC – New License
469.875~ FCC – New License

Patapsco & Back Rivers Baltimore, Maryland
160.590 161.520 Ch 1 Road, Yard, and Car Dept.
160.845 160.215 Ch 2 MofW
452.325 457.325 FCC – Mobiles
452.375 457.375 FCC – Mobiles
452.425 457.425 FCC – Mobiles
452.475 457.475 FCC – Mobiles
452.775 457.775 FCC – Mobiles
452.825 457.825 FCC – Mobiles
452.925 457.925 FCC – Remote control locomotives

Pearl – Pittsburgh

Pearl River Valley   Picayune, Mississippi
461.450~ 466.450~ FCC – Mobiles/MR
461.700~ 466.700~ FCC – Mobiles/MR

Pecos Valley Southern   Pecos, Texas
161.100   General operations

Pee Dee River   Bennettsville, North Carolina
161.280   Ch 1 Work trains
160.530   Ch 2 Seldom used
161.310   Ch 3 General operations

Pend Oreille Valley   Newport, Washington
161.415 160.245   General operations

Peninsula Terminal   Portland, Oregon
457.775   General operations

Peoria & Pekin Union   Creve Coeur, Illinois
160.470   Ch 1 Road and dispatcher
160.500   Ch 2 Switching
160.530   Ch 3 Switching and MofW
160.545   Ch 4 Switching
161.235   Ch 5 Administration
461.1375   FCC
462.7875   FCC

Philadelphia, Bethlehem & New England   Bethlehem, Pennsylvania
160.575   Road and yard
160.695   Supervisory
161.565   MofW
160.215   FCC – 7 Base and mobile
161.280   FCC – 7 Base and mobile
452.925 457.925   FCC – Remote control locomotives

Pickens Railroad   Pickens, South Carolina
161.280   General operations

Pigeon River   South Milford, Indiana
461.825   General operations

Pioneer Railroad – West Jersey Division   Salem, New Jersey
161.025   General operations

Pioneer Valley   Westfield, Massachusetts
160.335   Ch 1 General operations – Holyoke Branch
161.085   Ch 2 General operations – Easthampton Branch
161.025   FCC – Base and mobile

Pittsburg & Shawmut   Kittanning, Pennsylvania
161.160   General operations
160.740   Interdepartmental

Pittsburgh & Ohio Valley   Neville Island, Pennsylvania
161.370   General operations

Pittsburgh, Allegheny & McKees Rocks
McKees Rocks, Pennsylvania
160.425 General operations

Pittsburgh, Chartiers & Youghiogheny
Pittsburgh, Pennsylvania
160.590 General operations

Pocono Northeast – see Luzerne & Susquehanna, page 85

Point Comfort & Northern Lolita, Texas
160.500 General operations

Port Bienville Bay St. Louis, Mississippi
160.695~ G – 1 Base and mobiles

Port Everglades Port Authority Fort Lauderdale, Florida
158.995~ 159.255~ FCC – 1 MR and 25 mobiles
155.985~ FCC – 6 mobiles
158.925~ FCC – 1 base and 30 mobiles

Port Jersey Bayonne, New Jersey
472.5625~ 475.5625~ FCC – 25 Mobiles/1 MR
467.750~ FCC – 11 mobiles

Port Manatee Piney Point Florida
155.955 Ch 1 General operations

Port of Catoosa Tulsa, Oklahoma
464.600 469.600 Ch 1 Administration

464.975 Ch 2 Intra-plant switcher

Port of Tillamook Bay Tillamook, Oregon
161.070 General operations
161.055 160.305 General operations

Port Railroads Exeter, California
Operated by San Joaquin Valley Railroad
160.365 General operations

Port Royal Railroad Port Royal, South Carolina
160.980 General operations

Port Terminal Railroad Association of Houston
Houston, Texas
160.710 General operations
160.650 Joint operations with Santa Fe
161.550 Joint operations with Southern Pacific
161.070 Switching
161.145 Switching
161.265 MofW
160.845 Administrative

Port Terminal Railroad of South Carolina
Charleston, South Carolina
160.980 General operations

Port Utilities Commission of Charleston
Charleston, South Carolina
160.980 General operations

Portland – Reading

Portland Terminal Company   Portland, Maine
161.250   General operations

Portland Terminal Railroad   Portland, Oregon
161.490   General operations

Poseyville & Owensville – operated by Indiana Hi-Rail

Presidents Island Terminal   Memphis, Tennessee
161.355~   G – FCC

Providence & Worcester   Worcester, Massachusetts
160.650   Ch 1 Road
161.100   Ch 2 Yard
161.325   Worcester Yard
160.755 160.890 Police/MofW/Signal Dept.
452.9125   End-of-train devices

Quebec North Shore & Labrador   Sept-Iles, Quebec
159.810   Ch 1 Road
159.930   Ch 2 Yard
160.335   Ch 3 Dispatcher
160.215   Ch 4 Switching
160.365   Ch 5 MofW
160.290   Ch 6 Yard

Queen Anne's   Lewes, Delaware
160.455   Trackage on Delaware Coast Line

Quincy Bay Terminal   Quincy, Massachusetts
160.215   General operations

R. J. Corman
Bardstown, Kentucky
160.845 161.235 General operations
Celina and St. Marys, Ohio
160.455 161.385~ General operations

Rail Link Inc. (Commonwealth Railway) Midlothian, Virginia
469.550~   FCC – USA

Rail Switching Services   Dothan, Alabama
469.325~   FCC – Camden, Arkansas; Foley, Panama City(2), Florida; Dublin, Macon, Savannah, Georgia; Hammond, Indiana; Bastrop, Mansfield, Taft, Louisiana; Cincinnati, Ohio; Memphis, Tennessee; Longview, Texarkana, Texas; Green River(3), Wyoming

Rarus Railroad   Anaconda, Montana
160.320   Road
160.380   Service and administration

Reading, Blue Mountain & Northern Reading, Pennsylvania
161.250   General operations
161.370   FCC
160.470   FCC
160.770   FCC

Red River Valley & Western Breckenridge, Minnesota

161.295		Ch 1 Switching
160.440		Ch 2 Switching
160.365		Ch 3 Road
160.530	161.445	Ch 4 Mof W
160.530		Ch 8 MofW
161.445	160.230	Road – Tuttle, North Dakota
161.445	160.230	Road – Veblen, South Dakota

(controlled from Breckenridge, Minnesota)

Red Springs & Northern Parkton, North Carolina

160.980 General operations

Richmond Belt Richmond, California

160.770 General operations

Richmond, Fredericksburg & Potomac Richmond, Virginia

Although the RF&P has been absorbed by CSX, these frequencies were still in use at the end of 1994.

161.100△		Future road
161.550△		Ch 1 Road and dispatcher to train
161.355	161.460	Ch S Police and supervisory
161.490△		Ch 2 Train to dispatcher

Richmond – Acca Yard

160.350	Yard engine 81
160.980	Yard engine 83
161.010	Yard engine 84
160.650	Car Dept.
160.860	Bryan Park engine terminal

River Terminal Cleveland, Ohio

161.370 General operations

Roberval & Saguenay Jonquiere, Quebec

161.145	160.185	Road
160.145	159.945	Yard
160.350	161.385	Inter-plant switching
160.830	160.230	MofW
419.000		Dispatchers link – Alma to Arvida

Alma

160.020	Road – Alma & Jonquiere Railway
160.650	Yard – Alma & Jonquiere Railway
160.725	Dispatcher – Alma & Jonquiere Railway

Arvida

160.605	Yard
160.725	Yard
160.995	Intra-plant switching

Port Alfred

160.605	Yard
160.725	Yard

Rochester & Southern Retsof, New York

160.770	161.445	Road and repeater (Rochester & Southern)
160.500		Road (Genesee & Wyoming)
160.590		Shop and MofW
161.100		Yard

Caledonia, New York
452.9125 457.9125 Rochester/Caledonia link

Rockdale, Sandow & Southern   Rockdale, Texas
160.500	General operations
160.410	UP Trackage
160.575	MofW

Rocky Mountain Railcar & Railroad   Henderson, Colorado
160.815~	G – FCC

Commerce City, Colorado
160.305 161.385	General operations
160.815	General operations

Sedalia, Colorado
463.600 468.600	General operations
463.6375~	FCC

Romaine River   Havre-St.-Pierre, Quebec
160.650	General operations

Sabine River & Northern   Orange, Texas
161.445	Road and repeater output
161.445 160.695	Road repeater

Saginaw Valley   Bad Axe, Michigan
161.400	General operations

St. Lawrence   Norfolk, New York
161.160	Ch 1 Dispatcher
160.260	Ch 2 Road and yard

St. Lawrence & Atlantic   Berlin, New Hampshire
160.965	Ch 1 Road

160.815	Ch 2 Administration
464.500	FCC

St. Maries River   St. Maries, Idaho
160.275 161.055	General operations

St. Marys Railroad   St. Marys, Georgia
160.620	General operations
160.560	General operations

Salt Lake, Garfield & Western   Salt Lake City, Utah
160.305	General operations
161.070	General operations

San Diego & Imperial Valley   San Diego, California
160.455	General operations
161.505	General operations

San Joaquin Valley   Exeter, California
160.365	General operations
452.9125	Dispatcher link – Pampa Peak and Joaquin Ridge
457.9125	Dispatcher link – Trains to Base

San Luis Central   Monte Vista, Colorado
160.680	General operations

San Manuel Arizona   San Manuel, Arizona
161.460	General operations
457.900	Remote data links

San Pedro & Southwestern — Benson, Arizona
160.935   Switching
160.440   161.520   General operations

Sand Springs — Sand Springs, Oklahoma
160.230   General operations

Sandersville Railroad — Sandersville, Georgia
160.860   General operations

Santa Fe Southern — Santa Fe, New Mexico
160.290   General operations

Santa Maria Valley — Santa Maria, California
160.770   Road and repeater output
160.770   161.175   Road repeater

Savannah State Docks — Garden City, Georgia
807.4375   General operations
852.4375   General operations

Seaview Transportation Corp. — North Kingston, Rhode Island
160.845   General operations

Seminole Gulf — Fort Myers, Florida
160.710   161.550   Road and dispatcher
161.100   CSX coordinated operations
161.235   Switching
160.275   MofW

Sequatchie Valley — South Pittsburg, Tennessee
154.600   Road
464.700   469.700   Dispatcher link

Shamokin Valley — Northumberland, Pennsylvania
160.455   General operations

Shore Fast Line — Pleasantville, New Jersey
160.335   Road
161.385   Switching

Sidney & Lowe — Sidney, Nebraska
463.325   468.325   FCC

Sierra Railroad — Oakdale, California
160.590   General operations

Sisseton – Milbank — Sisseton, South Dakota
461.950   466.950   General operations

Sisseton Southern — Chamberlain, South Dakota
161.415   160.500   FCC – Mobiles/repeater

Somerset Railroad — Lockport, New York
160.380   161.040   General operations

Soo Line (CP Rail System) — Minneapolis, Minnesota
161.370   Ch 1 Road
161.520△   Ch 2 Road
161.085   Ch 3 Road

Soo Line

160.770△		Ch 4 Road
161.430		Ch 5 Yard
160.725		Ch 6 Yard
160.530		Alternate Yard
160.920		Alternate Yard
160.350		MofW – Wisconsin, west of Milwaukee
160.260		Police – Former Soo Line, systemwide, except Chicago
160.440		Police – Former Milwaukee Road north of Chicago
161.205		Police – Mutual aid
161.400	160.260	PBX – Glenwood, Minnesota

Iowa

Davenport
161.430	Ch 5 Nahant Yard
160.530	West Davenport Yard and MofW

Muscatine
161.430	Ch 5 Yard

Ottumwa
161.430	Ch 5 Yard

Illinois

Chicago
161.205		Police – Mutual aid
161.235		Police
452.875	457.875	Milwaukee Road trucks

Chicago – Bensenville Yard
160.515		Hump
161.430		Ch 5 Yard
160.620		Locomotive hostler
160.395		Car Dept.
160.470	161.145	Car Dept.

Savanna
161.430	Ch 5 Yard

Minnesota

Appleton
161.430	Ch 5 Yard

Glenwood
160.725	Ch 6 Yard

Minneapolis
160.440	Police
161.205	Police – Mutual aid

Minneapolis – General Office Bldg
161.325	Janitors

Minneapolis – Shoreham Yard
160.980	Intermodal facility

St. Paul
160.440	Police
161.205	Police – Mutual aid

St. Paul – Pig's Eye Yard
160.680		Hump
161.430		Ch 5 Yard
160.530		Roundhouse
160.230	161.400	Car Dept.
160.920		Rip track

North Dakota

Harvey
161.520	Ch 2 Yard

Wisconsin

Madison
160.770	Ch 4 Yard

Milwaukee
160.920	Burnham Bridge Yard

161.430	Ch 5 Other yards
160.350	MofW
160.440	Police
Superior	
160.680	Yard
161.430	Ch 5 Yard
West Allis	
160.440	Police

South Branch Valley Moorefield, West Virginia

853.1625 808.1625	Trunked operation
853.4875 808.4875	Trunked operation

South Brooklyn Brooklyn, New York

161.505	Road and dispatcher to train
158.775	Train to dispatcher
160.845	Yard

South Buffalo Lackawanna, New York

161.190	Road and yard
161.280	MofW

South Carolina Central Hartsville, South Carolina

161.175	General operations

South Central Florida Clewiston, Florida

161.250 160.830	General operations

South Central Tennessee Centerville, Tennessee

161.355	General operations

South Kansas & Oklahoma Coffeyville, Kansas

160.785	General operations

South Orient San Angelo, Texas

160.440	General operations
161.490	FCC – 1 BM

South Shore Louisiana

160.230~	EE

Southeast Kansas Coffeyville, Kansas

160.785	General operations
160.845	General operations

Southeastern Rail Columbus, Mississippi
(now operated by Kansas City Southern)

161.085	General operations
160.920	Illinois Central Road Ch 2
Artesia, Mississippi	
161.355	Active

Southern Alabama Troy, Alabama

154.600~	FCC

Southern Pacific San Francisco, California

161.550Δ	Road
160.290Δ	Road – Alternate, east of El Paso, Texas
160.590Δ	Road – Alternate, east of El Paso, Texas
160.320Δ	Road – Alternate, west of El Paso, Texas
161.280Δ	Road – Kansas City to Chicago and St Louis

Southern Pacific

160.650		Road – AT&SF
160.890	161.040	PBX P-8 – West of Houston, Texas
160.950	161.160	PBX P-9 – West of Houston, Texas
160.680	161.400	PBX P-10 – East of Houston, Texas
160.800	161.490	PBX P-11 – East of Houston, Texas
161.220	160.320	PBX P-12 – Kansas City; Topeka; San Francisco
161.340	160.365	PBX P-13 – Kansas City
160.350	160.980	PBX P-14 – Houston, San Antonio, Texas
161.220	160.800	PBX – San Francisco
160.275	160.815	PBX – Mount Vaca, California
160.395	161.235	PBX – Palmdale, California (Mount Emma)
161.400		Administration/Police/MofW – Systemwide
160.860		Police

St. Louis Southwestern Territory (Cotton Belt)

160.305		Yards
160.395		MofW
161.355		Yards

Arizona
Tucson

161.100	Yard	
161.430	160.470	Pacific Fruit Express
160.320	161.130.	Car Dept.

Tucson Division

161.205	Police

Yuma

161.400	Yard

Arkansas
North Little Rock

161.100	Yardmaster
160.230	Car Dept.

Pine Bluff

160.530	Hump

161.100		Yard – Red
160.440		Yard – Blue
1160.230	161.160	Car Dept.

Texarkana

160.500	161.190	Car Dept.

California
Bakersfield

161.430		Yard
160.275	161.310	Car Dept.
160.470	161.220	Pacific Fruit Express

Berkeley

160.320	PMT Trucking

Fresno

160.275	161.310	Car Dept.
161.220	160.470	Car Dept.
160.410		Pacific Fruit Express
161.400		PMT Trucking

Los Angeles

161.100	Shops Yard
160.530	Shops Yard intermodal facility
161.205	Police
161.220	Police

Mojave

161.430	Yard

Oakland

161.100		Switching and crew caller
160.275	161.310	Car Dept.
160.320		PMT Trucking

Redwood City

160.725	PMT Trucking

Roseville

161.220	Police

Roseville – Antelope Yard
160.980		Hump
160.470		Switching
160.620		Switching
161.100		Switching
161.430		Switching
160.275	161.310	Car Dept.
160.335		Car Dept.
161.340	160.800	Car Dept. – Receiving yard
160.350	161.130	Car Dept. – Departure yard
160.410	160.725	Rehab and Maintenance Center
161.490		Purchases and Materials

Sacramento
160.470		Switching
160.215		Car placement notification
161.490		Car placement notification
161.250		Stores Dept.
161.520	160.425	Mechanical Dept.
160.800		PFE Terminal
160.290		PMT Trucking

Salinas
160.470	161.340	Pacific Fruit Express
160.845		PMT Trucking

San Francisco
160.980		Yard and utility
160.845	161.130	Car Dept.
160.290		PMT Trucking

San Jose
160.470	161.340	Car Dept.
160.290		PMT Trucking

Southern California
161.220		Police

West Colton
160.470	160.845	Hump and switching
161.100		Switching – Trim yard
161.430		Switching – Receiving yard
160.620		Yard and utility
452.900	457.900	Car Dept. – Receiving yard
160.380	160.920	Car Dept. – Departure yard

Western Division
161.400		Police

Wilmington
160.305	161.310	Light Rail operations

Wilmington – ICTF Yard
161.400		Yard switcher
160.350		Intermodal facility
161.205		Security

Illinois

East St. Louis
160.875		Yard
161.280		Yard
160.305	161.355	Mechanical Dept.
161.220		Mechanical Dept.
161.340		Mechanical Dept.
161.400		Mechanical Dept.
161.205		Police

Louisiana

Lafayette Division
161.205		Police

New Orleans
160.860		Police

SOUTHERN PACIFIC

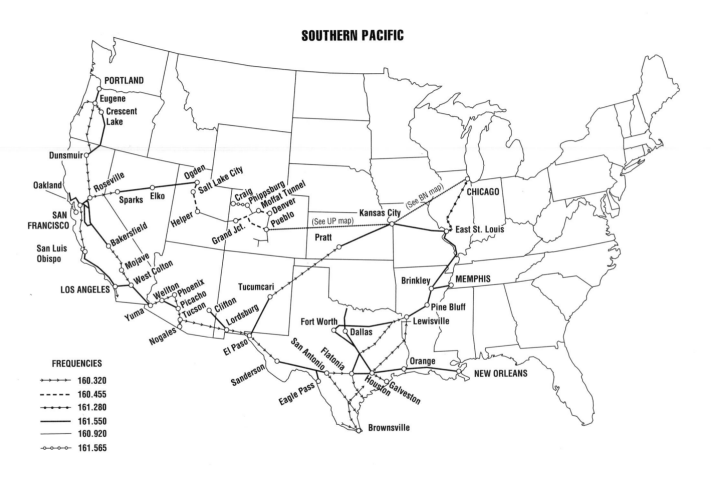

PORTLAND
Eugene
Crescent Lake
Dunsmuir
Oakland
Roseville
SAN FRANCISCO
Sparks
Elko
Ogden
Salt Lake City
Craig
Phippsburg
Moffat Tunnel
Denver
Helper
Pueblo
Grand Jct.
(See BN map)
CHICAGO
Kansas City
(See UP map)
East St. Louis
Pratt
San Luis Obispo
Bakersfield
Mojave
West Colton
LOS ANGELES
Wellton
Phoenix
Picacho
Yuma
Tucson
Clifton
Lordsburg
Tucumcari
Brinkley
MEMPHIS
Pine Bluff
Fort Worth
Lewisville
Nogales
Dallas
El Paso
San Antonio
Flatonia
Orange
Sanderson
Houston
Galveston
NEW ORLEANS
Eagle Pass
Brownsville

FREQUENCIES

→→→	160.320
- - -	160.455
•-•-•	161.280
———	161.550
———	160.920
∘-∘-∘	161.565

New Orleans – Avondale Yard
161.430   Yard
160.710   Yard
Shreveport
161.100   Yard
Missouri
Kansas City
160.365   Police
161.205   Police
161.265   Police – Mutual aid
854.8625 809.8625 Mobile data terminals
Kansas City – Armourdale Yard
161.400   Yard
161.070   Car Dept.
Nevada
Sparks
160.320   161.130   Car Dept.
Oregon
Eugene
160.410   Hump
160.470   Yard
161.310   Yard
161.430   Yard
161.400   Diesel maintenance
160.260   160.770   Car Dept.
150.290   PMT Trucking
Klamath Falls
161.310   160.575   Car Dept.

Tennessee
Memphis
161.205   Police
Texas
160.860   Police – Mobile to mobile, statewide
Beaumont
160.710   Yard
Dallas
160.230   Yard
160.290   Intermodal facility
160.860   Police – Mobile to mobile
El Paso
160.350   Yard
161.430   Miller Yard
160.380   160.590   Car Dept.
Ennis
160.230   Yard
Hearne
160.230   Yard
Houston
161.310   Police
Houston – Englewood Yard
161.400   Yard
161.430   Yard
San Antonio – Kirby Yard
160.740   Yard
160.845   161.460   Diesel service
160.980   160.230   Car Dept.
San Antonio Division
161.400   Police

111

Southern – Stockton

Strang
| 161.280 | | Yard |

Utah

Ogden
| 161.400 | 160.470 | Car Dept. |

Dispatcher links
160.320	Alturas to Likely Mountain, California
160.485	Mt. Lemmon (Tucson) to Sibyl, Arizona (east of Benson)
160.485	Mt. Tassajara to San Luis Obispo, California
160.485	Oak Creek Pass to Monolith, California
160.575	Oak Creek Pass to Newhall, California
160.575	Williams Hill (Lockwood) to Bradley, California
160.770	Coquille to Coos Bay, Oregon
160.770	Mt. Emma, California (Palmdale)
160.845	Tucumcari to Santa Rosa, New Mexico
160.845	Lordsburg, New Mexico
160.845	Vail, Arizona
161.220	Walong Siding, California
161.310	Cliff Siding to Pama Peak, California

Southern Railroad Co. of New Jersey   Winslow, New Jersey

| 160.335 | 161.385 | General operations |

Southern Railway of British Columbia (former BC Hydro)
Vancouver, British Columbia

160.275	Ch 1 Dispatcher
160.515	Ch 2 MofW and yard
160.545	Ch 3 Road and yard – Line-ups on Ch 3 at 0800 and 1230 hrs
160.605	Ch 4 Yard and Car Dept.

North Vancouver – Trapp Yard
| 160.725 | CP Ch 78 – Yard transfer |

Southwest Railroad   Longview, Texas

| 466.850 | General operations |

Southwestern Railroad   Whitewater, New Mexico

| 160.380 | General operations |

Spokane International (UP)   Spokane, Washington

160.560	Road
160.320	Road (UP)
160.740	Road (UP)

Springfield Terminal (Guilford Transportation Industries)

| 161.400 | Road and yard |

Steelton & Highspire   Steelton, Pennsylvania

161.190		General operations
160.740		General operations
452.325	457.325	Inter-plant switching
452.375	457.375	Inter-plant switching
452.425	457.425	Inter-plant switching
452.475	457.475	Inter-plant switching
452.775	457.775	Inter-plant switching
160.425		FCC – Base and mobiles
452.925	457.925	FCC – Remote control locomotives

Stockton Terminal & Eastern   Stockton, California

| 160.455 | Road and yard |
| 161.235 | MofW |

Tacoma Municipal Belt Line   Tacoma, Washington
161.070   Switching
161.145   Switching
161.295   Switching

Tennessee Southern   Pulaski, Tennessee
160.755   General operations

Tennken   Dyersburg, Kentucky
160.365   Road
160.935   Yard

TennRail   Counce, Tennessee
160.605   General operations
161.400   General operations
161.370

Terminal Railroad Association of St. Louis
Granite City, Illinois
160.500∆   Road
160.845   160.290   PBX
161.205   Police mutual aid
161.310   Police and MofW
Madison, Illinois – Madison Yard
160.650   Hump
160.425   Pulldown
452.875   457.875   Car Dept.
St. Louis, Missouri – Harlem Yard
161.535   Switching

Terminal Railway Alabama State Docks   Mobile, Alabama
161.100   Ch 1 General operations
161.070   Ch 2 General operations

Texas & New Mexico   Hobbs, New Mexico
161.520   General operations

Texas & Northern   Lone Star, Texas
153.200~   FCC – Base and mobiles
153.230~   FCC – Base only
154.490~   FCC – Base only
161.100~   FCC – Base only

Texas & Western   Plainview, Texas
160.305~   FCC – Base only
161.175~   FCC – Base only

Texas City Terminal   Texas City, Texas
160.620   Ch 1 General operations
160.725   Ch 2 General operations

Texas, Gonzales & Northern   Gonzales, Texas
160.455   General operations

Texas Mexican   Laredo, Texas
161.220   160.695   Road and dispatcher
161.130   Yard

Texas North Western   Etter, Texas
160.455   General operations

Texas – Trona

Texas Northeastern   Sherman, Texas
160.815   General operations

Texas, Oklahoma & Eastern   De Queen, Arkansas
160.230 161.445 Ch 1 Road repeater
160.230   Ch 2 Road and repeater output
160.605   Ch 3 Yard
160.785   Ch 4 Yard

Texas South-Eastern   Diboll, Texas
160.920   General operations

Texas Southern   San Antonio, Texas
160.215   Ch 4 Yard

Thermal Belt   Bostic, North Carolina
161.175   FCC – BM

Three Rivers – see CSX

Thurso & Nation Valley (Chemin de fer Thurso)
                                Thurso, Quebec
160.245   Ch 1 Road and repeater output
160.245 160.965 Ch 2 Road repeater and dispatcher

Tioga Central – see Owego & Harford

Toledo, Peoria & Western   East Peoria, Illinois
160.245 161.535 PBX
161.400   Road

160.440   Norfolk Southern coordinated operations
160.800   Conrail coordinated operations

Tomahawk Railway   Tomahawk, Wisconsin
160.290   General operations
160.740   FCC

Tonawanda Island   North Tonawanada, New York
27.125   CB Ch 14 General operations

Toronto Terminals Railway (Union Station) Toronto, Ontario
461.2125 466.2125 Stationmaster – Arrivals and departures
461.0125 466.0125 Security

Tradewater Railway   Sturgis, Kentucky
160.635   General operations

Transkentucky Transportation   Paris, Kentucky
160.665   Road
161.265   Yard
161.445   Dispatcher
161.190   General operations

Trinidad Railway   Trinidad, Colorado
161.250 160.710 Road – Jansen to New Elk Mine

Trona Railway   Trona, California
161.085   General operations
161.550   Southern Pacific interchange
160.320   Southern Pacific interchange

Tulsa-Sapulpa Union   Sapulpa, Oklahoma

161.070   General operations

Turtle Creek Industrial   Export, Pennsylvania

468.700   Road and yard
463.800   Dispatcher

Tuscola & Saginaw Bay   Owosso, Michigan

Vassar, Michigan
160.575   Ch 1 Road and dispatcher
Millington, Michigan
161.100   Ch 2 Road and dispatcher
Durand, Michigan
160.590   Grand Trunk Western interchange

Twin Cities & Western   Minneapolis, Minnesota

160.875   Ch 1 Yard – Hopkins to Appleton, Minnesota
161.460   Ch 2 Road – Hopkins to Appleton, Minnesota
160.860   MofW – occasional use

Twin States   St. Johnsbury, Vermont

160.230   General operations
161.340   General operations
160.230   161.340   Repeater (use undetermined)

Tyburn Railroad   Penndel, Pennsylvania

160.335   Road and yard
161.385   MofW

Union Pacific   Omaha, Nebraska

160.410   Ch 1 Road
160.470   Ch 2 Road
160.515   Ch 3 Road
160.740   Ch 4 Road
160.680   Ch 5 Road
160.980   Ch 6 Road
160.605   MofW – Simplex
160.290   161.520   Administration PBX
                 Arkansas: Van Buren
                 California: Los Angeles, Oakland, Oroville, Portola, Sacramento, Stockton, Yermo
                 Colorado: Denver, Julesburg, La Salle
                 Iowa: Council Bluffs
                 Idaho: Blackfoot, Eastport, Idaho Falls, Montpelier, Nampa, Pocatello, Rupert, Soda Springs, Twin Falls
                 Missouri: Kansas City
                 Kansas: Marysville, Topeka
                 Montana: Dillon, Silver Bow
                 Nebraska: Grand Island, North Platte, South Morrill
                 Nevada: Elko, Las Vegas, Winnemucca
                 Oregon: Barnes, Hinkle, La Grande, Portland, The Dalles
                 Utah: Ogden, Salt Lake City, Wendover
                 Washington: Fife, Seattle, Spokane
                 Wyoming: Cheyenne, Green River, Kemmerer, Laramie
160.605   161.025   PBX – Mof W

160.665	161.430	Administration PBX – Former Missouri Pacific, Dolton, Illinois
161.280	160.785	Administration PBX – Former Western Pacific
160.755	161.325	Administration PBX – Former Missouri Pacific
		Arkansas: Bald Knob, Little Rock, McGehee, Texarkana, Wynne
		Illinois: Benton, Chester, Findlay, Mt. Vernon, Salem, Villa Grove
		Kansas: Osawatomie
		Louisiana: Addis, Alexander, Kinder, Monroe, New Orleans, Shreveport
		Missouri: Carthage, Pleasant Hill, Poplar Bluff, St. Louis, Sedalia
		Tennessee: Memphis
		Texas: Beaumont, Fort Worth, Harlingen, Longview, San Antonio
161.325	160.215	Administration PBX – Kemmerer, Wyoming
161.205		Police – Mutual Aid
457.9375		End-of-train telemetry

Arkansas
North Little Rock

161.190	Hump
161 455	Cab Signal (hump control)
160.815	Pulldown
160.935	Industrial yard
161.040	Car Dept.
161.370	Crew cabs
160.665	Jenks Shop
161.250	Maintenance Director
161.430	Store room
161.355	Wrecker

160.080	MoPac Trucking Lines No. 1
160.470	Yard

Texarkana
| 161.116 | Yard |

Van Buren
| 160.680 | Yard |

California
Los Angeles
160.410		Hump
160.680		Yard
161.340	160.590	Car Dept.
160.710		UP Motor Freight

Milpitas
| 160.830 | Yard |
| 161.115 | Yard |

Oakland
| 160.620 | Yard |
| 160.680 | Yard |

Oroville
| 160.380 | Yard |
| 160.740 | Yard |

Sacramento
| 160.740 | Yard |

Sierra Peak
| 161.175 | Intermodal facility and railroad trucks |

Stockton
160.530	Yard
160.620	Yard
160.680	Yard
160.740	Yard
160.770	Yard

161.115		Yard
161.460		Yard
160.830		West end switcher
160.920		Terminal superintendent
160.380		Work channel
160.995		UP Fruit Express
161.280		UP Trucking Line
161.100		Active

Yermo

160.680		Yard
160.740		Yard
161.115		Signal Dept.

Colorado

Denver

160.410		Yard
160.680		Yard
161.070		Car Dept.

Idaho

Blackfoot

160.680		Yard

Idaho Falls

160.680		Yard

Montpelier

160.470		Yard
160.515		Yard
160.680		Yard
160.740		Yard

Nampa

160.410		Yard
160.680		Yard

Pocatello

160.860		Hump
160.680		Yard
160.800		Yard
160.350		Car Dept.
161.070	160.590	Car Dept.
160.650		Car Dept.
160.980	161.400	UP Fruit Express
160.905		UP Fruit Express
161.340		UP Fruit Express

Soda Springs

160.680		Yard

Twin Falls

160.680		Yard

Illinois

Chicago

160.035		MoPac Trucking Lines
161.145		Yard
160.470		Ch 2 MofW
161.430	160.655	PBX – Executive

Dupo

160.590		Yard engines
160.470		Yardmaster
160.080		Intermodal facility and railroad trucks

Kansas

Kansas City

160.680		Kansas City terminal – West

Marysville

160.680		Yard
160.740		Yard

Salina

160.410		Yard

Union Pacific

160.470		Yard
160.680		Yard
Topeka		
160.410		Yard
160.470		Yard
160.680		Yard
160.980		Kansas City dispatcher
Wichita		
160.515		Yard
160.875		Link to Rosalia
161.250		Car Dept.
161.385		Link to Conway Springs
161.475		Link to Rosalia
Louisiana		
Alexandria		
161.070		Yard
Livonia		
160.410		Yard
160.470		Yard
161.115		Yard
New Orleans		
160.770		MP Trucking Lines
Shreveport		
161.265		Yard
Missouri		
Kansas City		
160.065		MP Trucking Lines
160.980		Kansas City terminal – East
Kansas City – Neff Yard		
160.395		East hump
160.815		East pulldown
160.950		East pulldown
160.590		Yard
160.875		Car Dept.
160.425		Mechanical Dept.
Kansas City – Quindero Yard		
160.830		Yard
St. Louis		
160.740		MofW (main line)
160.410		MofW (yard)
160.410		Car Dept.
160.590		Dupo yard engines
160.470		Dupo yardmaster
160.080		MP Trucking Lines
Nebraska		
Grand Island		
160.680		Yard
North Platte		
160.350		East hump
160.410		West hump
161.445	160.440	East Yard pulldown 1
160.500		East Yard pulldown 2
160.230		West Yard pulldown 1
160.530	161.550	West Yard pulldown 2
160.680		Yard
160.740		Yard
161.190	161.565	East Car Dept.
161.070	160.590	West Car Dept.
160.800		Shop Foreman
160.650		Diesel tower
160.890		Hostler shop
161.475		Hostler service

UNION PACIFIC

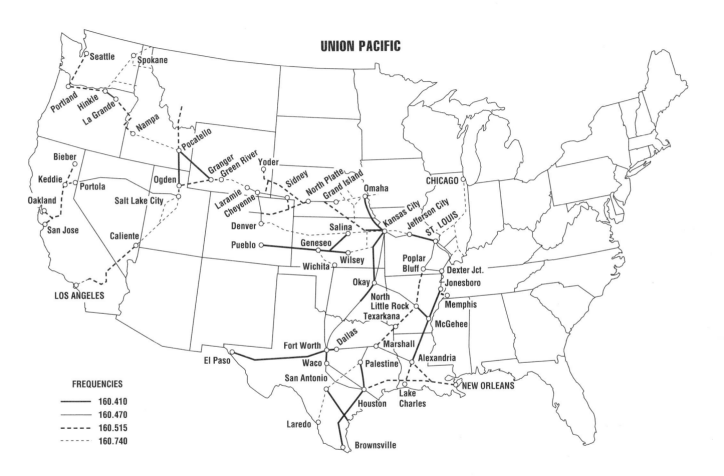

FREQUENCIES

——	160.410
—	160.470
- - -	160.515
- - - -	160.740

Union Pacific

161.325		Crew Caller
161.145		Signal Dept.
161.250		Store room
160.980	161.400	UP Fruit Express
Omaha		
160.350		Yard
160.470		Yard
160.515		Yard
160.650		Yard
160.680		Yard
160.770		Yard
160.830		Yard
160.860		Yard
160.905		General use
161.115		General use
160.980	161.445	Store room
161.310		UP Motor Freight
854.8875		FCC
South Morrill		
160.740		Yard
854.8875		FCC
Nevada		
Elko		
160.680		Yard
160.740		Yard
Winnemucca		
160.380		Yard
160.515		Yard
160.740		Yard

Oregon		
Barnes		
160.230		Switching 1
160.350		Switching 2
160.410		Switching 3
160.800		Switching 5
160.860		Switching 6
161.145		Switching 8
160.680		Yard
161.265		Yard
161.355		Yard
Hermiston – Hinkle Yard		
160.470		Hump
160.830		Pulldown 2
160.230		Switching 1
160.680		Yard
161.340	160.890	Car Dept.
160.650		Hostler
160.350		Signal Dept.
La Grande		
160.680		Yard
Portland		
160.230		Switching 1
160.350		Switching 2
160.410		Switching 3
160.800		Switching 5
160.860		Switching 6
160.680		Yard
161.310	160.980	Car Dept.
160.830		UP Motor Freight

The Dalles
160.680 Yard
Tennessee
Memphis
161.355 Yard
160.350 MoPac Trucking Lines
Texas
Dallas
160.635 Yard and switching
161.310 Yard
161.280 MoPac Trucking Lines
Fort Worth
160.830 Hump – Centennial Yard
161.250 160.905 Pulldown
161.115 Yard and Switching
160.770 Mechanical Dept. – Yard Train Inspection
160.665 Diesel Shop
Laredo
161.310 Yard
Palestine
160.770 Car Dept.
San Antonio
161.280 MoPac Trucking Lines
161.310 Yard
Whitesboro
160.410 Yard
Utah
Ogden
160.410 Yard
160.680 Yard
160.710 161.190 Car Dept.

160.995 UP Fruit Express
160.350 Active
Salt Lake City
160.680 Yard 1
160.710 Yard 2
160.800 Yard 3
160.860 Yard 4
160.230 Yard 5
160.380 Yard 6
161.340 160.620 Car Dept.
160.650 Diesel shop
160.310 UP Motor Freight
Wendover
160.515 Yard
160.740 Yard
Washington
Fife
160.410 Yard
160.680 Yard
Seattle
160.230 Switching 1
160.350 Switching 2
160.410 Switching 3
160.860 Switching 6
160.740 Switching 9
160.680 Yard
160.800 Yard
161.340 160.890 Car Dept.
160.950 UP Motor Freight
Spokane
160.680 Yard

Union – Vancouver

Wyoming
Cheyenne
160.650		Yard
160.680		Yard
160.770		Yard
161.070	160.590	Car Dept.

Green River
160.650		Yard
160.680		Yardmaster
161.070	160.590	Car Dept.
160.350	161.325	MofW – Special, Kemmerer
161.145		Signal Dept. – Evanston

Kemmerer
160.470		Yard
160.515		Yard
160.680		Yard
160.740		Yard

Laramie
160.680		Yard
160.230		Rail plant
160.800		Rail plant

Sherman Hill
452.900	457.900	Road repeater

Dispatcher links
161.265		Gurdon, Ozark, Van Buren, Arkansas
161.355		Almond, Newport, Arkansas
161.385		Concordia, Conway Springs, Downs, Wichita, Kansas
161.385		Eunice, New Mexico; Monahans, Texas
161.445		Cotter, Matney Knob, Newport, Arkansas
452.825	457.825	Sherman Hill – Hermosa to Tie Siding

452.875	457.875	Sherman Hill
452.900	457.900	Sherman Hill – Granite

Union Railroad   East Pittsburgh, Pennsylvania
160.260	Ch 1 Road/Dispatcher

West Mifflin – Clairton Yard
160.500	Ch 2 Yard – Duquesne, Edgar, and Irvin Works
160.620	Ch 3 Yard – Homestead and Rankin
160.350	Ch 4 Hump – Clairton Works
160.395~	FCC
161.550~	FCC

Upper Merion & Plymouth   Conshohocken, Pennsylvania
160.485	General operations

Utah Railway   Martin, Utah
160.560		General operations
161.145		General operations
452.375	457.375~	FCC
452.775	457.775~	FCC

Utah Western   Pleasant Grove, Utah
161.370	General operations

Valdosta Railway   Lake Park, Georgia
160.680	General operations
160.590	CSX trackage
160.950	Norfolk Southern trackage

Vancouver Wharves Ltd.   Vancouver, British Columbia
464.225	Yard

460.800	465.800	Car Dumper/Ship Loading
464.375		Yard
464.625		Yard
464.775		Yard

Vandalia Railroad　　　　　　　Vandalia, Illinois
160.545　　　General operations

Ventura County　　　　　　Oxnard, California
161.355　　　General operations

Vermont Railway　　　　　Burlington, Vermont
161.010	160.290	Ch 1 Dispatcher
160.440		Ch 2 Road and yard
160.710		Ch 2 Road and yard
161.250		Car Shop, Burlington

VIA Rail Canada　　　　　Montreal, Quebec
Systemwide
418.050　　Ch S1 On-board services/station services
451.850　　Ch S2 On-board services/station services
456.8625　Ch S3 On-board services/station services
British Columbia
Vancouver
452.6625 457.6625 Car and diesel shop
469.3875　Vancouver Maintenance Centre
Ontario
Toronto – Union Station
461.2125 466.2125 Stationmaster arrival and departure

Quebec
Dorval
418.050　　Ch S1 Stationmaster
Montreal – Pointe St. Charles Yard
160.245　　Coach yard
160.275　　Diesel shop
160.725　　Coach yard
160.665　　Diesel shop switch tender
161.025　　Diesel shop switch tender
Montreal – Central Station
161.295　　Station switcher
451.850　　Ch S2 Stationmaster
456.8625　Ch S3 Stationmaster

Virginia Railroad Bureau
151.685~　FCC – Mobiles Only

Virginia Southern　　　　Keysville, Virginia
161.310　　General operations

Virginian Transportation Corp.　Kenbridge, Virginia
160.755~　G – FCC

Wabash & Grand River　　Chillicothe, Missouri
161.025　　General operations

Waccamaw Coast Line　　Conway, South Carolina
461.450~ 466.450　FCC

Walking Horse & Eastern　Shelbyville, Tennessee
154.600~　FCC

123

Warren & Saline River   Warren, Arkansas
    451.625 456.625   General operations

Washington Central   Yakima, Washington
    160.770 161.295   General operations
    160.440   Yard
    Ellensburg
    161.130 160.545   BN Ch 5 PBX
    Parker
    160.665 161.505   BN Ch 3 PBX

Washington County   Barre, Vermont
    161.190   Road and repeater output
    161.190 160.470   Road repeater

Washington Terminal   Washington, D. C.
    160.290 161.370   Ch 1 Road and Car Dept.
    160.350 161.145   Ch 2 Baggage and Maintenance
    160.440 161.445   Ch 3 Police

Washington Western   Clifton, Louisiana
    160.755   Green Bros Sand & Gravel

WCTU Railway   White City, Oregon
    160.680   Switching
    160.800   Switching

Wellsboro & Corning   Wellsboro, Pennsylvania
    160.455   General operations
    161.070   Conrail trackage rights

West Jersey   Salem, New Jersey
    161.025   General operations

West Shore   Mifflinburg, Pennsylvania
    154.600~   G – FCC
    154.570~   G – FCC
    Local sister railroads use 160.455 and 160.725

West Tennessee   Trenton, Tennessee
    160.560   General operations
    160.290   Dispatchers link
    161.070   Dispatchers link

Western Railroad   New Braunfels, Texas
    160.335   General operations

Wheeling & Lake Erie   Brewster, Ohio
    161.025   Ch 1 Road – Former Pittsburgh & West Virginia
                       lines
    161.250   Ch 2 Road – Former Nickel Plate lines
    160.440   Former Akron, Canton & Youngstown line
    160.665   Yard
    161.565   Yard
    855.8875 810.8875 Yard clerk data terminals

Wichita, Tillman & Jackson   Wichita Falls, Texas
    161.265   General operations
    160.275 161.265   General operations

Willamette & Pacific Albany, Oregon
160.770   General operations
160.365 161.355 PBX – Marys Peak, Eugene
160.215 161.175 PBX – Prospect Peak, Salem

Willamette Valley Independence, Oregon
161.475 160.560 General operations
161.070   FCC – B&M
160.530   FCC – B&M

Willamina & Grand Ronde Willamina, Oregon
160.530   General operations

Wilmington & Western Wilmington, Delaware
160.755   General operations

Winamac Southern Kokomo, Indiana
160.455   Ch 1 General operations
161.295   Ch 2 General operations

Winchester & Western Winchester, Virginia
Bridgeton, New Jersey
161.310   General operations

Winchester, Virginia
160.920   General operations

Winston-Salem Southbound Winston-Salem, North Carolina
160.590   Joint operations with CSXT
161.250   Joint operations with NS
72.68   Dispatchers link
75.74   Dispatchers link

Wiregrass Central Enterprise, Alabama
160.500   Road
161.190   Illinois Central trackage rights

Wisconsin & Calumet Monroe, Wisconsin
160.215   General operations

Wisconsin & Michigan Bessemer, Michigan
161.265   General operations

Wisconsin & Southern Horicon, Wisconsin
160.575   Ch 1 Road
161.145   Ch 2 MofW

Wisconsin Central

Wisconsin Central   Stevens Point, Wisconsin

160.785	Ch 1 Road
160.260	Ch 2 Yard
161.295	Ch 3 Road
160.335 ·	Ch 1 Fox River Valley, Road
160.845	Former Fox River Valley
161.250	Former Green Bay & Western
161.070	Former Green Bay & Western
161.385	Former Green Bay & Western
161.445	Former Green Bay & Western

Michigan
Gladstone
160.260	Yard

Wisconsin
Fond du Lac – Shops Yard
160.260	Yard

Green Bay – Terminal Area
160.785	Road within yard limits
161.295	Yard – Oakland Avenue Yard

Neenah
160.260	Yard

Stevens Point
160.260	Yard

Wisconsin Rapids
160.260	Yard
160.785	Yard

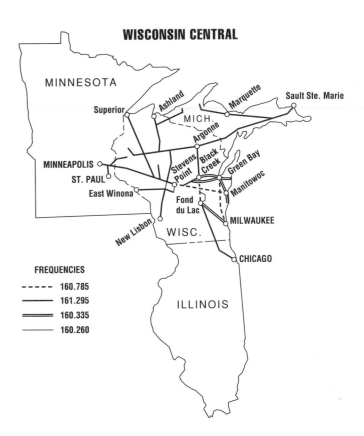

WISCONSIN CENTRAL

FREQUENCIES

- - - - 160.785
——— 161.295
═══ 160.335
——— 160.260

Wyoming Colorado Laramie, Wyoming
160.380   General operations

Yadkin Valley Rural Hall, North Carolina
160.980   General operations
452.9125   FCC – Mobiles
457.9125   FCC – Mobiles

Yolo Shortline West Sacramento, California
160.260   General operations

Yorkrail West York, Pennsylvania
160.500   Road
161.370   Yard and MofW

Youngstown & Austintown Austintown, Ohio
160.845   General operations

Youngstown Southern Youngstown, Ohio
160.995   General operations

Yreka Western Yreka, California
161.070   General operations

INDUSTRIAL RAILROADS

A&K Railroad Material
Edwardsville, Illinois
463.200~ 468.200~ FCC
Salt Lake City, Utah
462.025~ 467.025~ FCC

Acme Steel   Riverdale, Illinois
153.200   Plant switching

Agrico Chemicals Company   South Pierce, Florida
158.430~   FCC-3 base and 15 mobiles
451.900~ 456.900~ FCC-95 Mob-6 CO/1 MR

Alabama By-Products   Birmingham, Alabama
31.20   General operations
35.32   General operations
35.84   General operations

Alcoa Terminal   Alcoa, Tennessee
153.080   General operations

Algoma Steel Company   Sault Ste. Marie, Ontario
149.020   Plant switching
154.570   Plant switching
160.650   Plant switching
165.720   Plant switching

Allied Chemical Corp.
Jamesville, New York
153.170~   FCC-6 base and 75 mobiles
Solvay, New York
151.865   Inter-plant switching
153.110   Administration and car placement

AMAX Coal Company   Terre Haute, Indiana
151.895   Mine switching

American Can of Canada Ltd   Marathon, Quebec
160.650   General operations

American Cast Iron Pipe   Birmingham, Alabama
153.155   Plant switching

American Cyanamid   Brewster, Florida
451.775   456.775   General operations

American Maize Company   Hammond, Indiana
469.875~   FCC – Switching~

Anheuser-Busch Brewing   Merrimack, New Hampshire
153.170   Plant switching

Archer Daniels Midland   Peoria, Illinois
160.635   Plant switching

Armco Steel   Middletown, Ohio

Hamilton, Ohio
153.290		Plant switching and blast furnace operations

Middletown, Ohio
855.6375	810.6375	Plant switching
461.100	466.100	Steel processing and narrow gauge Switching

Asbestos Corporation (Normandie)   Black Lake, Quebec
158.430	Switching
163.260	Switching

Association of American Railroads (AAR)

AAR Railroad Test Center, Pueblo, Colorado
172.700	173.6375	Ch 1 Road dispatcher and security
173.150		Ch 2 Switching
173.050		Ch 3 Testing
172.825		Ch 4 Testing
171.650		Ch 5 Hazardous material training
172.300	170.750	Ch 6 Facilities, fire, and safety
171.2375		Ch 7 Phone patch
173.9125		Ch 8 Fire and safety
166.025		Ch 12 Hazardous Materials Staff (Hazmat Ch 2)

Chicago, Illinois
160.995	Research & Test Dept. – Illinois Inst. of Technology
161.055	Research & Test Dept. – Illinois Inst. of Technology

Nationwide
160.995	Track testing with test car AAR-100
161.055	Track testing with test car AAR-100

935.8875	Advanced Train Control – trunked wayside data link
935.9375	Advanced Train Control – trunked wayside data link
935.9875	Advanced Train Control – trunked wayside data link
936.8875	Advanced Train Control – trunked wayside data link
936.9375	Advanced Train Control – trunked wayside data link
936.9875	Advanced Train Control – trunked wayside data link
	400 base stations are now in use on Union Pacific – packet format, 4800 baud.

Atlas Steel   Welland, Ontario
149.020	Plant switching
154.570	Plant switching
165.720	Plant switching

Babcock & Wilcox   Barberton, Ohio
153.110	Plant switching
153.320	Plant switching
462.300~	FCC-1 base and 12 mobiles

Beaver Creek Logging   Weogufka, Alabama
48.88	Plant switching

Bethlehem Steel

Navy Shipyard, Sparrows Point, MD
153.140	158.430	Plant switching

Burns Harbor, Indiana
153.290	Ch 2 dock and car dumper
154.570	Ch 3 dispatcher/MofE/MofW
161.010	CSS&SB interchange
161.070	Conrail interchange
462.325	Ch 1 dispatcher and yard

Leary Bros Company, Burns Harbor, Indiana
49.59   "OX" scrap yard switching
Levy Company, Burns Harbor, Indiana
44.02   Slag pit switching

Black Mesa & Lake Powell   Page, Arizona

151.625   General operations

Blue Diamond Mining   Knoxville, Tennessee

161.235   PT – Mobiles

Branford Steam Railroad   Branford, Connecticut

47.48   Quarry switching

Buchannan Forest Products   Thunder Bay, Ontario

152.420   Plant switching
152.990   Plant switching
153.230   Plant switching

Bucyrus Erie   South Milwaukee, Wisconsin

462.450   Plant switching

Bunker Hill Company   Smelterville, Idaho

153.260   Plant switching

Byers   Sarnia, Ontario

148.165   Plant switching
452.5125   Plant switching
452.7125   Plant switching
452.8625   Plant switching
452.9375   Plant switching

C & P Ore Dock Terminal   Cleveland, Ohio

160.650   Ore dock switching

Canadian Forest Products

Vancouver Island, British Columbia
160.650   Ch 1 Road and repeater output
160.650   161.295   Ch 2 Dispatcher
165.540   Yard
La Tuque, Quebec
160.770   157.590   Yard

Canadian Occidental Petroleum   North Vancouver, British Columbia

458.3375   Plant switching

CF Chemicals Corp.

Bartow, Florida
153.275~   FCC – 1 base and 36 mobiles
462.375~   FCC – 1 base and 1 mobile
462.500~   467.500~   FCC – 8 CO 80 mobile/1 MR
Plant City, Florida
153.110~   FCC – 1 base and 36 mobiles

Checker Cab Company   Kalamazoo, Michigan

160.395   Plant switching

Cheney Lime & Cement   Graystone, Alabama

154.570   FCC
154.600   FCC

Chicago Railway Equipment   Chicago, Illinois
464.975~   FCC

Ciment St-Laurent   Joliette, Quebec
142.455   Plant switching

Climax Molybdenum Company   Climax, Colorado
Climax, Colorado
152.870~   FCC – 1 base and mobiles
451.825~ 456.825~ FCC – Mobiles/1 base
Crested Butte, Colorado
152.870~   FCC – 1 base and 50 mobiles
Empire, Colorado
152.870~   FCC – 1 base and 50 mobiles
Heeney, Colorado
451.825~ 456.825~ FCC – 18 mobiles/1 MR
Silverthorne, Colorado
151.520~ 150.020~ FCC – 100 mobiles/9 MR

Conners Steel Corp.   Birmingham, Alabama
462.375   General operations

Consolidated Coal Corp.   Lynco, West Virginia
49.52~   FCC
49.58~   FCC

Coors Brewery   Golden, Colorado
462.475 467.475 Plant switching

Copper Range   White Pine, Michigan
152.480~   FCC
152.870~   FCC
158.400~   FCC

Corn Products   Argo, Illinois
153.200   Plant switching

Crop Mate Inc.   Brimfield, Illinois
160.590   Plant switching

Crown Zellerbach Vancouver Island, British Columbia
160.650   General operations

Crucible Specialty Metals   West Syracuse, New York
462.325 467.325 Railroad operations and motor pool

Cyprus Northshore Mining Company Babbitt, Minnesota
451.725   Road and yard
451.950 456.950 Road repeater link
457.9375   End-of-train telemetry
461.100   Yard and dock

Delta Railroad Construction   Ashtabula, Ohio
151.505   Track maintenance

Deseret-Western Railway   Bonanza, Utah
457.000   Power plant switching

Dofasco – Ebenezer

Dofasco (Dominion Foundry & Steel)   Hamilton, Ontario

153.575   Plant switching

Dominion Coal   Vansant, Virginia

461.700   Plant switching

Dominion Terminal Association   Newport News, Virginia

464.4875~469.4875~	FCC
464.5125~469.5125~	FCC
464.5375~469.5375~	FCC
464.5625~469.5625~	FCC
464.5875~469.5875~	FCC
464.6125~469.6125~	FCC
464.6375~469.6375~	FCC
464.6625~469.6625~	FCC
464.6875~469.6875~	FCC
464.7125~469.7125~	FCC
464.7375~469.7375~	FCC
72.48~	FCC – Remote control locomotives~
72.56~	FCC – Remote control locomotives~
75.44~	FCC – Remote control locomotives~
75.60~	FCC – Remote control locomotives~

Domtar Ltd.

Cochrane, Alberta
165.000~   1 base and 3 mobiles
Edmonton, Alberta
464.350~   1 base and 5 mobiles
New Westminster, British Columbia
153.680~   1 base and 6 mobiles

Prince George, British Columbia
173.880~   2 mobiles
Tie Treating Plant, Delson, Quebec
151.055~   1 base and 12 mobiles
Wood Plant, Truro, Quebec
157.620~   1 base and 4 mobiles

Dow Chemical (Texas)

160.905   MR

Duke Power & Light Co.

River Bend Plant, Mt. Holly, North Carolina
47.98~   FCC
48.08~   FCC
48.12~   FCC
Marshall Steam Plant, Terrel, North Carolina
47.98~   FCC
48.12~   FCC

DuPont   Sarnia, Ontario

151.580   Plant switching
152.045   Plant switching
152.105   Plant switching
152.405   Plant switching
159.120   Plant switching

Eastman Kodak   Rochester, New York

160.305   Plant switching

Ebenezer Railcar Service   East Aurora, New York

461.8625~   FCC – low power

461.9875~   FCC – Low Power

Econo Rail Corp
466.6125   FCC – Mobiles, Victoria City, Texas
466.7875   FCC – Mobiles, Victoria City, Texas
853.4875   FCC – Mobiles, Texas, statewide

E. B. Eddy   Hull, Quebec
46.16   Plant switching

Electro-Motive Division   La Grange, Illinois
153.080~   FCC – 1 base and 20 mobiles
158.460~   FCC – 1 base Pager
462.225~   467.225~   FCC – 50 mobiles/1 MR

Elk Run Coal Company   Sylvester, West Virginia
47.52~   FCC – 1 base and 10 mobiles

Federal Railroad Administration
– See U. S. Department of Transportation

Gardinier Phosphoric   South Tampa, Florida
462.200   467.200   Ch 1 Plant foreman
462.350   467.350   Ch 2 Plant switching

General Chemical   Amherstburg, Ontario
159.435   Plant switching
149.290   Plant switching

General Electric
Somersworth, New Hampshire

153.380   Plant switching
Schenectady, New York
153.200   Plant switching
Toledo, Ohio – Railcar Services
151.655   Plant switching

General Motors, Diesel Division   London, Ontario
164.840   Plant switching
168.030   Plant switching
468.9625   D.O.C. licensed

Georgia Marble Company   Tate, Georgia
43.14   Plant switching

P. H. Glatfelter Pulp & Paper   Spring Grove, Pennsylvania
451.475~   456.475~   FCC
451.650~   456.650~   FCC

W. R. Grace Phosphate Company   Bradley, Florida
151.490~   FCC – 1 base and 55 mobiles
151.595~   FCC – 3 Bases and 64 mobiles
457.725~   FCC – 10 mobiles

Granite City Steel   Granite City, Illinois
153.230   Plant switching

Granite Mountain Quarry   Little Rock, Arkansas
457.525~   FCC
461.025~   FCC
467.775~   FCC

Great – International

Great Lake Coal & Dock St. Paul, Minnesota
151.775	Switching

Great Lakes Steel (Division of National Steel)
Detroit, Michigan
153.050	Joint operations with Delray Connecting
153.080	Joint operations with Delray Connecting
153.320~	FCC – 20 mobiles

Great Miami Inc. Hamilton, Ohio
151.625	Plant switching – Champion Paper Mill

Hines Lumber Company Burns, Oregon
153.170~		FCC – 1 base and 100 mobiles
452.100~	457.100~	FCC – 100 mobiles/1 MR

Hulcher Emergency Railroad Service Virden, Illinois
43.00	Mobile railroad wrecker service – nationwide

IMC Phosphate
Mulberry and Bartow, Florida
152.960~		FCC – 4 bases and 170 mobiles
153.110~		FCC – 2 bases and 30 mobiles
153.245~		FCC – 1 base and 25 mobiles
462.200~	467.200~	FCC – 2 CO and 150 mobiles/1 MR
462.250~	467.250~	FCC – 20 mobiles/1 MR
462.325~	467.325~	FCC – 2 CO and 150 mobiles/1 MR
462.425~	467.425~	FCC – 2 CO and 150 mobiles/1 MR

Nichols, Florida
452.900~	457.900~	Fixed base

South Tampa, Florida
153.200~	Plant switching

Indusmin Ltd. Acton Limestone Quarry, Acton, Ontario
166.620	Plant switching

International Nickel of Canada Copper Cliff, Ontario
463.2875	Ch 1 Dispatcher
463.4625	Ch 2 Dispatcher
463.5125	Ch 3 Dispatcher
463.5625	Ch 4 Switching
463.6125	Ch 5 Switching
463.6625	Ch 6 Switching
463.8125	Ch 7 Switching
463.8625	Ch 8 Switching
463.9375	Ch 9 Switching
463.9875	Ch 10 Switching
464.0375	Ch 11 Switching
464.1375	Ch 12 Switching
464.1875	Ch 13 Switching
464.2875	Ch 14 Switching
464.3375	Ch 15 Switching
464.4625	Ch 16 Switching
464.5125	Ch 17 Switching
464.5625	Ch 18 Switching
464.6125	Ch 19 Switching
464.6625	Ch 20 Switching
464.7125	Ch 21 Switching
464.7625	Ch 22 Switching
464.8625	Ch 23 Switching
464.9125	Ch 24 Switching

ITT Rayonier   Aberdeen, Washington
48.68   General operations

James River Marathon   Marathon, Ontario
160.650   Plant switching

Kennecott Copper   Salt Lake City, Utah
451.950   456.950   General operations
452.175   457.175   General operations
Bingham Canyon
451.850   456.850   General operations

Keystone Steel & Wire   Peoria, Illinois
153.380   Plant switching

Texas Gulf Ltd. – Kidd Creek Mine   Timmins, Ontario
158.400   Road and dispatcher
158.550   Yard

La Clede Steel Company   Alton, Illinois
158.280~   FCC – Base and mobiles
462.275~ 467.275~ FCC – Base and mobiles

Lake Ontario Steel Company Ltd.   Whitney, Ontario
151.115   Plant switching

Lehigh Portland Cement   Union Bridge, Maryland
451.725~   FCC – 5 mobiles
462.225~   FCC – 1 base and 15 mobiles

Lone Star Steel Company   Lone Star, Texas
153.200~   FCC – Base and mobiles
153.230~   FCC – Base and mobiles
154.490~   FCC – Base and mobiles

Loram Rail Service   Hamel, Minnesota
151.625   Rail grinding train (nationwide)

LTV Steel
Babbitt, Minnesota
152.990   Road and yard
467.850   End-of-train telemetry
Hoyt Lakes, Minnesota
152.900   Pit locomotives

Macmillan Bloedel Ltd   Harmac, British Columbia
Pulp Mill, Harmac, British Columbia
150.815   Plant switching
160.635   General operations
Pulp Mill, Port Alberni, British Columbia
161.055   Plant switching

Marine Industries   Sorel, Quebec
153.020   Plant switching

Metropolitan Sanitation District of Chicago Chicago, Illinois
453.925   458.925   Railroad operations

Metropolitan Stevedore Company Long Beach, California
151.715   Plant switching

Minnesota – Pennsylvania

Minnesota Mining & Manufacturing   Little Rock, Arkansas
152.930   Quarry switching

Morrison-Knudsen   Boise, Idaho
152.870~   FCC – 1 base and 600 mobiles
451.800~ 456.800~   FCC – 100 mobiles/1 MR

NASA – Kennedy Space Center   Cape Kennedy, Florida
170.175   Railroad operations

National Coal Company   Dayton, Tennessee
463.550~   FCC

Neptune Terminals   Vancouver, British Columbia
460.0875 465.0875   CN Ch 512 operations
464.750   Switching
464.100   Coal handling
464.425   Terminal operations

Northern Rail Service   Midland, Michigan
461.475~ 466.475~   FCC

Northwestern Steel & Wire   Sterling, Illinois
158.310   Plant switching

Northwood Pulp & Timber Co.   Fraserview, British Columbia
165.330   Switching

Novacor   Sarnia, Ontario
464.0625   Plant switching

464.2125   Plant switching
464.6125   Plant switching
464.7375   Plant switching
464.8625   Plant switching
469.1500   Plant switching

Ontario Locomotive   Western New York
464.550~   FCC

Ortner Car Company   Mount Orab, Ohio
154.515   Plant operations
154.570   Plant operations

Pacific Elevators   British Columbia
165.450   Remote control locomotives
458.9875   Switching

Peavey   Shakopee, Minnesota
469.5625   Plant switching

Pennsylvania Truck Lines (Conrail)
Junction Yard, Detroit, Michigan
160.155   Intermodal trucks
160.905   Van site
St Louis, Missouri
160.485~   G – Base and mobile
161.070~   G – Mobiles only
New England
160.410~   G – Base and mobile
160.980~   G – Mobiles only

Bergen, New Jersey
160.740~   G – 1 base and mobile
160.860~   G – Mobiles only
South Kearny, New Jersey
160.740~   G – Base and mobile
160.860~   G – Mobiles only
Buckeye Yard, Columbus, Ohio
160.740   Van site
160.980~   G – Mobiles only
Toledo, Ohio
160.740~   G – Base and mobile
160.860~   G – Mobiles only
Morrisville, Pennsylvania
160.470~   G – Base and mobile
160.980~   G – Mobiles only

Phelps Dodge Copper   Morenci, Arizona
151.505   Road, Morenci to Clifton
153.380   Mine Switching at Morenci

Pioneer Grain   North Vancouver, British Columbia
809.9875 854.9875 Primary switching
810.2375 855.2375 Primary switching
810.4875 855.4875 Primary switching
811.7375 856.7375 Primary switching
811.2375 856.2375 Primary switching
811.9875 856.9875 Primary switching
812.2375 857.2375 Primary switching
813.2375 858.2375 Switching
813.4875 858.4875 Switching
813.7375 858.7375 Switching

813.9875 858.9875 Switching
814.2375 859.2375 Switching

Ports Canada   Montreal, Quebec
159.63   Dispatcher
159.99   Yard
167.610   D.O.C. Licensed – 1 base and 29 mobiles

Port Stanley Terminal Rail   Port Stanley, Ontario
160.575   General operations

PPG Industries
Barberton, Ohio
153.260~   FCC – 1 base, 40 mobile, 10 pagers
154.600   Ch 2 Switching and MofW
158.295~   FCC – 1 base, 10 mobile, 80 pagers
Crystal City, Missouri
154.570   Ch 1 Switching

Proctor & Gamble
Cincinnati, Ohio
457.5625   Plant switching
Shaver, Alberta (Cellulose)
464.075   Plant switching

Produits Forestieres Daishowa   Quebec City, Quebec
47.26   Plant switching

Quebec & Ontario Paper
Thorold, Ontario
167.940   Yard

Rail – Shell

171.855	Yard	
451.0625	Yard	
451.7875	Yard	
Baie Comeau, Quebec		
160.605	Yard	
160.995	Yard	

Rail Services Inc Calvert City, Kentucky
151.745~ FCC

Rail-to-Water Transfer Chicago, Illinois
464.875~ FCC Switching~

Railroad Car Service Indianapolis, Indiana
463.325~ 468.325 FCC
483.325~ FCC

Rescar
Pennsylvania – Statewide
464.1125~ FCC
464.1375~ FCC
Texas – Statewide
462.150~ FCC
Longview, Texas
151.775~ FCC
152.360~ FCC
Orange, Texas
461.925~ FCC
Saginaw, Texas
160.995 Grain switching

Reynolds Metals Co.
Bauxite and Alexander, Arkansas
153.140~ FCC – 1 base and mobiles
43.18~ FCC – 1 base and mobiles
462.225~ FCC – 1 base and mobiles
467.300~ FCC – 1 base and mobiles
Gregory, Texas
462.200~ 467.200~ FCC
462.250~ FCC
462.800~ FCC
48.84~ FCC

Ringling Bros., Barnum & Bailey Circus
151.625 Loading/unloading train (nationwide)

Roberts Bank Coal Port Roberts Bank, British Columbia
164.850 Operations
140.160 142.815 CP Rail remote locomotive control
140.700 142.815 CP Rail remote locomotive control
164.940~ License 2 mobiles only
165.255~ License 2 mobiles only

Rock of Ages Websterville, Vermont
153.080~ FCC – 1 base and mobiles

Shaw Pipe Welland, Ontario
159.765 Plant switching

Shell Oil Company of Canada Ltd Pecten, Alberta
161.580 Plant switching

Simpson Timber   Shelton, Washington
   160.440   PBX
   161.085~   PT – FCC
   161.340   Road – repeater output
   49.20   General operations

South East Coal   Irvine, Kentucky
   160.515~   FCC – 1 base and 10 mobiles
   451.775~   FCC – 1 base and 10 mobiles

South Milford Grain   South Milford, Indiana
   461.825   Grain elevator and locomotive

Southern California Edison   Los Angeles, California
   161.445~   RW

Southwest Portland Cement   Fairborn, Ohio
   152.870   Inter-plant switching

Spruce Falls Power & Paper Co.   Kapuskasing, Ontario
   156.990   General operations

Steam Locomotive Corp. of America Hagerstown, Maryland
   160.500~   EE

Stelco (Steel Company of Canada)   Hamilton, Ontario
   461.100   Yardmaster

Stelpipe   Welland, Ontario
   151.055~   1 base and 4 mobiles

   152.990~   1 base and 13 mobiles
Page Hersey Works
   469.1000~   2 mobiles

Stockham Valve & Fitting   Birmingham, Alabama
   153.050   Plant switching

Sullivan Lumber   Preston, Georgia
   49.34~   FCC

Swift Agri-Chemicals   Agricola, Florida
   463.250~ 468.250   FCC – 2 Base and 80 mobiles

Swindell-Dressler Energy Supply Co.   Amarillo, Texas
   460.550   466.550   Plant switching

Tenneco Oil   Lavaca and Victoria, Texas
   452.900   457.900   Plant switching

Tennessee Valley Authority
   Huntsville, Alabama
   166.275   Switching – Widows Creek Steam Plant
   Sheffield, Alabama
   166.275   Switching – Wilson Dam
   Grahamville, Kentucky
   166.275~   Switching – Shawnee Steam Plant
   Cumberland, Tennessee
   166.275~   Switching – Cumberland Steam Plant
   Gallatin, Tennessee
   166.275~   Switching – Gallatin Steam Plant

Harriman, Tennessee
166.275   Switching – Kingston Steam Plant
Johnston, Tennessee
166.275   Switching – John Sevier Steam Plant

Texas Utilities

Monticello to Mt. Vernon, Texas
451.875   456.875   Inter-plant switching
Fairfield and Thermo, Texas
451.975~ 456.975   FCC

Chemin de fer Thurso   Thurso, Quebec

160.275   Plant switching

Transco Company   Bucyrus, Ohio

151.625   Plant operations

Trinity Industries   Fort Worth, Texas

469.6375   Trackmobile, Plant 26, NE 28th St.
469.7375   Switcher, Plant 25, 287 Peden Rd.
469.9375   Switcher Plant 109, East Bailey-Boswell Rd.

U. S. Air Force

Rome, New York: Griffiss AFB
162.015   Railroad operations
Oscoda, Michigan: Wurtsmith AFB
163.500   Railroad operations

U. S. Army

Anchorage, Alaska: Fort Richardson,
164.625   Railroad operations

Anniston, Alabama: Anniston Army Depot,
173.025   Railroad operations
173.4625~   Railroad operations
Anniston, Alabama: Fort McClellan
165.5375
Aviation Material Readiness Command
165.1625   General operations
Bayonne, New Jersey: Military Ocean Terminal
165.0375
Chattanooga, Tennessee: Voluntary Army Ammunition Plant
173.4625
Colorado Springs, Colorado: Fort Carson,
139.000   Railroad operations
Forest Park, Georgia: Fort Gillem
165.0375
Harrisburg, Pennsylvania: New Cumberland Army Depot
148.675   Railroad operations and motor pool
Hinesville, Georgia: Fort Stewart
165.1125   Railroad operations
Huntsville, Alabama: Redstone Arsenal
163.5375
Killeen, Texas: Fort Hood
165.1875   Railroad operations and motor pool
McAlester, Oklahoma: McAlester Army Ammunition Plant
143.520   Railroad operations
Radford, Virginia: Radford Army Ammunition Plant
163.5875
Rock Island, Illinois: Rock Island Arsenal
165.1875   Motor pool and maybe railroad
Romulus, New York: Seneca Army Depot
163.5625   Railroad operations and motor pool

Watervliet, New York: Watervliet Arsenal
173.4625   Railroad operations and motor pool

U. S. Department of the Interior
167.125   Helium Fields general operations
Amarillo, Texas: Helium Fields operations
415.150   General operations

U. S. Department of Transportation,
Federal Railroad Administration   Washington, DC
163.100   General Office Building

U. S. Navy
Bremerton, Washington: Puget Sound Naval Ship Yard
148.325   Railroad operations
Earle, New Jersey: Earle Naval Weapons Station
140.025   Railroad operations
Yorktown, Virginia: Naval Ship Yard
138.840   Railroad operations

U. S. Department of Energy
Portland, Oregon
172.500   168.300   Emergencies
Portland, Oregon: Bonneville Power Administration
172.525   168.325   Operations
Barnwell, South Carolina: Savannah River Plant
164.275   Railroad operations

U. S. Gypsum   Plaster City, California
151.595   General operations

U. S. Pipe & Foundry   Birmingham, Alabama
153.260   Plant switching
153.305   General operations

U. S. Steel   Minntac Mine, Mountain Iron, Minnesota
152.990~   FCC – Base and mobiles
151.925   West Pit Locomotives
152.960   West Pit Locomotives
154.490   East Pit Locomotives
451.825~   456.825~   FCC – Base and mobiles
452.025~   457.025~   FCC – Base and mobiles

U. S. Sugar Corp   Bryant, Florida
451.775   456.775   Plant switching
451.925   456.925   Ch 1 Road
451.925   Ch 2 Road – Talk-around

Union Carbide   Welland, Ontario
464.950   Plant switching

Union Tank Car Company   Marion, Ohio
154.655   Plant operations

United Aggregates   Acton, Ontario
166.620   Plant switching

Utah International   Fruitland, New Mexico
451.725~   456.725~   FCC – 75 mobiles/1 MR
451.850~   FCC – 75 mobiles
452.125~   457.125~   FCC – 100 mobiles/1 MR

VMV – Yankeetown

456.850~   FCC – 75 mobiles

VMV Enterprises   Paducah, Kentucky
160.215   Shop operations and switching

Vulcan Materials Rail Operations   Grand Rivers, Kentucky
151.535   Switching

Weyerhaeuser Corp.
Longview, Washington
160.245   160.995   Road – Curtis, Milburn & Eastern and
                    Chehalis Western
Curtis, Washington
160.425   161.385   Road – Columbia & Cowlitz

Wheeling Pittsburgh Steel
Steubenville, Ohio
153.110   Plant switching
Monessen, Pennsylvania
153.185~   158.415   FCC – Repeater

Winters Railway Service   North Collins, New York
35.96   Mobile railroad wrecker service

Yankeetown Dock   Yankeetown, Indiana
152.870   General operations
461.325~   466.325~   FCC – Base and mobiles
463.3125~   FCC – Mobiles
463.3375~   FCC – Mobiles
463.800~   468.800~   FCC – Base and mobiles
463.875~   468.875~   FCC – Base and mobiles

TRANSIT SYSTEMS AND COMMUTER AUTHORITIES

Baltimore Mass Transit Administration   Baltimore, Maryland

160.395	Ch 1 Subway road
161.475	Ch 2 Subway yard
161.085	Ch 3 Subway Police
161.565	Ch 4 Subway MofW
160.905	Ch 5 Light Rail yards, Canton and Timonium
161.010	Ch 6 Light Rail road
39.10	State Police
47.32	SHA
44.46	Mobility

Bay Area Rapid Transit   San Francisco, California

160.410	161.505	Ch 1 Road – duplex
160.860		Ch 2 Road
160.455		Yard
160.845		Administration
43.78		Power Dispatcher and MofW
453.150	458.150	Ch 1 Police
453.425	458.425	Ch 2 Police – Special operations
453.975	458.975	Yard and Shop
154.295	153.770	Emergency fire channel

Calgary Transportation Department   Calgary, Alberta

460.1250	465.1375	1 MR and 986 mobiles
460.1750	465.1875	1 MR and 986 mobiles
460.2500	465.2625	1 MR and 986 mobiles
460.3000	465.3125	1 MR and 136 mobiles
460.3500	465.3625	1 MR and 986 mobiles
460.575	465.5875	1 MR and 136 mobiles
460.6250	465.6375	1 MR and 136 mobiles
460.6750	465.6875	1 MR and 136 mobiles

CalTrain   San Francisco, California

160.485	Ch. 1 Road
160.815	Ch. 2 General purpose
160.320	Ch. 3 SP Road

Chicago Commuter Rail Service Board (Metra)   Chicago, Illinois

161.025		Road – Former Illinois Central Electric
161.340		Road – Former Rock Island
160.605		Police
160.635		Signal Dept and Police mobiles
160.680	161.220	PBX
161.280		MofW
161.610		Police and yard

Chicago Transit Authority   Chicago, Illinois

470.5375	473.5375	F1 Supervisor: Southside
470.9875	473.9875	F2 Road control and emergency calling
472.9375	475.9375	F3 CPD MDT transit units (Buses)
470.6375	473.6375	F4 Supervisor: Northside
471.0375	474.0375	F5 Congress/Douglas O'Hare (Blue)

Cleveland – McKinney

471.0625	474.0625	F6 Englewood/Jackson Park (Green), Lake, Midway (Orange)
471.0875	474.0875	F7 Ravenswood (Brown), Evanston (Purple), Skokie (Yellow)
471.1125	474.1125	F8 Howard-Dan Ryan (Red)
472.2375	475.2375	National K9 Contracted Security Police
460.350	465.350	City Police Ch 5

Cleveland Regional Transit Authority   Cleveland, Ohio

453.050	458.050	Police and MofW
453.850	458.850	Road

Duke University Medical Center   Durham, North Carolina

452.900	457.900	People Mover operations

Edmonton Transit Authority   Edmonton, Alberta

413.3875	418.3875	Road and dispatcher
413.4375	418.4375	MofW and buses

GO Transit   Toronto, Ontario

161.295		Road
413.9375	418.9375	Mimico Yard and Shop
419.4375		Willowbrook Shops

Los Angeles Metro Rail   Los Angeles, California

160.635	160.425	Ch 1 MofW/ET/C&S
160.755	160.695	Ch 2
160.425		Ch 3 MofE
160.695	161.265	Ch 4
161.505		Ch 5 Yard
160.725		Ch 6

160.935~		G – FCC
161.145~		G – FCC
471.3375	474.3375	Road – Blue Line
472.4875	475.4875	Yard control

Massachusetts Bay Transportation Authority
Boston, Massachusetts

30.90		MofW
31.14		MofE – inspection and repair
44.43		Power Director
44.46		Engineering
453.900	458.900	Administration
470.4125	473.4125	Red Line
470.6125	473.6125	Orange Line
470.6375	473.6375	Green Line
470.6625	473.6625	Police
470.6875	473.6875	Blue Line
472.5875	475.5875	Trackless trolleys and buses

Routes from North Station

160.320		Road and dispatcher
161.460~		G – FCC

Systemwide

160.590		Road and Dispatcher to train
161.490		Train to dispatcher
160.875		Yard
160.695	161.565	MofW/C&S – Primary
160.695		MofW/C&S – Talk-around

McKinney Avenue Transit Company   Dallas, Texas

452.825	457.825	General operations

Metra   See Chicago Commuter Rail Service Board

Metrolink   Los Angeles, California

161.415•	Ch 1 Road, Pomona – Mission Tower
160.815•	Ch 2 Yard and Mechanical, Taylor Yard
160.545•	Ch 3 Unassigned
160.995•	Ch 4 Maintenance of Way
160.320•	Ch 5 SP Road, Burbank Jct. to Santa Clarita
161.550•	Ch 6 SP Road, Mission Tower to Moorpark
160.515•	Ch 7 UP Road, Los Angeles to Riverside
160.560•	Ch 8 AT&SF Road, Mission Tower to San Bernardino
160.650•	Ch 9 AT&SF Road, Mission Tower to San Diego
161.190•	Ch 10 AT&SF Road, Lambert to San Bernardino
160.455•	Ch 11 Amtrak yard

Metropolitan Atlanta Rapid Transit Authority
Atlanta, Georgia

453.725	458.725	F1 Road – City-wide
453.700	458.700	F2 A-Division – East
453.775	458.775	F3 B-Division – North/West
453.875	458.875	F4 C-Division – Control/West
453.950	458.950	F5 Road – City-wide
453.925	458.925	F6 Administration
452.875	457.875	MofE
452.475	457.475	Police
452.375	457.375	Former road
452.775	457.775	Former road

Metro-North Railroad   New York, New York

160.950	Ch 1 Road and dispatcher – Hudson Division
161.280	Ch 2 Road and dispatcher – Harlem Division
160.545	Ch 3 Road and dispatcher – New Haven Division
160.410	Ch 4 MofW – Harlem and Hudson Divisions
161.160	Ch 5 MofW – New Haven Division
160.770	Ch 6 Shop
160.860	Stores Dept – Harmon Shop
161.070	Yard
161.220	Police

Grand Central Terminal

160.335	Tunnel emergency channel
160.770	Stationmaster

Metropolitan Transit Authority   New York, New York

Subways

156.105		C&S
160.305		Ch 5 Police – common
160.695		Ch 6 Police – patrol cars
160.845		Yard
470.3875	473.3875	ET, MofE, Administration
470.4875	473.4875	MofW

IRT subway lines (Division A)

158.880	Train to dispatcher
161.190	Road and dispatcher to train

BMT subway lines (Division B1)

158.775	Train to dispatcher
161.505	Road and dispatcher to train

IND subway lines (Division B2)

Miami – New Jersey

158.805		Train to dispatcher
161.565		Road and dispatcher to train
160.395		Coney Island Yard
160.875		Coney Island Yard
161.025		Coney Island Yard

Brooklyn

151.310		Ch 1 Police – Car to base
160.305		Ch 1 Police – Base to car

Bronx

151.190		Ch 2 Police – Car to base
160.500		Ch 2 Police – Base to car

Queens

151.145		Ch 3 Police – Car to base
160.965		Ch 3 Police – Base to car

Manhattan

151.340		Ch 4 Police – Car to base
160.905		Ch 4 Police – Base to car

Staten Island Rapid Transit

160.485		Yard and MofW
470.4375	473.4375	Road, Dispatcher and Police

Buses

161.175		Buses – Flushing and Fresh Pond
161.250	160.260	Bus telemetry
161.355		Bus telemetry
161.520	160.530	Buses – Staten Island
452.9125	457.9125	Buses – Staten Island

Miami Metro Rail   Miami, Florida

452.825	457.825	Road

452.375	457.375	Yard, ET, Train Intercom
452.425	457.425	Ch 3 Yard
452.325	457.325	B&B and MofE
452.475	457.475	Portable telephone
452.700	457.700	Metromover – operations
452.875	457.875	Metromover – telemetry

Montreal Urban Community Transportation Commission
Montreal, Quebec

141.465	Surface train operations and mobiles
142.545	Surface train operations and mobiles
165.330	Subway operations
169.440	Subway operations
169.905	Subway operations
169.440	Utility
169.905	Utility

New Jersey Transit   Newark, New Jersey

Hoboken

161.235	Road – Raritan Valley Route – NJ Transit
161.070	Road – Raritan Valley Route – Conrail
161.235	Road – North Jersey Coast – NJ Transit
160.860	Road – North Jersey Coast – Conrail
161.235	Road – Princeton Line
161.400	Road – Hoboken Division
161.400	Road – Atlantic City Route
161.355	Road – FCC
160.890	Mechanical
160.770	Electric/EMU Mechanical
160.410	Electric Power Control
160.440	Signal Dept. Trouble Desk

160.680		Ch 3 Police – Conrail
161.145		Ch 3 Police – Conrail
160.830		Police
160.830	160.215	Police – vehicular repeater
161.520		Buses
161.475~		

Newark
161.460		Newark City Subway – Road and dispatcher
161.370		Newark City Subway

Niagara Frontier Transportation Authority Buffalo, New York

453.275	458.275	Road and dispatcher
453.475	458.475	Yard and Shop
453.775	458.775	MofW
453.800	458.800	Police

Port Authority of Allegheny County Pittsburgh, Pennsylvania

160.515		Police
453.700	458.700	Trolleys
453.750	458.750	Trolleys
470.4125	473.4125	Ch 1 Transit Police and county sheriff
470.4375	473.4375	Ch 2 Transit Police and county sheriff
470.6125	473.6125	Ch 1 Digital data
470.6375		Dispatcher Link
470.6625	473.6625	Ch 2 Road
470.6875	473.6875	Ch 3 Police MW and utility
470.7375	473.7375	Ch 4 Yard

Port Authority Trans-Hudson Corp. New York, New York

New York, New York
160.470		Ch 1 Road and dispatcher

161.040		Ch 2 Police
161.460		Ch 3 MW/emergency channel

Newark, New Jersey
160.425		Shop
161.535		Ch 4 Car Shop
452.875	457.875	Yard

Port Authority Transit Camden, New Jersey

Philadelphia, Pennsylvania
500.8125	503.8125	Ch 1 Police
500.8375	503.8375	Ch 2 Power Director and MofW
500.8875	503.8875	Ch 3 Administration
500.9125	503.9125	Ch 4 Road

Lindenwold, New Jersey
453.675		People-mover operations

Sacramento Regional Transit Sacramento, California

453.525	458.525	General operations

San Diego Trolley San Diego, California

160.380		Ch 1 Operations
160.665	160.935	Ch 2 Operations
160.530		Ch 3 Unknown
160.710		Ch 4 MofW
160.905		Ch 4 MofW
161.415		Ch 4 MofW
161.565		Ch 4 MofW

San Francisco Municipal Railway San Francisco, California

484.6625	487.6625	Cable Car and Light Rail Vehicle operation

Santa Clara County Transit   San Jose, California
488.6375   Trolleys

Southeastern Pennsylvania Transportation Authority
                                    Philadelphia, Pennsylvania
Railroad Division
160.800   Ch 1 Conrail lines
160.350   Ch 2 Road – Main Line, Zoo to Tunnel, Airport,
                   Chestnut Hill West, Ivy Ridge, West Chester
160.395   Ch 3 Yards at Paoli, Frazer, Powelton Avenue,
                   Roberts Avenue, and Wayne Electric
161.460   Ch 4 Road – Tunnel to Lansale, Chestnut Hill
                   East, Norristown, Doylestown, Warminster,
                   and Neshaminy
160.290   Ch 5 ET Power/Signal Dept./MofW
161.070   Ch 6 Conrail road
160.920   Ch 7 Amtrak road
161.325   Car Dept – Suburban Station
Red Arrow Division
30.08   Philadelphia & Western
30.98   Ch 1 Red Arrow Division
31.14   Ch 2 Maintenance trucks and Shop
31.10   Ch 3 Maintenance trucks and Shop
30.89   Ch 4 Red Arrow Division
Blue Line Subway (Market-Frankford)
453.350   458.350   Transit Division City Police – Western Precinct
453.950   458.950   Transit Division City Police – Northwestern
                    Precinct
453.300   458.300   Transit Division City Police – Eastern Precinct
502.7125 505.7125 Ch 11 Subways

Orange Line Subway (Broad Street)
155.070   Transit Division City Police
System-Wide
502.6375 505.6375 Ch 8 Telemetry
502.6625 505.6625 Ch 9 Supervision – South End
502.6875 505.6875 Ch 10 Police
502.7375 505.7375 Ch 12 Emergencies
502.7625 505.7625 Ch 13 Police and MofW
502.7875 505.7875 Ch 14 Supervision – North End
504.1375   Ch 15 Car-to-car
160.275   Police
160.275   M.U. Car Inspectors
161.235   PBX
Subway-Surface trolleys use induction train phones

Tandy Center Subway   Fort Worth, Texas
461.200   Security
464.425   Operations

Toronto Transit Commission   Toronto, Ontario
412.0375   Ch 1 Operations Control
412.0625   Ch 2 Secondary operations
412.1125   Ch 3 Secondary operations
412.6125   Ch 4 Secondary operations
412.5875   Ch 5 Road – Scarborough line
151.925   MofW – trolley lines
410.5875   Telemetry
410.6125   Telemetry
410.7625   Telemetry
412.1375   Telemetry

Tri-County Metro Transit District   Portland, Oregon

452.325	457.325	Road
452.875	457.875	Yard

Tri-County Commuter Rail Authority (Tri-Rail)
Fort Lauderdale, Florida

161.100	Road
160.320	Dispatcher

(CSX frequencies – Tri-Rail has applied for its own.)

Vancouver Sky Train   Vancouver, British Columbia

157.650		Transit Police
410.0625	415.0625	Ch 2 Road – in subway
410.2875	415.2875	Ch 1 Road – above ground
410.4875	415.4875	Ch 3 Yard and Shop – Burnaby Maintenance Center
410.7875	415.7875	Telemetry
411.0625	416.0625	Dispatcher-Passenger intercom
460.3375	465.3375	Station maintenance

Virginia Railway Express   Springfield, Virginia

160.950	Norfolk Southern road
160.830	Norfolk Southern train to dispatcher
160.245	Norfolk Southern dispatcher to train
161.550	CSX road and dispatcher to train
161.490	CSX train to dispatcher
161.355	CSX police and supervisory

Washington Metropolitan Area Transit Authority
Washington, DC

160.260		Ops 1 Road and dispatcher – Red Line, Union Station to Silver Spring, Maryland
160.380		Ops 2 Road and dispatcher – Orange Line, New Carrolton, Maryland, to Ballston, Virginia
160.620		Ops 3 Road and dispatcher – Blue Line, Seat Pleasant, Maryland, to National Airport
161.025		MofW and ET
161.235		Yard 1
161.385		Ch 1 Police
161.385	160.725	Ch 2 Police

Brentwood, Maryland

161.235	Yard 1 – Car Dept.

New Carrolton, Maryland

160.605	Yard 2 – Car Dept. and train testing

Wheaton, Maryland

161.415	Start-up control network

Alexandria, Virginia

161.235	Yard 1

Falls Church, Virginia

161.235	Yard 1
161.415	Start-up control network

MUSEUMS AND TOURIST RAILROADS

Adirondack Scenic Railroad   Thendara, New York
160.440   Tourist operations

American Association of Railroaders
151.625   FCC
151.925   FCC

Association of American Railcar Operators   Nationwide
151.625   Track car operations

B&O Railroad Museum   Baltimore, Maryland
464.575   FCC
464.875   FCC
467.025   FCC

Bay Area Electric Railroad Association
San Francisco, California
161.355~   RW-Mobiles

Berkshire Scenic Railway   Lenox, Massachusetts
161.400   Tourist operations

Billy Jones Wildcat Railroad   Los Gatos, California
151.775   Amusement park train

Bluegrass Railroad Museum   Lexington, Kentucky
160.275   Switching
462.1625   Tourist operations

Boone & Scenic Valley Railroad   Boone, Iowa
463.800   Tourist operations

Boothbay Railway Village   Boothbay, Maine
151.715   Museum operations

Brackenridge Park Railroad   San Antonio, Texas
464.325   Amusement park train

Branson Scenic Railway   Branson, Missouri
160.635   Road
151.625   On-board services

British Columbia Forest Museum
Cowichan Valley, British Columbia
162.765   Tourist operations

Busch Gardens/The Dark Continent   Tampa, Florida
153.050   Monorail and steam trains
153.260   Monorail and steam trains
154.515   Monorail and steam trains
154.570   Monorail and steam trains
463.425   FCC
463.575   FCC
463.775   FCC

California State Railroad Museum   Sacramento, California
160.440   Ch. 1 Excursion trains
160.335   Ch. 2 Administration

Canadian Railway Museum Delson, Quebec
167.280   Museum operations

Cape Cod Railroad Buzzards Bay, Massachusetts
160.725   Dinner train

Carthage, Knightstown & Shirley Shirley, Indiana
160.695   Tourist operations

Cass Scenic Railroad Cass, West Virginia
31.98   General operations
Division of West Virginia Department of Natural Resources

Catskill Mountain Railroad Shokan, New York
160.365   Tourist operations
160.530   FCC – BM

Central Ohio Railfans Association Ohio
151.925   FCC
151.955   FCC

Connecticut Electric Railway Association
East Windsor, Connecticut
161.145   Museum operations

Conway Scenic Railroad North Conway, New Hampshire
161.250   General operations

Coopersville & Marne Coopersville, Michigan
160.695   Tourist operations

Cripple Creek & Victor Narrow Gauge Railroad
Cripple Creek, Colorado
452.325 457.325 Tourist operations

Cuyahoga Valley Line Peninsula, Ohio
160.230   Ch 1 Road – CSX
160.965   Old Ch 2 Yard
160.575   Ch 2 Yard

Cumbres & Toltec Scenic Railroad Chama, New Mexico
161.505 160.305 Road Repeater

Delaware & Ulster Rail Ride Arkville, New York
161.385   Tourist operations

Detroit Metro Zoo Detroit, Michigan
151.205 159.405 Amusement park train
151.205 159.300 Amusement park train

Disneyland Anaheim, California
464.4875   Monorail and steam trains
464.7625   Steam trains

Dodge City, Ford & Bucklin Railroad Dodge City, Kansas
154.570   General operations

Durango & Silverton Narrow Gauge Railroad
Durango, Colorado
160.860   Road
161.295   Police/Ticket Sales

East – Housatonic

East Broad Top Railroad   Orbisonia, Pennsylvania
154.570~   FCC
461.950   Tourist operations

Fort Smith Trolley Museum   Fort Smith, Arkansas
151.745   Trolley operations

Fox River Trolley Museum   South Elgin, Illinois
160.905   Trolley museum operations
Inductive train phones also in use

Fremont & Elkhorn Valley Railroad   Fremont, Nebraska
160.245   Tourist operations
161.265   Tourist operations

Fort Wayne Railroad Historical Society New Haven, Indiana
151.625   Excursion service
151.925   FCC

Georgetown Loop Railroad   Silver Plume, Colorado
161.115   General operations

Gold Coast Railroad Museum   Miami, Florida
160.245   Road and yard
161.295   Road
161.310   Road and yard

Golden Cat Railroad Museum   Cape Girardeau, Missouri
160.695   Tourist operations

Golden Spike National Historic Site   Promontory, Utah
171.675   Monument operations

Grand Canyon Railway   Williams, Arizona
160.350   Ch. 1 Road
160.350   161.565   Ch. 2 Road repeater
160.485   Ch. 3 Yard
160.830   Ch. 4 Yard
157.680   FCC

Halton County Radial Railway Museum   Rockwood, Ontario
154.490   Trolley museum operations

Hawaiian Railway Society   Honolulu, Hawaii
160.215   Museum operations

Heber Creeper Scenic Railroad   Heber, Utah
151.865   Tourist operations

Hobo Railroad   Lincoln, New Hampshire
160.470   General operations
161.550   160.560   Road repeater

Hocking Valley Scenic   Nelsonville, Ohio
161.355   Tourist operations

Housatonic Railroad   Canaan, Connecticut
160.395   Road & repeater output
160.395   161.505   Road repeater

Huckleberry Railroad   Flint, Michigan
Genesee County Parks & Recreation Dept
155.745   155.040   Tourist operations

Huntsville Depot   Huntsville, Alabama
160.425   Joint frequency with city park

Illinois Railway Museum   Union, Illinois
160.275   Ch. 1 Dispatcher
154.515   Ch. 2 Miscellaneous
154.540   Spare

Indiana Transportation Museum   Noblesville, Indiana
49.89   Trolley operations

Indiana Railway Museum   French Lick, Indiana
160.635   Tourist operations

Ironworld USA   Chisholm, Minnesota
453.225   458.225   Tourist operations

Junction Valley Railroad   Bridgeport, Michigan
27.015   CB Ch 5 General operations

Kalamazoo, Lake Shore & Chicago   Paw Paw, Michigan
160.815   Ch. 1 Road
160.215   Ch. 2 On-board services

Kentucky Railway Museum   New Haven, Kentucky
160.545   Tourist operations

Knott's Berry Farm   Buena Park, California
154.570   Amusement park trains
154.600   Amusement park trains

Knox, Kane & Kinzua   Kane, Pennsylvania
161.235   Tourist operations

Lahaina, Kaanapali & Pacific Railroad   Lahaina, Hawaii
154.540   Tourist operations

Lake Shore Railway Historical Society
    North East, Pennsylvania
154.570   FCC

Lake Superior & Mississippi   Duluth, Minnesota
160.380   General operations

Leadville, Colorado & Southern   Leadville, Colorado
161.565   Tourist operations

Lewis & Clark Railway   Battle Ground, Washington
464.225   469.225   Tourist operations

Little River Railroad   Coldwater, Michigan
152.915   Current channel
160.755   Future channel

Little Traverse Scenic Railway   Emmet City, Michigan
154.570   FCC
154.600   FCC

Mad River & Nickel Plate Railroad Museum   Bellevue, Ohio
151.625	FCC
153.625	Museum operations
154.570	FCC

Manitou & Pikes Peak Railway   Manitou Springs, Colorado
161.550 160.230 General operations

Mid-Continent Railway Museum   North Freedom, Wisconsin
| 151.625 | Tourist operations |
| 161.355 | Tourist operations |

Midland Railway   Baldwin City, Kansas
161.055   Tourist operations

Midwest Railway Historical Society   Cuyahoga Falls, Ohio
161.415   Tourist operations

Minnesota Transportation Museum   Minneapolis, Minnesota
| 161.355 | Jackson Street Roundhouse |
| 161.295 | Train operation at Osceola, Wisconsin |

Minnesota Zephyr   Stillwater, Minnesota
160.290   Dinner train operations

Monticello Railway Museum   Monticello, Illinois
160.635   FCC

Mount Rainier Scenic Railroad   Elbe, Washington
| 160.635~ | Tourist operations |
| 161.385~ | Switching |

Mount Washington Cog Railway   Mount Washington, New Hampshire
160.410   General operations

Mystic Valley Railway Society   Mattapan, Massachusetts
151.625   Excursion Service

National Railway Historical Society (NRHS)

Atlanta Chapter, Duluth, Georgia
160.605   Excursion service
Boston Chapter, Boston, Massachusetts
158.285   Excursion service
Bluewater Chapter, Detroit, Michigan
463.250   Excursion service
East Carolina Chapter, Apex, North Carolina
(North Carolina Railroad Museum)
160.425   Excursion service
Heart of Dixie Chapter, Birmingham, Alabama
154.515   Ch 1 Excursion service
154.540   Ch 2 Excursion service
Huntington Chapter, Huntington, West Virginia
159.270   Excursion service
Lancaster Chapter, Lancaster, Pennsylvania
151.925   Excursion service
Old Dominion Chapter, Richmond, Virginia
151.625   Museum/Excursion service
Pacific Northwest Chapter, Portland, Oregon
464.500   Excursion service
Roanoke Chapter, Roanoke, Virginia
151.925   Excursion service

Rochester Chapter — Rochester, New York
160.440 Train operations
160.470 Car hosts

Nevada Northern — Ely, Nevada
161.370 160.260 Tourist operations

Nevada State Railroad Museum — Carson City, Nevada
453.2375 Museum operations

New Hope Valley — Apex, North Carolina
160.425 General operations

New Jersey Museum of Transportation
Farmingdale, New Jersey
159.375 Tourist operations
159.465 Tourist operations

Niles Canyon Scenic Railway — Sunol, California
160.695 Tourist operations

North Alabama Railroad Museum — Huntsville, Alabama
452.325~ 457.325~ FCC
461.100~ 466.100~ FCC

North Carolina Transportation Museum
Spencer, North Carolina
155.145 General operations

North Shore Scenic Railroad — Duluth, Minnesota
160.920 Tourist operations

Old Colony & Newport Railway — Portsmouth, Rhode Island
160.395 Museum and dinner train operations

Omaha Zoo — Omaha, Nebraska
160.500 Zoo train
160.815 Zoo train

Orange Empire Railway Museum — Perris, California
151.625 Ch 1 Administration
151.700 Ch 2 Dispatcher
161.525 Ch 3 General operations

Oregon Electric Railway Historical Society
Glenwood, Oregon
464.550 Trolley operations

Osceola & St. Croix Valley Railway — Osceola, Minnesota
161.295 Road – Wisconsin Central trackage rights
161.355 Alternate

Pacific Railroad Society — South Pasadena, California
161.205 Police

Pennsylvania Trolley Museum — Washington, Pennsylvania
462.8125 Museum operations

Philadelphia Zoo — Philadelphia, Pennsylvania
151.805 Safari monorail

Portola – Silver

Portola Railroad Museum   Portola, California
161.010   Museum operations

Port Stanley Terminal   Port Stanley, Ontario
160.575   Tourist operations

Puget Sound & Snoqualmie Valley RR   Snoqualmie, WA
161.355   Museum operations
161.385   MofW

Railroad Museum of Pennsylvania   Strasburg, Pennsylvania
453.725   Museum operations

Railroaders Memorial Museum   Altoona, Pennsylvania
464.050   FCC
467.850   Museum operations
467.900   Museum operations

Riverside & Great Northern   Wisconsin Dells, Wisconsin
151.955   Tourist operations

Roaring Camp and Big Trees   Felton, California
151.910~   FCC
151.925   Tourist operations

Rockhill Trolley Museum   Rockhill, Pennsylvania
151.625   Museum operations

Rocky Mountain Railroad Club   Denver, Colorado
161.040   Tourist operations

Royal Gorge Scenic Railway   Canon City, Colorado
151.925   Amusement park trains

St. Louis & Chain of Rocks Railroad   St. Louis, Missouri
151.655   Tourist operations

St. Louis, Iron Mountain & Southern   Cape Girardeau, Missouri
160.845   Tourist operations

St. Louis Steam Train Association   St. Louis, Missouri
154.600   Operation of Frisco 1522

San Diego Railroad Museum   Campo, California
160.455 161.505 Museum operations

Santa Cruz, Big Trees & Pacific Railway   Felton, California
151.910   Tourist operations
161.550   Joint operations with Southern Pacific

Seashore Trolley Museum   Kennebunkport, Maine
160.470   Museum operations
160.500   Museum operations

Sierra Railway   Jamestown, California
160.590   Sierra Railroad trackage rights
452.900 457.900 Tourist operations

Silver Creek & Stephenson   Freeport, Illinois
154.570   Tourist operations

Silverwood Amusement Park   Athol, Idaho
160.845   Tourist operations

Smoky Hill Railway & Museum Association   Belton, Missouri
151.685   Tourist operations
151.955   Tourist operations

South Carolina Railroad Museum   Rockton, South Carolina
151.865   Tourist operations

Steamtown National Historical Site   Scranton, Pennsylvania
164.175   163.175   Railroad operations
164.475   Park rangers and law enforcement

Stone Mountain Scenic Railroad   Stone Mountain, Georgia
160.845   Tourist operations

Stourbridge Line   Honesdale, Pennsylvania
160.455   Tourist operations

Strasburg Railroad   Strasburg, Pennsylvania
161.235   Tourist operations

Sumpter Valley Railroad   Baker, Oregon
160.365~   Tourist operations

Tennessee Central Railway Museum
         Chattanooga, Tennessee
154.570   Excursion service

Tennessee Valley Railroad   Chattanooga, Tennessee
160.425   Tourist operations
463.225   468.225   Tourist operations

Texas State Railroad Historical Park   Rusk, Texas
151.340   Tourist operations

Tioga Central   Wellsboro, Pennsylvania
160.455   Road
151.955   On-board services

Tweetsie Railroad   Blowing Rock, North Carolina
468.400   Tourist operations
468.900   Tourist operations
464.475   FCC
468.8875   FCC

Twentieth Century Railroad Club   Chicago, Illinois
151.625   FCC – Mobiles

Valley Railroad   Essex, Connecticut
160.695   Tourist operations
152.360   Train to boat captain

Wabash, Frisco & Pacific Railway   Glencoe, Missouri
151.955   Tourist operations

Walt Disney World   Lake Buena Vista, Florida

462.550		Operations Ch 1 Staff paging
462.575	467.575	Operations Ch 2 Monorail and trains
462.625	467.625	Operations Ch 3 Transportation
462.650	467.650	Maintenance Ch 1

Washington Park & Zoo Railroad   Portland, Oregon

151.655	Amusement park trains

Western Maryland Scenic Railroad   Cumberland, Maryland

154.600	On-train portables

White Pass & Yukon Route   Skagway, Alaska

160.305	Ch 1 Road
160.170	Ch 2 Dispatcher
160.425	Ch 2 Yard

160.695	FCC - Active
160.800	FCC - Active
160.320~	FCC
160.350~	FCC
151.805~	FCC

Whitewater Valley Railroad   Connersville, Indiana

160.650	Tourist operations

Winnipesaukee Railroad   Meredith, New Hampshire

160.470	Tourist operations

Yosemite Mountain-Sugar Pine Railroad
Fish Camp, California

151.655	Tourist operations

RAILROADS OUTSIDE THE U. S. AND CANADA

MEXICO

Former Ferrocarril de Chihuahua al Pacifico

173.225		Ch 1 Road and dispatcher to Train
173.600		Ch 2 Train to dispatcher

Former Ferrocarril del Pacifico

167.100		Ch 1 Road
167.150		Ch 2 Yard
167.625	167.100	Active – Use undetermined

Former Ferrocarril Sonora Baja California

167.100		Yard
167.150		Road
167.625	167.100	Yard

Ferrocarriles Nacionales de Mexico

173.225	Ch 1 Road and dispatcher to Train
173.325	Ch ? Formerly Ch 2
173.450	Ch 3
173.600	Ch 2 Train to dispatcher

AUSTRALIA

Future allocations for all Australia

410.625	Yard
410.800	Yard
410.925	Yard
411.050	
411.175	Yard

411.325		
411.375		Yard
411.475		Yard
411.525		End to end, train to wayside
411.550		End to end, train to wayside
411.625		Yard
416.975	407.525	Low power, non-train
417.000	407.550	Cranes, forklifts, tractors
417.075	407.625	Low power, non-train
417.125	407.675	Low power, non-train
417.200	407.750	Low power, non-train
417.250	407.800	Low power, non-train
417.275	407.825	Yard/industrial switching
417.375	407.925	Yard switching and Pulldown
417.425	407.975	Number taking
417.500	408.050	Remote control yard locos
417.550	408.100	Road and dispatcher
417.850	408.400	Road and dispatcher
418.150	408.700	Road and dispatcher
418.175	408.725	MofW – Track
418.425	408.975	Road and dispatcher
418.450	409.000	Road and dispatcher
418.475	409.025	MofW – Electric Traction
418.725	409.275	Road and dispatcher
418.750	409.300	Road and dispatcher
418.775	409.325	MofW – Signals
419.025	409.575	Road and dispatcher

Australia

419.050	409.600	Road and dispatcher
419.075	409.625	MofW – Power and Light
419.325	409.875	Road and dispatcher
419.350	409.900	Road and dispatcher
419.375	409.375	Diesel Maintenance
419.600	410.150	Management police paging
419.625	410.175	Road and dispatcher
419.650	410.200	Road and dispatcher
419.900	410.450	Management police paging
419.925	410.475	Road and dispatcher
419.950	410.500	Road and dispatcher

Australian Iron & Steel Ltd.   Port Kembla, New South Wales

170.700	Intra-plant switching
170.760	Intra-plant switching

Australian National Railways   Keswick, South Australia

157.480		Parcel delivery trucks
162.310		Police
162.640		MofW
166.630	170.940	Dispatcher – Mt. Gambier to Millicent
167.530		Mechanical/electrical service trucks
168.370		Yard
168.520		Yard
168.580		Road – main line in South Australia
168.640		Dispatcher
168.700		Dispatcher at Launceston
168.910		Yard
168.910		Dispatcher – Tarcoola to Alice Springs
418.175		Tank car maintenance
418.475		Rescue and emergency units

450.200	Police
469.500	Dispatchers Link to 168.7
471.300	Yard
471.375	Yard
471.400	Yard
471.425	Yard
471.500	Yard
471.525	Yard
471.575	Yard
471.650	Yard
471.700	Yard
471.725	Yard
471.775	Yard
471.850	Yard

Former Tasmanian Government Railway (Tasrail)

168.520	Road and yard

Australian Railway Historical Society

450.025	Tourist operations

B.H.P. Steel   Newcastle, New South Wales

83.10	Plant switching

Bellarine Peninsula Railway   Queenscliffe, Victoria

80.43	Tourist operations

Castlemaine & Malden Railway   Malden, Victoria

80.43	Tourist operations

Emerald Tourist Railway   Victoria

77.69   Puffing Billy Train

Emu Bay Railway Co.   Burnie, Tasmania

163.180   Yard
165.205   166.045   Road – north territory
165.535   166.375   Road – south territory

Goldsworthy Railway   South Hedland, Western Australia

162.610   Ch 1 and 2 Train to dispatcher – systemwide
169.300   Ch 2 Dispatcher to train – Goldsworthy, W Australia
169.660   Ch 1 Dispatcher to train – Finucine Island and Shay Gap
Ore Loading Site
162.820   Train to yardmaster
169.930   Yardmaster to train

Hamersley Iron Ore Railways   Dampier, Western Australia

482.100   Ch 19 Common Simplex
482.150   Ch 15 Observer
485.500   480.300   Ch 16 Yard 1
485.800   480.600   Ch 17 Yard 2
486.100   480.900   Ch 18 Yard 3
Western Creek and Mt. Lois
486.425   481.225   Ch 11a Road
486.725   481.525   Ch 12a Services
487.025   481.825   Ch 13a Track maintenance
487.325   482.125   Ch 14a Spare

Dampier, Chichester, and Mt. Nameless
486.400   481.225   Ch 11b Road
486.700   481.525   Ch 12b Services
487.000   481.825   Ch 13b Track maintenance
487.300   482.125   Ch 14b Spare
Cherratte, Kanjenjie, and Doballs
486.450   481.225   Ch 11c Road
486.750   481.525   Ch 12c Services
487.050   481.825   Ch 13c Track maintenance
487.350   482.125   Ch 14c Spare

Perisher Ski Tube   Snowy Mountain, New South Wales

173.010   168.460   Ski Trains
173.160   168.610   Ski Trains

Queensland Government Railways

168.520   Ch 1 Road, yard, dispatcher, police
168.565   Ch 3 Road, yard, dispatcher, police
168.640   Ch 2 Road, yard, dispatcher, police
168.775   Ch 4 Road, yard, dispatcher, police
Acacia Ridge Yard
464.250   454.750   Yard and servicing
Townsville Yard
467.375   457.875   Yard
Whinstanes Yard
467.450   457.950   Yard
Willowburn Yard
464.250   454.750   Yard
Moolabin
467.450   457.950   Yard and servicing
Brisbane: North of Roma Street Station

Australia

499.875	494.675	Ch 1 Road, yard, and MofW
499.875	494.775	Ch 2 Road, yard, and MofW
499.875	495.150	Ch 3 Road, yard, and MofW
Brisbane: Roma Street Yard		
467.375	457.875	Yard
Brisbane: South of Roma Street Station		
499.150	494.925	Ch 1 Road, yard, and MofW
499.150	494.875	Ch 2 Road, yard, and MofW
499.150	494.750	Ch 3 Road, yard, and MofW
Mayne		
464.250	454.750	Yard and shop
Rockhampton		
467.375	457.875	Yard

State Railway Authority (New South Wales)
Sydney, New South Wales

168.140		Locomotive/mechanical/yard call system
168.640		MofW
411.550		Suburban operations
411.625		Yard
411.625		Yard
411.625		Yard
411.625		Yard
411.625		Yard
414.475	405.025	Engineers link
415.125	405.675	TX Site
416.975	407.525	Yard
416.975	407.525	Yard
417.275	407.825	TX Site
418.125	408.675	TX Site
418.125	408.675	TX Site

418.125	409.675	TX Site
418.150	408.700	Active – use undetermined
418.150	408.700	TX Site
Sydney to Newcastle		
418.300	408.850	TX Sites
418.325	408.875	TX Sites
418.400	408.950	TX Sites
418.425	408.975	TX Sites
418.450	409.000	TX Sites
418.850	409.500	TX Sites
Wollongong to Moss Vale		
418.475	409.025	TX Sites
418.500	409.050	TX Sites
418.725	409.275	TX Sites
418.750	409.275	TX Sites
418.750	409.30	TX Sites
418.775	409.325	TX Sites
418.800	409.350	TX Sites
Other areas		
419.100	409.650	TX Sites
419.400	409.950	TX Sites
419.600		TX Site
419.700	410.250	TX Sites
419.900	410.450	TX Site
419.900	410.450	TX Site
419.900	410.450	TX Site
419.925	410.475	TX Sites
450.050		Road
455.200		Railex
455.975		Locomotive testing shop
463.300	453.800	Active – use undetermined

463.475		Police
463.625	454.125	Active – use undetermined
465.200	455.700	Coal loader
465.475	455.975	Yard
465.525	456.025	Yard
476.625		Car Shop/Signal/Communications
476.875		Car Shop/Signal/Communications
477.125		Signals and Communications
485.075		Yard
485.200	480.000	MofW
485.500	480.300	Engineers
485.975	480.775	Electricians
486.050	480.850	Engineers
486.050	480.850	Engineers
494.250	499.450	Electricians

Dural, Razorback, and Sydney

505.550	515.550	PBX
505.800	515.800	PBX
506.100	516.100	PBX
506.450	516.450	PBX
516.750	516.750	PBX

Cowan, Glenbrook, and Heathcote

505.575	515.575	PBX
505.825	515.825	PBX
506.125	516.125	PBX
506.475	516.475	PBX
506.775	516.775	PBX

Chullora, Mount Penang, and Woonona Mountain

505.600	515.600	PBX
505.675	515.675	PBX
505.850	515.850	PBX

505.925	515.925	PBX
506.150	516.150	PBX
506.500	516.500	PBX
506.200	516.200	PBX
506.575	516.575	PBX
506.800	516.800	PBX
506.875	516.875	PBX

Future Use

505.625	515.625	PBX
505.875	515.875	PBX
505.900	515.900	PBX
506.225	516.225	PBX
506.175	516.175	PBX
506.525	516.525	PBX
506.550	516.550	PBX
506.825	516.825	PBX
506.850	516.850	PBX
515.650	505.650	PBX
82.260	73.280	Electric, mechanical, communications, and signals

Acdep Yard

469.625		Yard

B.H.P. Steel Works

83.10		Plant switching

Broadmeadow Yard

417.075	407.625	Yard
438.475		Loco
484.850		Yard
410.925		Active – use undetermined
411.175		Active – use undetermined
450.200		Car shop

Australia

471.275		Remote control locomotives
471.275		Remote control locomotives
471.275		Remote control locomotives
Coal Cliff Collery		
467.500	458.000	Coal loader
Cooks River Yard		
465.525	456.025	Yard
Cringila Yard		
465.575		Yard
456.075		Yard
Enfield Yard		
161.140		Yard call system
410.625		TX Site
416.975	407.525	Yard
476.675		Loco shop
476.875		Locomotives, signals, communications
Goulburn Yard		
161.140		Yard call system
465.200	455.700	Yard
Grafton Yard		
463.5625	468.6875	Yard and data
468.6875	463.5625	Yard and data
Junee Yard		
494.875		Yard
Lithgow Yard		
418.150	408.700	TX Site
451.625		Coal trains
465.200	455.700	Yard
Parkes Yard		
411.625		Yard
450.200		Yard
Penrith Yard		
450.200		Yard
Port Kembla Yard		
161.140		Yard call system
418.200	408.750	Active – use undetermined
465.475	455.975	Yard
474.825		Coal loader
Port Waratah Yard		
451.625		Coal trains
465.475	455.975	Yard
Redfern Yard		
469.625		Yard
Rozelle Yard		
465.575	456.075	Yard
Saleyards		
495.025		Yard
Sydney Produce Market		
450.250		Car shop
463.550	454.050	Yard
Sydney Yard		
464.150	454.650	Yard
Tarre Yard		
468.6875	463.5625	Yard
Trackfast Center		
411.525		Terminal operations
412.525	403.075	Yard
Werris Creek Yard		
494.875		Yard
Wollongong Yard		
474.825		Special work
XPT Maintenance Center		

450.075   Yard

TNT Harbour Link   Sydney, New South Wales

485.250	480.050	Monorail operations
485.550	480.350	Monorail operations
486.400	481.200	Monorail operations
489.375	484.175	Monorail operations

Victoria State Transport Authority   Melbourne, Victoria

170.820		MofW
417.550	408.100	Ch 9 Train/dispatcher – Brooklyn Loop Area
417.850	408.400	Ch 1 Train/dispatcher – Geelong to Warrnambool, North Geelong to Gheringhap
418.150	408.700	Ch 3 Train/dispatcher – Gheringhap to Ballarat to Mildura, Ouyen to Pinnaroo, Maryborough to Ararat
418.450	409.000	Ch 7 Train/dispatcher – Gippsland Area
418.750	409.300	Ch 8 Train/dispatcher – Mornington Peninsula and Long Island
419.050	409.600	Ch 4 Train/dispatcher – Melbourne to Bendigo to Swan Hill, Bendigo to Echuca to Deniliquin, Echuca to Moulamein, Dunolly to Inglewood, Castlemaine to Maryborough
419.350	409.900	Ch 2 Train/dispatcher – Melbourne to Ballarat to Ararat, Gheringhap to Maroona to Ararat, Maroona to Portland, Heywood to Mt. Gambier
419.650	410.200	Ch 6 Train/dispatcher – Melbourne to Albury, Ararat to Wolseley, Yaapeet Branch
419.950	410.500	Ch 5 Train/dispatcher – Melbourne to Wodonga and Albury, Goulburn Valley and

		Branches
450.875		Unknown use
457.750		Unknown use
465.400	456 .400	Ch 4 End to end
465.550	456 .050	Ch 3 End to end
467.150	457 .650	Ch 6 End to end
469.700		Ch 1 End to end
469.725		Ch 2 End to end
470.375	475 .575	Unknown use
473.375	478 .575	Unknown use
473.550	478 .750	Unknown use
77.24	82.86	Phone Patch

Gippsland Brown Coal Electric

166.330		Power plant
166.420		Power plant
166.480		Power plant
166.600		Power plant
166.690		Power plant
166.750		Power plant
77.24		Power plant

Melbourne

468.300	458.800	Dynon goods yard
469.600		Jolimont electric running depot
469.500		Spencer Street platforms/information
469.675		Spencer Street coach yard car checkers

Metropolitan Transit Authority   Melbourne, Victoria

465.875	456.375	Suburban
481.650		Trams – Inspectors
481.925		Trams – Preston Workshops
481.975		Trams – Inspectors

Australia, Britain

486.850	481.650	Metro – active
487.125	481.925	Metro Ch 3
487.175	481.975	Metro Ch 1
487.925	482.725	Metro – active
507.200	517.200	Automatic vehicle monitor

Western Australia Government Railways
Perth, Western Australia

168.520		Ch 1 Road and dispatcher
168.580		Ch 2 Road and dispatcher
168.610		Ch 3
168.640		Ch 4 Yard
168.550		Ch 5 Loading
168.700		Ch 6 Yard
168.670		Ch 7 Loading
168.730		Ch 8
168.430		Ch 9 Yard
168.790		Ch 10 Loading
169.000		Ch 11
169.030		Ch 12 Loading
169.060		Ch 13
169.090		Ch 14 Yard
169.120		Ch 15 Yard
169.150		Ch 16 Loading
169.180		Ch 17 Yard
169.210		Ch 18 Loading
169.240		Ch 19 Yard
169.270		Ch 20 Yard
172.830	170.310	Ch 21 Engineering
172.860	170.340	Ch 22 Engineering
172.890	170.370	Ch 23 Engineering
172.980	170.460	Ch 24 Engineering
172.800	170.670	Ch 25 Engineering
173.190	170.730	Ch 26 Engineering

Zig Zag Railway
Lithgow, New South Wales

484.825	Tourist operations

BRITAIN

British Railways

204.850	196.850	Ch 1 Traffic
204.900	196.900	Ch 2 Traffic
204.950	196.950	Ch 3 Traffic
205.000	197.000	Ch 4 Traffic
205.050	197.050	Ch 5 Traffic
205.100	197.100	Ch 6 Traffic
205.150	197.150	Ch 7 Traffic
205.200	197.200	Ch 8 Early warning
205.250	197.250	Ch 9 Early warning
205.300	197.300	Ch 10 Early warning
205.350	197.350	Ch 11 Traffic
205.400	197.400	Ch 12 Traffic
205.600	197.600	Ch 13 Traffic
205.650	197.650	Ch 14 Traffic
205.675	197.675	Ch 15 Emergency
205.700	197.700	Ch 16 Traffic
205.725	197.725	Ch 17 Control
205.750	197.750	Ch 18 Traffic
205.800	197.800	Ch 19 Traffic
205.8375	197.8375	Ch 20 Control
205.850	197.850	Ch 21 Traffic

205.900	197.900	Ch 22 Traffic
205.950	197.950	Ch 23 Traffic
206.000	198.000	Ch 24 Traffic
206.100	198.100	Ch 25 Traffic
206.150	198.150	Ch 26 Traffic
206.250	198.250	Ch 27 Control
206.300	198.300	Ch 28 Traffic
453.550		Yard, MofW, and Stations
453.775		Yard, MofW, and Stations

GERMANY

German Federal Railway

Trunked four-channel frequency groups

467.450	457.450	Ch 11	60-3			
467.475	457.475	Ch 12	60-2			
467.500	457.500	Ch 13	60-1	61-3		
467.525	457.525	Ch 14		61-2	71-3	
467.550	457.550	Ch 15	60-4	61-1	71-2	
467.575	457.575	Ch 16			71-1	72-3
467.600	457.600	Ch 17		61-4		72-2
467.625	457.625	Ch 18		73-3	71-4	72-1
467.650	457.650	Ch 19	62-3	73-2		
467.675	457.675	Ch 20	62-2	73-1		72-4
467.700	457.700	Ch 21	62-1		74-3	
467.725	457.725	Ch 22		73-4	74-2	
467.750	457.750	Ch 23	62-4		74-1	75-3
467.775	457.775	Ch 24		63-3		75-2
467.800	457.800	Ch 25		63-2	74-4	75-1
467.825	457.825	Ch 26	76-3	63-1		
467.850	457.850	Ch 27	76-2			75-4
467.875	457.875	Ch 28	76-1	63-4	64-3	
467.900	457.900	Ch 29		77-3	64-2	
467.925	457.925	Ch 30	76-4	77-2	64-1	
467.950	457.950	Ch 31	65-3	77-1		
467.975	457.975	Ch 32	65-2		64-4	
468.000	458.000	Ch 33	65-1	77-4		
468.025	458.025	Ch 34			78-3	
468.050	458.050	Ch 35	65-4		78-2	
468.075	458.075	Ch 36		79-3	78-1	
468.100	458.100	Ch 37		79-2		
468.125	458.125	Ch 38		79-1	78-4	
468.150	458.150	Ch 39	66-3			
468.175	458.175	Ch 40	66-2	79-4		
468.200	458.200	Ch 41	66-1	67-3		
468.225	458.225	Ch 42		67-2		
468.250	458.250	Ch 43	66-4	67-1		
468.275	458.275	Ch 44				
468.300	458.300	Ch 45	67-4			

IRELAND

Irish Rail (Iarnród Éireann)

453.025	459.525	Active – use undetermined
453.175	459.675	Active – use undetermined
453.225	459.725	Active – use undetermined

NEW ZEALAND

New Zealand Railways

153.4562		Ch 1 Road
153.7312		Ch 2 Train to dispatcher
151.950		Ch 2 Dispatcher to train
153.8312		Ch 3 Train to dispatcher
152.050		Ch 3 Dispatcher to train
153.1312		Ch 4 Train to dispatcher
152.350		Ch 4 Dispatcher to train
425.150	420.1375	Dispatcher link
425.650	420.6375	Dispatcher link
429.875	424.8625	Dispatcher link
453.3625		Yard
453.4875		Yard
453.5125		Yard
453.5625		Yard
84.5375		MofW – Low power – AM
85.71875	81.750	MofW – AM – Mobile telephone
85.73125	81.7625	MofW – AM – Mobile telephone
86.21875	82.250	MofW – AM – Mobile telephone
86.21875	82.3125	MofW – AM – Mobile telephone
86.33125	82.3625	MofW – AM – Mobile telephone
86.56875	82.600	MofW – AM – Mobile telephone
86.88125	82.9125	MofW – AM – Mobile telephone
86.96875	83.000	MofW – AM – Mobile telephone
87.15625	83.1875	MofW – AM – Mobile telephone
87.19375	83.225	MofW – AM – Mobile telephone
87.29375	83.325	MofW – AM – Mobile telephone
87.44375	83.475	MofW – AM – Mobile telephone
87.58125	83.6125	MofW – AM – Mobile telephone
87.66875	83.700	MofW – AM – Mobile telephone

SWEDEN

Stockholm Subway   Stockholm

167.0675	Ch 1 Surface
167.4375	Ch 2 Surface
166.7125	Ch 3 Surface
167.5375	Ch 1 Underground
166.7375	Ch 2 Underground
167.1125	Ch 3 Underground
167.1675	Ch 4 MofW

METROPOLITAN AREAS

ATLANTA

Amtrak
160.920△   Peachtree Station – Train and engine crews

Atlanta, Stone Mountain & Lithonia
161.025   General operations

CSX Transportation
160.590   Road – Former SCL
161.100   Road – Former SCL
161.520   Dispatcher – Former L&N
161.400   Yard – Former SCL
160.290   Yard – Former SCL
161.265   160.395   PBX
161.310   MofW – Former SCL
161.460   160.440   Car Dept. – Former SCL
161.040   Police
161.040   Police – Former SCL
161.205   Police mutual aid
Howells Yard
160.230   Pulldown
160.770   Hump
Hulsey Yard
161.310   Yard – Former Georgia Railroad
Tilford Yard
160.440   Pulldown

160.860   Yard
161.010   160.620   Car Dept.
161.610   Hump
452.950   Hump cab signals
160.785   Yard
161.370   Ch 1 Road and dispatcher to train
161.520   Ch 2 Train to dispatcher
161.310   Old Ch 1 Road
161.430   Old Ch 2 Yard

Metropolitan Atlanta Rapid Transit Authority
453.725   458.725   F1 Road – Citywide
453.700   458.700   F2 A Division – East
453.775   458.775   F3 B Division – North/West
453.875   458.875   F4 C Division – Control/West
453.950   458.950   F5 Road – Citywide
453.925   458.925   F6 Administration
452.875   457.875   MofE
452.475   457.475   Police
452.375   457.375   Former Road
452.775   457.775   Former Road

National Railway Historical Society, Atlanta Chapter
Duluth, GA

160.605   Excursion service

Norfolk Southern

160.830△		Ch 2 Train to dispatcher
161.490		Ch 3 Local switching
160.950△		Ch 5 Road (ex-Southern)
161.490		Ch 9 Yard
160.245△		Dispatcher to train
160.515	161.235	PBX 9
161.190		Signal maintainers and radio shop
161.535		Signal Dept. mobiles
160.365		Car Dept. (without repeater)
160.365	161.295	Car Dept. (with repeater)
160.650		Yard clerks
160.500		Traveling freight agents and wrecker
161.505		Wrecker
161.535		C&S mobile to mobile
161.475		Digital remote control of locomotives – eastbound
161.565		Digital remote control of locomotives – westbound
161.115		End-of-train telemetry
161.205		Police

Inman Yard

161.250		Yard
160.875	160.320	Hump
160.335	161.325	Pulldown
160.530	160.470	Pulldown
160.740	161.160	Pulldown
160.365	161.295	Car Dept.
160.635		Intermodal facility

Stone Mountain Scenic Railroad   Stone Mountain, Georgia

160.845	Tourist operations

U. S. Army   Forest Park, Georgia

165.0375	Fort Gillem

BALTIMORE

Amtrak

160.920		Road
160.455		Work trains and yard
160.515	161.115	MofW
160.650		Station services
160.815		Ch 2 Police – Car to car
161.295	160.365	Ch 3 Police – Base to car
161.205		Ch 4 Police – Car to car
160.365	457.900	Police – Portable/mobile repeater
452.900	161.295	Police – Portable/mobile repeater

Bethlehem Steel   Navy Shipyard, Sparrows Point

153.140	158.430~	Plant switching

Canton Railroad

160.980	General operations

Conrail

160.800△	Ch 1 Road
161.070△	Ch 2 Road and yard
160.860	Ch 3 Yard
160.980	Ch 4 Yard

161.130		Ch 3 MofW
161.130	160.710	Ch 4 PBX and MofW
160.680		Ch 3 Police – Car to car
160.560		Ch 4 Police – Base to car

Bayside Yard

| 161.325 | 160.275 | Car Dept. and car shop |

CSX Transportation

160.230	Road
160.320	Dispatcher
160.290	Yard
160.410	Yard
161.160	Yard
160.785	MofW
160.875	Police
161.205	Police mutual aid
160.740	Active
161.250	Active

Bay View Yard

| 160.530 | Ch 3 Yard |

Curtis Bay Yard

| 160.890 | Yard |
| 161.370 | Coal dock |

Locust Point Yard

| 160.470 | Yard |

Mass Transit Administration

160.395	Ch 1 Subway Road
161.475	Ch 2 Subway Yard
161.085	Ch 3 Subway Police
161.565	Ch 4 Subway MofW

160.905	Ch 5 Light Rail Yards, Canton and Timonium
161.010	Ch 6 Light Rail Road
39.10	State Police
47.32	SHA
44.46	Mobility

BIRMINGHAM

Alabama By-Products

31.20	General operations
35.32	General operations
35.84	General operations

American Cast Iron Pipe

| 153.155 | Plant switching |

Amtrak

| 160.920 | Switching |

Birmingham Southern

160.290	Road and dispatcher
160.425	Switching
160.560	Switching
160.575	Switching
160.755	Switching
160.815	Switching
161.325	Switching
161.385	Switching
161.445	Switching
161.535	Switching

Birmingham

160.890		MofW and dispatcher
161.025		34 St. Yard Ensley switcher
160.335		Koppers Coke Mill switcher

Burlington Northern

161.130	160.545	Ch 5 PBX
161.115		Police
East Thomas Yard		
160.530		Yard
160.635		Yard
160.710		Yard
160.875		Yard
160.965	160.485	Car Dept.
160.995		Intermodal facility – Dixie Hub
161.235		Yard
161.415		Yard

Conners Steel Corp.

462.375	General operations

CSX Transportation

161.370		Road – Former L&N
160.590		Road – Former SCL
161.100		Road – Former SCL
161.520		Dispatcher – Former L&N
160.380		Yard – Former L&N
160.620		Yard – Former L&N
161.280		Yard – Former L&N
161.400		Yard – Former SCL
161.265	160.395	PBX
161.205		Police mutual aid

161.205		Police
Boyles Yard		
160.305		Signal Dept.
160.860		Hump
161.010		Pulldown
161.055		Retarder tower
161.310	160.620	Car Dept.
452.950		Hump cab signals
Tote Yard		
160.440		Yard

Jefferson Warrior Railroad

153.260	General operations

National Railway Historical Society, Heart of Dixie Chapter

154.515	Ch 1 Excursion service
154.540	Ch 2 Excursion service

Norfolk Southern

160.830△		Ch 2 Train to dispatcher
160.950△		Ch 5 Road
160.245△		Dispatcher to train
160.275	161.235	PBX 10
160.365		Car Dept. (without repeater)
160.500		Traveling freight agents and wrecker
161.475		Digital remote control of locomotives – eastbound
161.505		Wrecker
161.565		Digital remote control of locomotives – westbound
161.115		End-of-train telemetry

172

161.205		Police

Norris Yard

161.250		Hump
160.320	160.740	Pulldown 1
161.145	160.770	Pulldown 2
161.430		Yard
160.665	161.085	Local yard
161.490		Ch 3 Yard
160.365	161.295	Car Dept.
160.650		Yard clerks
161.535		C&S Dept.

Stockham Valve & Fitting

153.050	Intra-plant switching

U. S. Pipe & Foundry

153.260	Intra-plant switching
153.305	General operations

BOSTON

Amtrak

160.920		Road
160.455		Work trains and yard
160.515	161.115	MofW
160.815		Ch 2 Police – Car to car
161.295	160.365	Ch 3 Police – Base to car
161.205		Ch 4 Police – Car to car
160.365	457.900	Police – Portable/mobile repeater
452.900	161.295	Police – Portable/mobile repeater

South Station

160.635		Commissary and station services

Southampton Yard

160.455		MofE

Bay Colony

160.305△		Ch 1 Road
160.305△	161.355△	Ch 2 Dispatcher
160.485		Spare channel
161.265		Active

Boston & Maine

161.520		Ch 1 Train to dispatcher
161.160		Ch 1 Dispatcher to train
161.400		Ch 2 Road and yard
161.370		Ch 3 MofW
161.250		Ch 4 Police
161.250	160.230	Police
160.440		Intermodal facility

Conrail

160.800△		Ch 1 Road
161.070△		Ch 2 Yard and road
160.860		Ch 3 Yard and road
160.980		Ch 4 Yard and road
161.130		Ch 3 MofW
161.130	160.710	Ch 4 PBX and MofW
160.680		Ch 3 Police – Car to car
160.560		Ch 4 Police – Base to car

Massachusetts Bay Transportation Authority

Transit
470.4125 473.4125 Red Line
470.6125 473.6125 Orange Line
470.6375 473.6375 Green Line
470.6875 473.6875 Blue Line
472.5875 475.5875 Trackless trolleys and buses

30.90	MofW
31.14	MofE – Inspection and repair
44.43	Power Director
44.46	Engineering
453.900 458.900	Administration
470.6625 473.6625	Police

Commuter Rail
North Station and East

160.320	Road and dispatcher
161.460	G – FCC

South Station

160.590	Dispatcher to train
161.490	Train to dispatcher

Systemwide

160.695 161.565	MofW/C&S – Primary
160.695	MofW/C&S – Talk-around
160.875	Yard

National Railway Historical Society, Boston Chapter

158.285	Excursion service

Quincy Bay Terminal

160.215	General operations

CHICAGO

Acme Steel

153.200	Plant switching

American Maize Company

469.875~	Switching

Amtrak

160.305	Commissary and terminal road
160.365 154.515	Union Station Police
160.740	Shop
161.205	Police mutual aid
161.265	Car Dept.
161.325 160.395	MofW and Signal Dept.

Association of American Railroads

160.995	Research & Test Dept. – Illinois Institute of Technology
161.055	Research & Test Dept. – Illinois Institute of Technology

Atchison, Topeka & Santa Fe

160.650	Road
160.830 161.490	PBX P-7
161.010	MofW
161.205	Police

Corwith Yard

160.785	Hump
160.995	Yard 3

| 161.385 | Intermodal facility |
| 159.705 | ATSF Trucking |

Belt Railway of Chicago

160.500	Road and dispatcher
161.445	East Yard
160.380	West Yard
160.695	MofW
161.205	Police mutual aid
Clearing Yard	
160.965	Hump
161.295	Car Dept. and Diesel Shop

Bethlehem Steel — Burns Harbor, Indiana

Burns Harbor Plant
153.290	Ch 2 Dock and car dumper
154.570	Ch 3 EJ&E Dispatcher/MofE/MofW
161.010	CSS&SB interchange
161.070	Conrail interchange
462.325	Ch 1 Dispatcher and yard

Leary Bros. Company
| 49.59 | "OX" Scrap Yard switching |

Levy Company
| 44.02 | Slag Pit switching |

Burlington Northern

161.100△	Ch 1 Road and dispatcher
161.160	Ch 2 Road and dispatcher
161.205	Ch 6 Police
160.425 160.935	Ch 8 PBX
452.9375 457.9375	Car Dept.

Cicero Yard
| 160.335 | Car Dept./Police/Hump |

Chicago Union Station
| 452.900 457.900 | Diesel shop |

Chicago & Chemung — Woodstock, Illinois

| 153.830 | General operations |

Chicago & North Western

160.890	Ch 1 Road
160.455	Ch 2 MofW and road
161.040	Ch 3 Road
160.980	IHB interchange

Global One
| 452.9125 | Intermodal facility |

Proviso Yard
161.175	Ch 4 Yard 1 – Intermodal facility
160.575	Ch 5 Yard 2 – Pulldown
160.815	Ch 5 Yard 2 – Pulldown
161.475	Ch 6 Hump – Mobiles only

Chicago Central & Pacific

| 160.755 | Road |

Chicago Commuter Rail Service Board (Metra)

161.340	Road – Former Rock Island
161.025	Road – Former Illinois Central electric
161.280	MofW
160.635	Signal Dept. and police mobiles
160.680 161.220	PBX
161.610	Police and yard
160.605	Police

Chicago

Chicago Rail Link

160.635	Road – Off Metra
161.340	Road – On Metra
Canal Street Yard	
160.035	Intermodal facility

Chicago Railroad Police Trunked System

939.7625
939.7750
939.7875
939.8000
939.8125
939.8250
939.8375
939.8500
939.8625
939.8750

Chicago Railway Equipment

464.975~	FCC

Chicago Short Line

160.335	General operations

Chicago SouthShore & South Bend

161.355	161.010	Ch 2 Road repeater – west of Gary, Indiana
161.025		Ch 3 Illinois Central trackage rights – Chicago to Kensington
161.100		Ch 4 MofW

Chicago Transit Authority

470.5375	473.5375	F1 Supervisor: Southside
470.9875	473.9875	F2 Road control and emergency calling
472.9375	475.9375	F3 CPD MDT transit units (Buses)
470.6375	473.6375	F4 Supervisor: Northside
471.0375	474.0375	F5 Congress/Douglas O'Hare (Blue)
471.0625	474.0625	F6 Englewood/Jackson Park (Green), Lake, Midway (Orange)
471.0875	474.0875	F7 Ravenswood (Brown), Evanston (Purple), Skokie (Yellow)
471.1125	474.1125	F8 Howard-Dan Ryan (Red)
472.2375	475.2375	National K9 Contracted Security Police
460.350	465.350	City Police Ch 5

Chicago, West Pullman & Southern

160.215	General operations

Conrail

160.800△		Ch 1 Road
161.070△		Ch 2 Road and yard
160.860		Ch 3 Yard and road
161.130		Ch 3 MofW
160.980		Ch 4 Yard and road
160.545		Ch 4 Police – Base to car
160.560		Ch 4 Police – Car to car
161.130	160.710	Ch 4 PBX and MofW
161.055		Intermodal facility
51st Street Yard		
160.860		Ch 3 Yard
Burns Harbor, Indiana		
160.860		Ch 3 Yard

CSX Transportation

160.230	Road – Former Chessie System
161.370	Road – Former L&N
160.290	Yard – Former Chessie System
160.320	Dispatcher – Former Chessie System
161.520	Dispatcher – Former L&N
160.530	Yard – Former Chessie System
160.785	MofW – Former Chessie System
160.875	Police – Former Chessie System
161.205	Police mutual aid

48th Avenue Yard
160.290	Ch 5 Yard

Ashland Avenue Yard
161.415	Yard clerks

Barr Yard
160.275	Car Dept. and intermodal facility
160.740	Ch 7 Yard

Dolton Yard
161.145	Yard

Halsted Street Yard
161.310	Clerks and crew van

Elgin, Joliet & Eastern

160.260	Yard
160.350	Road and dispatcher
160.725	Steel mill switcher
161.475	Car Dept. – Kirk Yard
161.550	MofW and Police

Electro-Motive Division, General Motors   La Grange, Illinois

153.080~	FCC – 1 base and 20 mobiles
158.460~	FCC – 1 base (pager)
462.225 467.225	FCC – 50 mobiles/1 MR

Fox River Trolley Museum   South Elgin, Illinois

160.905	Trolley Museum operations – Inductive train phones also used

Grand Trunk Western

160.590△	Ch 1 Road and dispatcher
160.530△	Ch 2 Road and dispatcher
160.845	Ch 3 Chicago Yard
160.950 160.845	PBX
160.950	MofW
160.905	Police
161.205	Police mutual aid

Illinois Central

160.920△	Ch 2 Road
161.205	Police

Markham Yard
161.505	Yard
160.815	Woodcrest Locomotive Shop
160.920	Car Dept.
161.280	Yard

Indiana Harbor Belt

160.545 463.4625	Police portable mobile repeater
160.545	Police

Chicago

160.980	Ch 1 Road
161.070	Ch 2 Road
161.400	MofW

East Blue Island yard

161.565	161.535	Car Dept.
161.565		Hump

Gibson Yard

160.665	Yard

Iowa Interstate

160.305	Ch 2 Yard – Chicago to Joliet
161.340	Metra trackage rights

Manufacturers' Junction

161.475	General operations

Metra – see Chicago Commuter Rail Service Board

Metropolitan Sanitation District of Chicago

453.925	458.925	Rail operations

Norfolk Southern

161.250		Ch 2 Road (former Nickel Plate)
160.440		Ch 3 Road (former Wabash)
160.365	161.445	PBX 13
160.950		MofW
160.440		Cummins Drawbridge
161.205		Police
160.620		Police – Car to car
161.115		End-of-train telemetry

Calumet Yard

160.485	Car Dept.
160.515	Intermodal facility

Landers Yard

161.415	Car Dept.

Rail-to-Water Transfer

464.875~	FCC (Switching)

Soo Line (CP Rail)

161.520Δ		Ch 2 Road
160.770Δ		Ch 4 Road
160.440		Police – Former Milwaukee Road
161.205		Police mutual aid
161.235		Police
452.875	457.875	Milwaukee trucks

Bensenville Yard

161.430		Ch 5 Yard
160.515		Hump
160.620		Hostler
160.395		Car Dept.
160.470	161.145	Car Dept.

Southern Pacific

161.280Δ	Road

Union Pacific

160.410		Ch 1 Road
160.470		Ch 2 MofW
161.430	160.665	Administration and PBX
160.605	161.025	MofW – PBX

160.035	MoPac Trucking Lines
161.205	Police mutual aid
161.370	Police
Dolton Yard	
161.145	Yard

Wisconsin Central

161.295	Ch 3 Road

DALLAS and FORT WORTH

Amtrak

160.440	Road and Car Dept.
160.500	Switching

Atchison, Topeka & Santa Fe

160.650		Road
161.010		MofW
160.425	161.295	PBX
159.585		ATSF Trucking
161.370		Yard
161.190		Zacha Junction intermodal facility
Saginaw Yard		
160.560		Yellow Switcher – 2
161.370		Yard
Cleburne		
160.275		Stores Dept.
160.875	161.505	Car Dept.

Fort Worth Belt

160.410	General operations

Fort Worth Western

160.215	General operations

Kansas City Southern

161.055	Local switching

McKinney Avenue Transit Company

452.825	457.825	General operations

Rescar

160.995	G – switching at Union Equity Coop Exchange

Southern Pacific

161.550Δ	Road
160.320Δ	Road – Alternate
160.290	Intermodal facility
160.860	Police – Mobile to mobile
Miller Yard	
160.230	Yard

Tandy Center Subway

461.200	Security
464.425	Operations

Union Pacific

160.410Δ		Ch 1 Road
160.470Δ		Ch 2 Road
160.515Δ		Ch 3 Road
160.605	161.025	MofW PBX
160.755	161.325	Administration PBX
161.025		MofW

161.205	Police mutual aid
160.905	Communications Dept.
160.935	Communications Dept.

Mesquite Intermodal Facility (Dallas)

161.280	Ch 1 MoPack Trucking Lines
161.310	Ch 2 Yard
160.635	Yard and switching

Centennial Yard (Fort Worth)

160.770		Ch 4 Car Dept. and Mechanical
160.830		Ch 5 Hump
161.250	160.905	Pulldown
160.665		Diesel shop
161.115		Yard

DETROIT and WINDSOR

Amtrak

161.505	160.245	Police

Detroit Metro Zoo

151.205	159.300	Amusement park train
151.205	159.405	Amusement park train

Delray Connecting

153.050	Mill operations
153.080	Plant switching

Canadian National   Windsor, Ontario

160.215	Ch 16 Yard and MofW
160.695	Ch 17 Yard

Conrail

160.800△		Ch 1 Road
161.070△		Ch 2 Road and yard
160.860		Ch 3 Yard and road
161.130		Ch 3 MofW
161.130	160.710	Ch 4 PBX and MofW
160.560		Ch 4 Police – Base to car
160.500		PBX – Administration
160.860		Towers south and west of West Detroit
160.980		Towers north and east of West Detroit
161.100		Yard
161.430		MofW
161.055		MofW – Special projects
161.325		Crew cabs
161.535		Police – Car to car
161.280		Police mutual aid

River Rouge Bridge

156.600	Bridge to river traffic

CP Rail   Windsor, Ontario

161.115	CP 4 Yard
161.265	CP 16 Yard
160.185	CP 56 Yard and intermodal facility
160.755	CP 79 Car Dept.
161.355	CP 99 Yard

CSX Transportation

160.230	Road
160.320	Dispatcher
160.290	Yard

160.530		Yard
160.890		Yard
160.410		Yard
160.665		Yard
160.695		Yard
160.725		Yard
161.160		Ch 4 Yard
160.785		MofW
160.875		Police
161.205		Police mutual aid
161.280		Police mutual aid

Essex Terminal — Windsor, Ontario

160.605	Yard
160.905	Road and dispatcher

Great Lakes Steel

153.050	Joint operations with Delray Connecting
153.080	Joint operations with Delray Connecting
153.320~	FCC-20 Mobiles

Grand Trunk Western

160.590∆		Ch 1 Road and dispatcher
160.530∆		Ch 2 Road and dispatcher
161.550	160.740	Chevrolet plant yard
160.950		MofW
160.920	160.260	PBX
161.385	160.335	PBX – Flat Rock
160.470		Police
161.280		Police mutual aid

Norfolk Southern

160.440		Ch 3 Road (ex-Wabash)
161.490		Ch 9 MofW
160.515	161.235	F9 PBX
161.115		End-of-train telemetry
161.205		Police
160.305		Police – Car to car
161.205		Police – Car to car
161.280		Police mutual aid
Melvindale Yard		
160.380		Car Dept.
160.620		Car Dept.
Oakwood Yard		
161.250		Yard

Pennsylvania Truck Lines — Junction Yard

160.905	Intermodal facility
160.155	Intermodal Trucks

KANSAS CITY

Amtrak

161.175	Car Dept.

Atchison, Topeka & Santa Fe

160.650		Road
160.335	161.460	PBX
161.220	160.320	PBX
161.340	160.365	PBX
161.205		Police

Kansas City

161.265		Police mutual aid

Argentine Yard

160.215		Eastbound hump
160.845		Westbound hump
161.370		Yard
160.905	161.535	Diesel shop
160.950	161.475	Eastbound Car Dept.
452.900	457.900	Westbound Car Dept.
161.040		Intermodal facility
159.555		ATSF Trucking

Burlington Northern

161.100	Ch 1 Yard
161.160	Ch 2 Road
160.650	Ch 4 Yard
160.695	Intermodal facility
160.620	Supervisory
160.935	Crew Cab
161.430	MofW
161.205	Ch 6 Police
161.265	Police mutual aid
161.415	Active – use undetermined
952.2375	Microwave data

10th Street Yard

160.275	Yard

19th Street Yard

160.800	Yard

Murray Yard

160.485	Hump
160.725	Diesel shop
160.995	Pulldown

161.235		Pulldown
161.355		Pulldown
161.385	160.710	Car Dept.

Chicago & North Western

160.890	Ch 1 Road
160.455	Ch 2 MofW and road

Gateway Western

161.280	Ch 1 Road
161.460	Ch 2 Road
161.025	Ch 3 MofE
161.010	Ch 4 Intermodal facility
160.725	Ch 5 Yard
161.295	Ch 6 Yard

Kansas City Public Service

161.055	General operations

Kansas City Southern

160.260	Ch 1 Road and dispatcher to train – Line-ups at 0630 and 1230 hrs.
160.350	Ch 2 Train to dispatcher
161.250	Ch 3 Mobiles
160.890	Ch 4 Supervisory – Mobiles
161.565	Remote control locomotives
160.860	KCS Trucks

Knoche Yard

160.305	Intermodal facility
161.055	Yard

Kansas City Terminal (operated by Gateway Western)

161.310	Ch 1 Road and yard
160.500	Ch 2 Engineering Dept.
161.010	Ch 3 Dispatcher/Police

Midland Railway   Baldwin City, Kansas

161.055	Tourist operations

Norfolk Southern

161.190		Ch 1 Yard
160.440		Ch 3 Road
160.785	161.415	PBX 12
161.115		End-of-train telemetry
161.265		Police mutual aid
161.445	160.575	Car Dept.

Claycomo Yard

160.380	Switching

Northeast Kansas & Missouri   Hiawatha, Kansas

160.815	General operations

Soo Line

160.770	Ch 4 Road

Southern Pacific

161.280	Road – Kansas City to Chicago
161.550	Road
160.365	Police
161.205	Police
161.265	Police mutual aid

Armourdale Yard

161.070	Car Dept.
161.400	Yard

Union Pacific

160.410Δ		Ch 1 Road
160.470Δ		Ch 2 Road
160.515Δ		Ch 3 Road
160.740Δ		Ch 4 Road
160.980		Kansas City terminal – east
160.680		Kansas City terminal – west
160.245		Diesel shop
160.620		Diesel shop
160.710		Diesel shop
160.290	161.520	Administration – PBX – Former UP
160.605	161.025	MofW – PBX
160.635		Terminal MofW
161.025		MofW (except Chicago)
160.080		Intermodal facility and trucks
160.065		MoPac Trucking Lines
161.205		Police mutual aid
161.265		Police mutual aid

Armstrong Yard

161.130	160.530	Car Dept.

Neff Yard

160.395	East hump
160.815	East pulldown
160.950	East pulldown
160.590	Yard
160.425	Mechanical Dept.
160.875	Car Dept.

Kansas City, Los Angeles

Quindaro Yard
160.830   Switching

Wabash & Grand River   Chillicothe, MO
161.025   General operations

LOS ANGELES

Amtrak
160.455   Terminal switching
161.055   161.475   Police
452.900   457.900   Car Dept

Atchison, Topeka & Santa Fe
160.650   Road
161.190∆   Ch 4 Road
161.010   MofW
160.260   161.490   PBX
161.205   Police
Hobart Yard
161.370   Yard
161.070   160.440   Car Dept
161.190   Intermodal facility

Harbor Belt Line
160.980   General operations

Los Angeles Metro Rail
160.695   161.265   Red Line – Road
161.505   Red Line – Yard

160.725   Red Line – FCC
471.2125 474.2125 Red Line – FCC
471.3375 474.3375 Red Line – FCC
471.9875 474.9875 Blue Line – Yard
472.4875 475.4875 Blue Line – Road
483.4625 486.4625 Blue Line – County sheriff and transit police
484.1625 487.1625 Blue Line – County sheriff and transit police
160.425   160.635   Red and Blue Lines – MofW
160.755   FCC
160.935   FCC
161.145   FCC

Los Angeles Junction
161.130   General operations

Metropolitan Stevedore Co.   Long Beach, CA
151.715   Plant switching

Southern California Metrolink
161.415   Ch. 1 Road, Pomona to Mission Tower
160.815   Ch. 2 Yard and mechanical, Taylor Yard, primary
160.545   Ch 3 Road, Palmdale Subdivision
160.995   Ch 4 Yard, secondary
160.320   Ch 5 SP Road, Burbank Jct. to Santa Clarita
161.550   Ch 6 SP Road, Mission Tower to Moorpark
160.515   Ch 7 UP Road, Los Angeles to Riverside
160.560   Ch 8 ATSF Road, Mission Tower to San Bernardino
160.650   Ch 9 ATSF Road, Mission Tower to San Diego
161.190   Ch 10 ATSF Road, Lambert – San Bernardino
160.455   Ch 11 Amtrak yard

Southern Pacific

161.550△	Road
160.320△	Road (alternate)
161.205	Police
161.220	Police

Shops Yard

160.530	Intermodal facility
161.100	Yard

Wilmington

160.305 161.310	Light Rail operations

Wilmington – ICTF Yard

160.350	Intermodal facility
161.205	Security
161.400	Yard switcher

Union Pacific

160.515△	Ch 3 Road
160.290 161.520	Administration – PBX
160.605 161.025	MofW – PBX
161.025	MofW
161.205	Police mutual aid
160.710	UP Motor Freight

East Yard

160.410	Hump
160.680	Yard
161.340 160.590	Car Dept.

Waterfront Area

160.980	Harbor channel

MEMPHIS

Burlington Northern

161.100	Ch 1 Yard
161.160	Ch A1 Road and yard
160.800	Ch A3 Yard
161.040	Ch A4 Yard
160.725	Ch B2 Yard
160.845	Ch B4 Yard
161.130 160.545	Ch 5 PBX
160.620	Supervisory
161.430	MofW
160.965 160.485	Police – PBX
160.995	C&S – Simplex PBX
161.430	MofW – Simplex PBX

Tennessee Yard

160.230	Hump
160.515	Yard
160.560	Yard
160.470	UP interchange
161.310 160.710	Car Dept.
161.385	Ch A2 Intermodal facility
160.905	Police

CSX Transportation

161.265 160.395	PBX
161.370	Road
161.520	Dispatcher
161.205	Police

Memphis

Leewood Yard

160.440		Yard – Primary
160.335		IC interchange
160.920		IC interchange

Illinois Central

161.190△		Ch 1 Road
160.920△		Ch 2 Road
161.205		Police
160.920		Road – Terminal area
161.205		Police

Johnston Yard

160.620		Yard
160.785		Yard
161.460		Ch 3 Yard
161.010		Ch 4 Yard
161.400		Locomotive service
160.590	161.280	Car Dept.
161.250		Active – "S5"
160.650		Active – Use undetermined
160.740		Active
161.280		Active

Norfolk Southern

160.245		Dispatcher to train
160.830		Ch 2 Train to dispatcher
161.475		Digital remote control of locomotives – eastbound
161.565		Digital remote control of locomotives – westbound
160.275	161.145	F8 PBX

161.535		C&S
160.365		Car Dept. (without repeater)
160.365	161.295	Car Dept. (with repeater)
161.505		Wrecker
161.115		End-of-train telemetry
161.205		Police

Forest Yard

161.490		Yard
160.470		UP interchange
161.550		SP interchange
160.365		Car Dept. – Simplex

Presidents Island Terminal

161.355~	G – FCC

Southern Pacific

161.550	Road
161.205	Police

Union Pacific

160.410		Ch 1 Road
160.470		Road – Terminal zone
161.025		MofW
160.605	161.025	MofW – PBX
160.755	161.325	Administration – PBX
161.205		Police mutual aid

Sargent Yard

160.350	MoPac Trucking Lines
161.355	Yard

MINNEAPOLIS and ST. PAUL

Burlington Northern

160.695	Road, southeast
160.920	Road, west
161.100	Road, northwest and northeast
161.160	Road, north and central
161.385	Road, northwest
160.335	OCS calling channel
160.500	Signal Dept.
160.830	Engineering Dept.
161.010	Telemetry – GPS in cab
161.250	Police and Administration Communication Center
452.900	Administration
855.1875 810.1875	Mobile data terminals

35th Avenue Tower

160.290 160.875	Machine Shop
160.365	Hump
160.410	Pulldown
160.590	Car Dept.
160.710	Fuel truck
452.950 457.950	Hump cab signals

Midway Yard

161.500	Intermodal

Northtown Yard

161.160	Yard and mainline hump dispatcher

Union Yard and others

160.650	Yard

Chicago & North Western

160.890	Ch 1 Road, south and east
160.455	Ch 2 MofW
161.040	Ch 3 Road, southwest
161.175	Ch 4 Yard
160.575	Ch 5 Yard
160.485	Ch 6 Police

Valley Park Yard

161.220	Yard

Dakota Rail

160.275	General operations

Great Lakes Coal & Dock

151.775	Switching

Minnesota Commercial

160.560	Ch 1 Road
160.740	Ch 2 Yard

Minnesota Transportation Museum

161.355	Jackson Street Roundhouse, St. Paul
161.295	Wisconsin Central trackage rights at Osceola, Wisconsin

Minnesota Zephyr

160.290	Dinner Train operations

MNVA Railroad

161.265 160.305	General operations

Osceola & St. Croix Valley

161.295	Wisconsin Central trackage rights at Osceola, Wisconsin
161.355	Alternate channel

Soo Line (CP Rail System)

161.370	Ch 1 Road outside terminal area, east and west
161.520	Ch 2 Road in terminal area, east and west
160.770	Ch 4 Road, south
161.430	Ch 5 Yard
160.440	Police

General Office Building

161.325	Janitors

Shoreham Yard

160.980	Intermodal

Pig's Eye Yard

160.230	161.400	Car Dept.
160.530		Roundhouse
160.680		Hump
160.920		Rip track
161.430		Yard

Twin Cities & Western

160.875	Ch 1 Yard
161.460	Ch 2 Road
160.860	Ch 3 MofW (occasional use)

NEW YORK

Amtrak

160.365	457.900	Police – Portable/mobile repeater
160.515	161.115	MofW
160.815		Ch 2 Police – Car to car
161.205		Ch 4 Police – Car to car
161.295	160.365	Ch 3 Police – Base to car
452.900	161.295	Police – Portable/mobile repeater

Penn Station

160.650		Station services
161.325	160.275	Car Dept.
452.900		Commissary and redcaps

Sunnyside Yard

160.650		Yard
160.755	160.245	Car Dept.

New York to Washington

160.920	Road
160.650	Station services

New York to New Haven

161.280	Road – Metro-North
161.160	Electric traction

West Side Line

160.920	Road

Conrail

160.800	Ch 1 Road
161.070	Ch 2 Road and yard
160.860	Ch 3 Yard and road
160.980	Ch 4 Yard and road
161.130	Ch 3 MofW

161.130	160.710	Ch 4 PBX and MofW
160.680		Ch 3 Police – Car to car
160.680		Ch 3 Police
160.560		Ch 4 Police – Base to car

Elizabethport, New Jersey
161.340	160.680	Police – PBX
160.770		Yard
161.430		Train Movement desk and taxi

North Bergen, New Jersey
160.740	Yard
160.665	Intermodal facility

Perth Amboy, New Jersey
161.355	Yard (former Raritan River Railroad)

Newark, New Jersey
160.560	Oak Island yardmaster

Long Island Rail Road

160.380	Ch 1 Road and towers
161.445	Ch 2 Dispatcher
161.265	Ch 3 Yard; Road on Port Jefferson Branch and Main Line east of Hicksville
161.385	Ch 1 Signal Dept. & ET
160.725	Ch 3 MofW – B&B Dept.
161.535	Ch 4 Car Dept., End to end, MofE
160.455	Ch 1 Police – Base to car
160.605	Ch 2 Police – Car to car
160.395	MofW – Mobiles
452.6375	457.6375 Low power use
452.6875	457.6875 Low power use
452.7625	457.7625 Low power use
452.8125	457.8125 Low power use

452.8625	457.8625 Low power use
452.9125	457.9125 Police – Mobile/portable repeater
75.44	Point-to-point link
75.60	Point-to-point link

Flatbush Avenue, Brooklyn
161.490	160.320	Ch 4 Police

Easthampton
160.620	Police link

Holbrook
160.620	Police link

Jamaica
160.335	Stationmaster

Mastic and Shirley
160.620	Police link

Penn Station, New York
160.320	161.490	Ch 3 Police

Speonk
160.620	Police link

Westhampton
160.620	Police link

Metro-North Railroad

160.950	Ch 1 Road and dispatcher – Hudson Division
161.280	Ch 2 Road and dispatcher – Harlem Division
160.545	Ch 3 Road and dispatcher – New Haven Division
160.410	Ch 4 MofW – Harlem and Hudson Divisions
161.160	Ch 5 MofW – New Haven Division
160.860	Stores Dept. – Harmon Shop
161.070	Yard
161.220	Police

New York

Grand Central Terminal
160.335	Tunnel emergency channel
160.770	Stationmaster

Metropolitan Transit Authority

Subways
156.105	C&S
160.305	Ch 5 Police – Common
160.695	Ch 6 Police – Patrol cars
160.845	Yard
470.3875 473.3875	ET, MofE, Administration
470.4875 473.4875	MofW

IRT subway lines (Division A)
158.880	Train to dispatcher
161.190	Road and dispatcher to train

BMT subway lines (Division B1)
158.775	Train to dispatcher
161.505	Road and dispatcher to train

IND subway lines (Division B2)
158.805	Train to dispatcher
161.565	Road and dispatcher to train
160.395	Coney Island yard
160.875	Coney Island yard
161.025	Coney Island yard

Brooklyn
151.310	Ch 1 Police – Car to base
160.305	Ch 1 Police – Base to car

Bronx
151.190	Ch 2 Police – Car to base
160.500	Ch 2 Police – Base to car

Queens
151.145	Ch 3 Police – Car to base
160.965	Ch 3 Police – Base to car

Manhattan
151.340	Ch 4 Police – Car to base
160.905	Ch 4 Police – Base to car

Staten Island Rapid Transit
470.4375 473.4375	Road, Dispatcher, and Police

Buses
161.175		Buses – Flushing and Fresh Pond
161.250	160.260	Bus Telemetry
161.520	160.530	Staten Island buses
452.9125	457.9125	Staten Island buses

New Jersey Transit
160.860		Road – North Jersey Coast – Conrail
161.235		Road – North Jersey Coast – NJ Transit
161.070		Road – High Bridge Branch – Conrail
161.235		Road – High Bridge Branch – NJ Transit
161.400		Road – Hoboken Division
160.410		Electric power control
160.440		Signal Dept. Trouble Desk
160.770		Electrical/EMU/Mechanical
160.890		Mechanical
161.520		Buses
161.370		Newark City Subway
161.460		Newark City Subway – Road and dispatcher
160.680		Ch 3 Police – Conrail
161.145		Ch 3 Police – Conrail
161.475		Ch 3 Police – Conrail
160.830		Police
160.830	160.215	Police – Vehicular repeater

New York Cross Harbor

160.590	General operations
156.650	Marine operations – Ch 13

New York, Susquehanna & Western Little Ferry, New Jersey

160.485	Ch 3 Road and dispatcher

Pennsylvania Truck Lines

Bergen, New Jersey

160.740~	Base and mobile
160.860~	Mobiles only

South Kearny, New Jersey

160.740~	Base and mobile
160.860~	Mobiles only

Port Authority Trans-Hudson

160.470	Ch 1 Road and dispatcher
161.040	Ch 2 Police
161.460	Ch 3 MofW/Emergency Channel

Henderson Yard

160.425		Shop
161.535		Ch 4 Car shop
452.875	457.875	Yard

Port Jersey Railroad Bayonne, New Jersey

472.5625~475.5625~	FCC – 25 mobiles/1 MR
467.750~	FCC – 11 mobiles

U. S. Army Bayonne, New Jersey

165.0375	Military Ocean Terminal

U. S. Navy Earle, New Jersey

140.025	Rail operations, Earle Naval Weapons Station

PHILADELPHIA

Amtrak

160.365	457.900	Police – Portable/mobile repeater
160.515	161.115	MofW
160.815		Ch 2 Police – Car to car
161.205		Ch 4 Police – Car to car
161.295	160.365	Ch 3 Police – Base to car
452.900	161.295	Police – Portable/mobile repeater
160.650		Station services
160.920		Road

Atlantic City Line

160.920		Road
161.355		Stationmaster/Station services

30th Street Station

160.350	161.265	Train Managers
160.455		Yard and work trains
160.650		Station services
161.505	160.965	MofE
452.900		Station administration

Conrail

160.800△		Ch 1 Road
161.070△		Ch 2 Road and yard
161.130		Ch 3 MofW
160.980		Ch 4 Yard and road
161.130	160.710	Ch 4 PBX and MofW

Philadelphia

161.010	Active
161.205	Police – CR and Amtrak
160.680	Ch 3 Police – Car to car
160.560	Ch 4 Police – Base to car
Coal Pier	
160.830	Yard
161.220	Yard
Race Street Yard	
161.520 160.275	Car Dept.
Reading Division	
160.350	Commuter trains (SEPTA)
South Philadelphia Yard	
160.860	Ch 3 Yard
160.260	Crew bus
161.430	Crew bus
160.590	Active – Use undetermined
160.995	Active – Use undetermined
161.190	Active – Use undetermined
161.340	Active – Use undetermined
Wayne Junction	
161.400	Signal Dept. Trouble Desk

CSX Transportation

160.230	Road
160.320	Dispatcher
160.530	Yard
161.160	Yard
160.380	Yard
160.785	MofW
160.410	Ch 6 MofW, locomotive service
160.875	Police

160.725	Police
161.205	Police mutual aid
Waterfront Area	
160.470	Ch Y Yard
160.890	Ch Y1 Yard

New Hope & Ivyland

152.960	General operations
161.475 160.425	General operations

New Jersey Transit

161.355	Road – Atlantic City line

Port Authority Transit

453.675	Operations, Lindenwold, New Jersey
500.8125 503.8125	Ch 1 Police
500.8375 503.8375	Ch 2 Power Director and MofW
500.8875 503.8875	Ch 3 Administration
500.9125 503.9125	Ch 4 Road

Southeastern Pennsylvania Transportation Authority

Railroad Division

160.800	Ch 1 Conrail Lines
160.350	Ch 2 Road – Main Line, Zoo to Tunnel, Airport, Chestnut Hill West, Ivy Ridge, West Chester
160.395	Ch 3 Yards at Paoli, Frazer, Powelton Avenue, Roberts Avenue, and Wayne Electric
161.460	Ch 4 Road – Tunnel to Lansdale, Chestnut Hill East, Norristown, Doylestown, Warminster, and Neshaminy
160.290	Ch 5 ET Power/Signal Dept./MofW

161.070		Ch 6 Conrail Road
160.920		Ch 7 Amtrak Road
161.325		Car Dept – Suburban Station

Red Arrow Division

30.08		Philadelphia & Western
30.98		Ch 1 Red Arrow Division
31.14		Ch 2 Maintenance trucks and shop
31.10		Ch 3 Maintenance trucks and shop
30.89		Ch 4 Red Arrow Division
502.6375	505.6375	Ch 8 Telemetry
502.6625	505.6625	Ch 9 Supervision – South end
502.6875	505.6875	Ch 10 Police
502.7375	505.7375	Ch 12 Emergencies
502.7625	505.7625	Ch 13 Police and MofW
502.7875	505.7875	Ch 14 Supervision – North end
504.1375		Ch 15 Car to car

Blue Line Subway (Market-Frankford)

453.350	458.350	Transit Division City Police – Western Precinct
453.950	458.950	Transit Division City Police – Northwestern Precinct
453.300	458.300	Transit Division City Police – Eastern Precinct
502.7125	505.7125	Ch 11 Subways

Orange Line Subway (Broad Street)

155.070		Transit Division City Police

System-Wide

160.275		Police
160.275		M.U. car inspectors
161.235		PBX

Upper Merion & Plymouth

160.485		General operations

SAN FRANCISCO

Alameda Belt Line

160.935		General operations

Amtrak

160.440		Car Dept.

Atchison, Topeka & Santa Fe

160.245	161.535	PBX P-2
160.650△		Ch 1 Road
161.010		MofW

Richmond Yard

161.190		Intermodal facility
161.370		Yard
161.145		Yard
160.785		Yard

Bay Area Electric Railroad Association

Western Railroad Museum, Rio Vista Junction

161.355		RW – Mobiles

Bay Area Rapid Transit

160.410	161.505	Ch 1 Road – Duplex
160.860		Ch 2 Road
160.455		Yard
453.975	458.975	Yard and shop

San Francisco, St. Louis

160.845		Administration
43.78		Power Dispatcher and MofW
154.295	153.770	Emergency fire channel
453.150	458.150	Ch 1 Police
453.425	458.425	Ch 2 Police – Special operations

CalTrain

160.485•		Ch. 1 Road
160.815•		Ch. 2 General purpose
160.320•		Ch. 3 SP Road

Napa Valley Railroad

160.575	161.475	F1 General operations
160.575		F2 Talk-around
161.085		F3 Simplex
161.175		F4 Simplex
452.9125	457.9125	F4 Simplex

Oakland Terminal

| 160.935 | General operations |

San Francisco Municipal Railway

| 484.6625 | 487.6625 | Cable Car and Light Rail Vehicle operations |

Southern Pacific

161.550△		Road
160.320△		Road (Alternate)
160.275	161.310	Car Dept.
160.320		PMT Trucking
161.100		Switching and crew caller

Union Pacific

160.515		Ch 3 Road
161.460		Yard – Green
161.115		Yard
160.785		Yard
160.605	161.025	MofW – PBX
161.025		MofW
161.205		Police mutual aid

ST. LOUIS

Alton & Southern

160.770	Ch 1 Road and dispatcher
160.335	Ch 2 Yard
160.560	Administration

East St. Louis, Illinois

160.905	North hump
161.445	South hump
161.145	Pulldown
161.175	Car Dept.

Amtrak

| 160.410 | Car Dept. |
| 452.900 | Terminal services |

Aviation Material Readiness Command

| 165.1625 | General operations |

Burlington Northern

| 161.100 | Ch 1 Yard |

194

161.160		Ch 2 Road
161.430		MofW
161.130	160.545	Ch 5 PBX
160.620		Supervisory
Lindenwood Yard		
160.665		Car Dept.
160.695		Yard
160.785		Yard
161.295		Intermodal facility
161.415		Yard

Chicago & North Western

160.890	Ch 1 Road
160.455	Ch 2 MofW and road

Conrail

160.800		Ch 1 Road
161.070		Ch 2 Road and yard
160.680		Ch 3 Police – Car to car
160.980		Ch 4 Yard and road
Brooklyn Yard		
160.485		Yard
Rose Lake Yard, Rose Lake, Illinois		
161.325	160.275	Yard
160.710		Yard
160.995		Yard
161.055		Yard
161.085		Yard

CSX Transportation

160.230	Road – Former Chessie System

161.370		Road – Former L&N
160.320		Dispatcher – Former Chessie System
161.520		Dispatcher – Former L&N
161.280		Yard – Former L&N
160.260		Yard
160.935		Yard
161.265	160.395	PBX
161.205		Police mutual aid
Cone Yard		
160.365		Yard
East St. Louis		
161.280		Yard
160.530		Ch 3 Intermodal facility
160.605		Remote control locomotives
160.875		Car Dept.
161.205		Police mutual aid

Gateway Western

161.280	Ch.1 Road (SPCSL)
161.460	Ch 2 Road (GWWR)
161.025	Intermodal facility
160.860	Intermodal facility
East St. Louis	
161.025	Ch 3 Mechanical Dept.
160.725	Ch 5 Yard
161.295	Ch 6 Yard
Venice, Illinois	
161.010	Intermodal facility

Granite City Steel — Granite City, Illinois

153.230	Plant switching

St. Louis

Illinois Central
160.920	Ch 2 Road
161.010	Ch 4 Yard
161.205	Police

Laclede Steel Co.   Alton, Illinois
158.280~	FCC – Base and mobiles

Manufacturers Railway
160.740	Road and yard
160.515	Administration
River Yard	
161.385	Car Dept.

Norfolk Southern
160.245		Dispatcher to train
160.830		Ch 2 Train to dispatcher
160.440		Ch 3 Road (former Wabash routes)
160.950		Ch 5 Road (former Southern Railway routes)
161.490		Ch 9 Yard
161.490		Ch 9 MofW
160.335		Illinois Terminal – 1
160.695		Illinois Terminal – 2 MofW
160.380	161.235	PBX 11
161.250		A. O. Smith Yard
160.350		Luther Yard
160.620		Yard clerks, East St. Louis
160.350		Trainmasters and WR Tower
161.475		Digital remote control of locomotives – eastbound

161.565	Digital remote control of locomotives – westbound
161.115	End-of-train telemetry
160.575	Police
161.205	Police

Pennsylvania Truck Lines
160.485~	G – Base and mobile
161.070~	G – Mobiles only

St. Louis & Chain of Rocks Railroad
151.655	Tourist operations

St. Louis Steam Train Association
154.600	Operation of Frisco 1522

Southern Pacific
161.550△		Road
161.280△		Road – Chicago to St. Louis
East St. Louis		
160.875		Yard
161.280		Yard
160.305	161.355	Mechanical Dept.
161.220		Mechanical Dept.
161.340		Mechanical Dept.
161.400		Mechanical Dept.
161.205		Police

Terminal Railroad Association of St. Louis
160.500△		Road
160.845	160.290	PBX

161.205		Police mutual aid
161.310		Police and MofW
Harlem Yard		
161.535		Switching
Madison Yard, Madison, Illinois		
160.425		Pulldown
160.650		Hump
452.875	457.875	Car Dept.

Union Pacific

160.590		Dupo yard engines
160.470△		Dupo yardmaster
160.410△		Car Dept. and yard MofW
161.025		MofW
160.605	161.025	MofW – PBX
160.740		Mainline MofW
160.755	161.325	Administration – PBX
161.205		Police mutual aid
160.080		MoPac Trucking Lines

ST. PAUL – see Minneapolis, page 187

TORONTO

Canadian National

161.415	Ch 1 Road
161.205	Ch 2 Dispatcher
160.935	Ch 3 Dispatcher
160.665	Ch 4 Yard
160.365	Ch 5 General terminal
161.025	Ch 8 Dispatcher

160.215		Ch 16 Yard
160.785		Ch 20 MofW
160.905		Ch 24 C&S
160.305		Ch 28 Yard
161.055		Ch 29 Yard
161.235		Ch 35 Police
160.455	161.085	Ch 81 MofW
160.215	160.905	Ch 82 MofW – PBX
160.515	161.505	Ch 83 MofW

Primary channels in use are 1–8 and 20. For track line-ups monitor channels 2, 3, 8, and 20 0700-0815, 1201-1315, and 1600-1630 hrs.

464.8625		Ch 411 – 1 base and 20 mobiles
459.2250		Ch 418 – 1 base and mobiles
469.9875		Ch 428 Yard
464.2000	469.7000	Ch 509 – 1 base and 20 mobiles
460.0875	465.0875	Ch 513 – 1 base and 1 mobile
MacMillan Yard		
160.665		Ch 4 Switch tenders
160.605		Ch 14 Intermodal facility
160.395	160.965	Ch 63 Car Dept.
460.2750	465.2875	Ch 503 Hump – Yellow/Red
460.6000	465.6125	Ch 504 Eastbound departure yard – Blue
460.9000	465.9125	Ch 505 Inspection and South Control – White
461.1250	466.1375	Ch 506 Train makeup – express yard
461.950	466.9625	Ch 507 Westbound departure yard – Green
Malport Yard		
160.665		Ch 4 Yard
160.365		Ch 5 Yard (Alternate)
Mimico Yard		
160.665		Ch 4 Yard

Toronto

CP Rail

161.475		CP 1 Road and dispatcher
161.475	161.535	CP 2 Train to dispatcher
161.475	160.425	CP 3 Train to dispatcher
161.115		CP 4 Road and dispatcher
161.325		CP 5 Road and dispatcher
161.325	160.425	CP 6 Train to dispatcher
161.535		CP 7 Road and dispatcher
161.535	160.425	CP 8 Train to dispatcher
161.115	160.425	CP 9 Train to dispatcher
160.725	160.425	CP 10 Train to dispatcher
160.845		CP 11 MofW
160.845	160.335	CP 12 Utility PBX
161.175		CP 13 MofW
161.175	160.335	CP 14 Utility PBX
160.845	160.245	CP 15 Utility PBX
161.265		CP 16 MofW
161.265		CP 16 Yard
161.265	160.245	CP 17 Utility PBX
161.175	160.635	CP 18 Utility PBX
161.505		CP 19 MofW
161.505	160.635	CP 20 Utility PBX
161.265	160.605	CP 21 Utility PBX
161.505	160.605	CP 22 Utility PBX
159.885		CP 51 Police
160.245		CP 58 Intermodal facility
160.545		CP 70 Police mutual aid
160.725		CP 78 Road and dispatcher
161.235		CP 96 Police
161.355		CP 99 Industrial yard

159.930	160.755	CP 112 Car Dept.
452.700		CP 440 Yard
456.2375		CP 451 Yard
457.4125		CP 457 Yard
464.550		CP 481 Yard

Agincourt Yard

161.325		CP 5 Yard
159.930		CP 52 Yard
160.050		CP 53 Locomotive shop/car planner
160.185		CP 56 Industrial yard
160.275		CP 59 Yard
160.335		CP 62 Diesel shop
160.725		CP 78 Yard
160.755		CP 79 Yard
160.875		CP 83 Hump
160.050	160.755	CP 114 Car Dept.
451.150		CP 429 1 base and 3 mobiles
451.2250	456.2375	CP 435 1 base and 5 mobiles
452.4000	457.4125	CP 438 1 base and 5 mobiles
452.7000	457.7125	CP 441 1 base and 5 mobiles
459.2000		CP 469 1 base and 19 mobiles

Cambridge Yard

160.815	CP 82 Yard

Obico Yard

161.145	CP 93 Yard

Oshawa Yard

160.995	CP 87 Yard

GO Transit

161.295	Road

Mimico Shops
413.9375 418.9375 Yard and shop
Willowbrook Shops
419.4375 Shops

Toronto Terminals Railway (Toronto Union Station)

461.0125 466.0125 Security
461.2125 466.2125 Stationmaster, arrival and departure

Toronto Transit Commission

412.0375	Ch 1 Operations control
412.0625	Ch 2 Secondary operations
412.1125	Ch 3 Secondary operations
412.6125	Ch 4 Secondary operations
412.5875	Ch 5 Road – Scarborough Line
151.925	MofW – Trolley Lines
410.5875	Telemetry
410.6125	Telemetry
410.7625	Telemetry
412.1375	Telemetry

VIA Rail Canada

461.2125 466.2125 Union Station — Stationmaster, arrival and departure

WASHINGTON

Amtrak

Washington Union Station
160.800 Road – Terminal area

160.290	161.370	Ch 1 Road
160.350	161.145	Ch 2 Car Dept.
160.440	161.445	Ch 3 Administration and redcaps
160.365	161.295	Police
Northeast Corridor		
160.365	457.900	Police – Portable/mobile repeater
160.455		Work trains and yard
160.515	161.115	MofW
160.815		Ch 2 Police – Car to car
161.205		Ch 4 Police – Car to car
161.295	160.365	Ch 3 Police – Base to car
452.900	161.295	Police – Portable/mobile repeater
160.650		Station services
160.920		Road

Conrail

160.800△		Ch 1 Road
161.070△		Ch 2 Road and yard
161.130		Ch 3 MofW
161.130	160.710	Ch 4 PBX and MofW
160.680		Ch 3 Police – Car to car
160.560		Ch 4 Police – Base to car
Benning Yard		
160.980		Ch 4 Yard

CSX Transportation

160.230	Road – Former Chessie System
160.320	Dispatcher – Former Chessie System
160.470	Yard – Former Chessie System
160.530	Yard – Former Chessie System
160.785	MofW – Former Chessie System

Washington

160.875	Police – Former Chessie System
160.890	Yard – Former Chessie System
161.160	Yard – Former Chessie System
161.205	Police mutual aid

Norfolk Southern

160.830△	Ch 2 Train to dispatcher
160.245△	Dispatcher to train
160.950△	Ch 5 Road
161.490	Ch 9 Yard
160.500	Traveling freight agents and wrecker
161.505	Wrecker
161.535	C&S Mobile to mobile
161.475	Digital remote control of locomotives – eastbound
161.565	Digital remote control of locomotives – westbound
161.115	End-of-train telemetry
161.205	Police

Richmond, Fredericksburg and Potomac (CSX)

161.100	Future Road
161.520	Future Dispatcher
161.550△	Ch 1 Road and dispatcher to train
161.355 161.460	Ch S Police and Supervisory
161.490△	Ch 2 Train to dispatcher

Virginia Railway Express   Springfield, Virginia

160.950	Norfolk Southern Road
160.830	Norfolk Southern Train to dispatcher

160.245	Norfolk Southern Dispatcher to train
161.550	CSX Road and dispatcher to train
161.490	CSX Train to dispatcher
161.355	CSX Police and Supervisory

Washington Metropolitan Area Transit Authority

160.260	Ops 1 Road and dispatcher – Red Line – Union Station to Silver Spring
160.380	Ops 2 Road and dispatcher – Blue and Orange Lines – New Carrollton, MD, to Ballston
160.620	Ops 3 Road and dispatcher – Blue Line – Seat Pleasant to National Airport
161.025	MofW and ET
161.235	Yard 1
161.385	Ch 1 Police
161.385 160.725	Ch 2 Police
Brentwood Yard	
161.235	Yard 1 – Car Dept.
New Carrolton Yard	
160.605	Yard 2 – Car Dept. and train testing
Wheaton	
161.415	Startup control network
Alexandria	
161.235	Yard 1
Falls Church	
161.235	Yard 1
161.415	Startup control network